AUTISM IN THE HOOD

*A Nice Jewish Boy's Nineteen Years
In the Hood*

Benjamin Wolfson

ISBN: 979-8-9896418-4-0 (Paperback Edition)
ISBN: 979-8-9896418-8-8 (Hardcover Edition)
ISBN: 979-8-9896418-3-3 (Ebook Edition)

Printed in the United States of America.

For a friend in Wisconsin.

Table of Contents

INTRODUCTION

This book is a chronicle of my work experience with children ages zero to three on the autism spectrum in the hoods of Brooklyn, New York from approximately the year 2000 to 2019. It's a recounting of my experiences interacting with children and parents in environments that few people like me—White, Orthodox Jewish, and middle class—are lucky enough to have been involved with. My life has been enriched in many ways for having had that opportunity.

I worked primarily in the "bad neighborhoods." These might be described as the hood, the ghetto, the projects, or "those parts of town." The children were mostly Black, the majority from "the Islands," with the occasional Latin child, Chinese, Pakistani, Bangladeshi, and, very rarely, a White or Orthodox Jewish child. Many were Muslim.

The primary reason I worked in neighborhoods of ethnicity is that most therapists did not want to go into them. The majority of therapists were White females who feared going into these neighborhoods. Black women therapists had no problem entering them, but there weren't a lot of Black women therapists. There were only a handful of White male therapists, and many of them also refused to work in the hoods. I had never, in all my time in New York, met a Black male therapist except for one. Unfortunately, he was not a very good one.

I will briefly describe how the services were rendered. A child aged zero to three was first evaluated, and from that initial evaluation, a diagnosis was given and recommendations for required services were written. He (I use male pronouns because autism is prevalent five to one in males) may be given special education, speech, physical therapy, occupational therapy, and anything else he might need, such as a feeding program. Services were given either in the EI (Early Intervention) Center or at home—sometimes both. If a child was getting services at the Center, his teacher wrote individualized programs for him. The assistants at the Center applied the programs. If the child also received home therapy (usually the case), the home therapist would implement the same programs at home. This is considered necessary because generalization of acquired skills usually do not transfer from one environment to another unless specifically taught. At least, that's a problem in autism. If the therapy was home-based, the home-based therapist would write and implement the programs. The child would have more than one home-based special education therapist, depending on how many hours he received. The child could receive up to twenty hours a week of special education. In addition, he could receive two to five, half-hour sessions a week of speech, occupational, and physical therapy. That's a lot of therapists trapsing through people's houses every day. All this for a child who was usually between eighteen and twenty months old when first diagnosed. The services were provided for free by the City of New York.

The method utilized was Applied Behavior Analysis, or ABA for short. Readers of this book will already know what ABA is, so I'll briefly mention here only that when therapists "apply" the methodology, what it usually involves is discrete trial teaching.

"DTT is a structured ABA technique that breaks down skills into small, 'discrete' components. Systematically, the trainer teaches these skills one by one. Along the way, trainers use tangible reinforcements for desired behavior. For example, a trainer teaching colors to a child might begin by teaching red. She would ask the child to point to red and then reward the behavior. She would then move on to teaching yellow by itself, reinforce that skill, and then ask about both colors. After the child learns all his colors, the trainer might teach the child to say each color's name."[1]

The children ranged in severity from "low functioning" to "high functioning." I never liked those terms. Low functioning usually meant that the child did not talk; respond to language; interact with peers or adults, including the parents; understand language; or engage in limited interests, such as lining up objects, turning in circles, or rocking. While all children engage in such behaviors, children on the spectrum had a "DIF." The "DIF" was Duration, Intensity, and Frequency. They would engage in these activities ceaselessly. Other issues included lack of self-help skills or daily living skills, food refusal or selectivity (only McDonald's pancakes), and other types of "strange" behaviors, such as staring at a corner in the ceiling out of his eye. Tantrums and aggressiveness were common.

Higher functioning children might talk or follow instructions yet have the other diagnostic symptoms that bring the diagnosis. Instruction was one-to-one—one child, facing one therapist. Often, therapists had children who were lower functioning. Occasionally, I would work with a higher functioning child. A few times, I was lucky enough to work with savants. A savant is someone who exhibits extraordinary skills utilizing remarkable memory, creativity, math, reading, or other skills.

Most of the families I worked with were poor, "lower socio/economic" people. Conditions were generally poor. The hoods were always NYCHA apartment buildings—New York City Housing Authority, called "Nischa" colloquially. Some were better than others, but the poorest had infestations of mice inside the apartments, rats outside, cockroaches, ants, falling plaster, lead paint chips, exposed electrical wires, broken windows, poor plumbing, heat brought by pipes that ran through rooms and were dangerous to touch, broken elevators, security doors that didn't work, no air conditioning, and no smoke alarms. As far as cleanliness, that was a personal thing. Most of the time, the places I worked in were very clean and tidy.

New York was a new world to me, having been raised in a small town in Wisconsin. All the preconceived notions I had of it were negative. Poverty, crime, filth, violence, and gangs are what I expected. People in Appleton, Wisconsin were White WASPS: White-Anglo-Saxon-protestants. There were no Black people, Chinese people, Jewish people, or Latin people. Everyone spoke English. It was mostly blue collar, where people took hunting and fishing seriously. This included deer, bear, elk, duck, partridge, and turkey, each in its own season. Not to be confused with rifle season, bow season, or muzzle-loader season. Fishing was just as important—walleye, musky, perch, large mouth, small mouth, sturgeon. Every living room proudly displayed the family gun rack and was adorned with the heads of "six-point bucks" or mounted muskies. People were union and conservative Democrats. How a nice Jewish boy born in Chicago ended up living there is for another book. So, arriving in New York City and beginning a new career in my early forties was like arriving on another planet.

In this book, I discuss many of the beliefs, myths, and mistakes about autism and about the application of the methodology of Applied Behavior Analysis. To this day, the "Autism Wars" continue between professionals, parents, and people on the spectrum about what autism is; which methodology is best used to teach people on the spectrum; whether medication is called for or to be strictly avoided; and whether, indeed, autism should even be considered an illness or a deficit or be listed in the DSM-V as a diagnosis. Do diets help? Should there be research for a cure? Are such people simply "neurodivergent?" Can an autistic person "recover?" Should they?

The other reason for writing is to show how different families dealt with the devastating news that their child, at age two, had been given such a diagnosis—and then the fear, or lack thereof, for their prognosis. Autism diagnosis was a great equalizer. Rich or poor, Black or White, autism was always an uninvited guest.

CHAPTER ONE

Some Successes

When children who are diagnosed as being on the spectrum respond to treatment such that their diagnosis falls away, I could never help but wonder, was the child really "autistic" or was there just some kind of delay in developmental milestones, in which case, the child would have improved with or without intervention. In the course of my work, some children improved so dramatically that it made me wonder. I would have loved to take the credit for their improvement: "Ah, I'm a miracle worker," or "I'm such a good therapist!" But then, you put the children who really changed on a scale of all the children who made no advances in cognition, language, social skills, or environmental awareness, and you know there's no miracles and you're not as good as you think. Some kids just do well, and some kids don't. Some kids "recover" and some kids don't.

In this chapter, I want to recall some of the children who "recovered." These are the rare few who exhibited all the symptoms of ASD—and surely the diagnosis was correct—yet, by the end of therapy, before age three, they became "TD," or typically developing. In other words, "normal." My apologies to those who think that the word "normal" is insulting to those who are "not normal" or to those in the neurodiversity group who believe that everyone is normal, just "normal different."

Maria

I received a phone call to take a new case in downtown Brooklyn. Downtown meant only one thing: no parking. I was very hesitant to take this kid. The City of New York pays over a hundred and twenty dollars an hour to service a child. Due to the parking situation, up to forty-five minutes of that hour could easily be consumed in finding a place to park. Bad enough there's no parking, but some genius in New York invented "alternate side parking." This means that on designated days of the week, twice a week, for ninety minutes, one cannot park on one side of the street so they can clean it. Alternate side made it just about impossible to make any appointments somewhere during the street cleaning hours. Or, of course, you could pay outrageous prices to park in the local pay for park areas in downtown Brooklyn. So, when the call came through, "Ben, got a kid on East Forth near Atlantic Avenue, can you take her?" I immediately said, "No, thank you." Ayelet, the service coordinator did not like to hear "no." Her job was to place therapists. Her phone never stopped ringing.

"There's no parking over there!" I exclaimed. As if she didn't know this!

"Aw c'mon, there's no parking anywhere, that's no excuse." She was right, but I knew that as bad as parking in New York was, downtown was worse. We'd done this dance many times before, and I always gave in if I had a break in my schedule. "Okay, how old is she?"

"Lemme look. Um, uh, seventeen months," Ayelet answered hesitantly. She knew....

"Seventeen months! What am I supposed to do with a seventeen-month-old baby? Who diagnosed her anyway? Ain't no assessment I know of that can diagnose a kid at seventeen months!"

"When can you start?" she asked cheerily. She had the hardest job in the world but was always in a good mood. Not normal. The child would be doing a home program. That meant four hours of ABA at home plus speech, PT, OT. Four hours a day for a seventeen-month-old child? There was no way I could write programs to fill that many hours in a day!

Nevertheless, I reluctantly started the next day. The area they lived in was called Park Slope. The rich and famous who did not want to live in Manhattan lived there. I found the address and drove around the block looking for a parking place. Once, twice, three times. Mind you, a "block" in New York is not like a "block" in Appleton, Wisconsin. It would take twenty minutes to drive around the block in downtown Brooklyn, assuming there was no construction going on, no garbage pickup, no school buses, and no eight million people crossing the street.

After forty-five minutes of trying to find a parking spot, I called the parents and told them that I was highly skeptical that I could fit their baby girl into my schedule if I had to spend an hour finding a parking spot. "Hey, no problem, get here when you can." It was the end of September.

The door was on a busy street between a barbershop and a locksmith in a three-story building that used to be a factory. The buzzer rang, and I entered to face a long staircase. They were on the third floor. Great, my knees were already just about gone. I'd have to shlep two bags up three flights every day. These are the dirty little secrets the service coordinators don't tell you. I was greeted at the door, breathing heavily, by the biggest dog I had ever encountered. Bella was not happy to see me, and she had to be locked up.

The apartment was amazing. A redesigned old warehouse with a magnificent view of Brooklyn. The girl's name was Maria—a beautiful little fluff ball of blond hair and blue eyes. She looked like a baby. She could neither walk nor talk, and she made no sounds unless angry—in which case she cried, tantrumed, banged her head, or threw things. She made no eye contact with me and was completely impervious to my presence. She also had "stims." This is self-stimulatory behavior—"higher order stims," like lining things up, and "lower order stims," like hand flapping and spinning in circles. She was able to crawl, and I was not sure why she wasn't walking. If you stood her up, she would stand on her toes against a piece of furniture.

I asked her mom why she wasn't walking. Did they rule out everything physical? She told me that the PT said, "weak muscle tone." I didn't buy it. There are a few catch phrases therapists use when they cannot explain something. One is, "weak muscle tone." Another is "sensory issues." ABA people will say things like, "child has difficulty attending" or "exhibits escape behavior" when in reality, the therapist is boring the poor child to death. Maria looked perfectly normal to me physically.

On my fifth day working with her, Mom, who usually worked days, was home, and I thought that we might try to get Maria to walk using the same technique they use to teach babies to swim. Mom is one foot away in the water, and they put the baby in the water facing her. The child will instinctively "swim" to her. (Don't try this at home!) We tried it at home. Mom kneeled one foot away from her as I stood Maria up and let go. She fell into Mom's arms. Repeat. Again. Again. Okay, now she knows how to do it. Mom moved back a half a foot. Again. Mom moved back a foot. Again. At the end of that first day trying this technique, Maria walked across the room. Mom was amazed. I wasn't. Pretty simple, really. Walking is hard. Why walk when you can crawl? But when you get powerful reinforcement for walking, and you are able to, you do. No miracles, no magic. The PT was just another professional blaming the victim. "Weak muscle tone." Yeah, sure.

Mom worked because Dad had a disability. His legs were not in good shape. He was a big Italian guy and really easy going and funny. There was also a seventeen-year-old brother labeled with, "Asperger's syndrome." He was not home much, as he attended college. Then there was Anthony—a cute, orange-haired, seven-year-old boy with two labels: ADHD and speech disorder (I could not understand a word he said). When he came home from school, it was "batten down the hatches."

Dad told me that Maria banged her head when angry. Or she bit herself. These are common behaviors often exhibited by non-verbal children on the spectrum. I soon saw these things. Part of my job as a behavior analyst was to figure out "the function" of these behaviors. Why does she do these things, under what conditions, when, and with whom? I needed to see the behavior "under controlled conditions."

So, next session, first thing, as she lay on the floor happily, I gave her a sucker (a "lolly" in NY) and then snatched it back from her. She fell over, and her head hit the floor with a thud. But she did not bang it over and over, which is what usually happens when we label a child "head banger." She just held it there while screaming. That told me that when she wants something, and can't get access to it, she will bang her head.

Her wrist biting happened when she couldn't escape. "Escape" in behavioral language means running away from or refusing to do something that you don't want to do. A good therapist knows when it's time to just back off and wait and start over, or having to set limits such that the child will be able to work on a schedule even when that work is not desired. Escape behaviors happen a lot when therapists lock children in high-chairs or behind a table and chair and then present a non-desired activity. Old school ABA used to advise that you trap them like that and "work through" the behavior. Okay, we were going to have to "replace" that head banging and wrist biting with an "appropriate" communication form of some kind. That would take time and patience.

I noticed by the end of our first month that Maria had some skills that suggested she was not as bad as her evaluations suggested. She repeated some sounds, did some imitation, and put together a three-piece puzzle. I could get her to look in my eyes. These were all good signs.

A few bad signs were that she would not sit in a chair at all, ever. A worse problem was that she did not like to have her hands touched. Using hand-over-hand modeling would be out, and settling in one place to hold her attention would be difficult.

One other problem was that I really wasn't sure where to start with such a young child. I knew one thing for sure: she was not very interested in me, and I'd have to change that. They teach in ABA that you must find "reinforcers"—that is, things that will inspire a child to perform some action with which you can encourage her to continue. That is partially true. The whole truth is that *you* must become the reinforcer. If the child doesn't like you, forget it. Take your fancy ABA certification and your master's degree and go home. You have to try various toys with each child that you hope might interest them. For children on the spectrum, you can make some educated guesses: tops, small windup toys, pull string toys, puzzles, magnets, alphabet pieces and numbers, shapes, anything that makes a pattern, and music.

With such a young child, the only approach was to not approach her. Just sit on the floor next to her, with no other objects of interest in the room to draw away her attention, and spin tops that made music and lit up. Or spin a slinky and sing, "wheels on the bus." She would have to come over to see what I was doing. If she did, then I knew that I had the right reinforcer. Hopefully, we could then move to playing with them while sitting at a table. I knew that once she was regularly sitting at the table, we could begin structured teaching.

Maria was smart! She took a few months to sit comfortably and respond, but once she did, she began to learn quickly. She began to imitate physically and verbally. Her eye contact improved, and she laughed a lot.

By November, she was able to do formal programming at the table. Certainly, there were not two hours' worth of programs for me and two hours for her morning ABA instructor, Nick. So, a lot of time was filled with taking data on how often she vocally imitated.

Nick wrote that she was imitating a funny whistle he'd made, and she was humming along to songs. Her tantruming continued when she was bored or hungry. But it was going well, and we were working on replacing those behaviors with pointing to things that she wanted.

By the end of December, she was imitating words more regularly. She would say, "Stop!" because a favorite activity of hers was that I would spin a musical top and then suddenly stop it and shout, "STOP!" She would roar with laughter. Through December and January, she was occasionally repeating the words of songs. I was hoping that her speech would have been better. In oral imitation, I would say to her, "Do this" and open my mouth or stick out my tongue or make raspberries, or a high, shrill "eee" sound. If she would "exhibit the behavior," I would reinforce it. Maria did not like imitation much—not physical, not oral. I could not get her to orally imitate upon command, but I could get her to join in a song or say the names of things that she wanted. We had to do it her way.

Through February and March, she was doing better with the programs, but the pace was slow. I was sure that she was far more capable, as she seemed to understand language well. Her verbal imitation was increasing, and her ability to do programs when she agreed was very good. But my little girl was moody. One day, she would be perfect, and the next, she would be screaming and head banging. I believed we should try to work in a back room with less distractions. It was a good idea! Less distracted, and my control of access to anything fun, meant she had to pay attention. My job was to keep her not only attending but to enjoy what we were doing. If she wasn't attending, that means I wasn't fun, and if I'm not fun, why would a child under two care to attend to me?

Still, there were skills she needed to learn, even when they weren't fun. Poor kid had two hours in the morning and two in the afternoon. I wondered what Nick was doing with her, as he was not writing in the communication book, and I didn't find any information from him. He did not answer his phone. I called the Center and asked what was up. They told me that Mom cancels Nick a lot because he's not so good. I asked Mom if it was true, and she said that Maria did not like Nick. "She tantrums or cries throughout their entire session."

I thought, *Oh. Great. She's losing valuable time.* Her participation was not so consistent with me, either. When it wasn't, she was usually sluggish, her head on the back of the chair. I began to try something that no good ABA therapist should do. I decided with Maria that when she got upset, I would hug her and sing until she calmed down. No! But-but you're reinforcing escape behavior! Horrors! "That's exactly the wrong thing to do," they taught us in the courses. Every time she does not want to do something, the story goes, she'll tantrum, and you will let her out of what she's supposed to do. She will "learn" that tantruming leads her to "evade" the program. With some children, that is true. I did not think Maria was tantruming to get out of work. I thought she was tantruming because she just could not tell me, "I'm bored! I hate imitation!"

Imagine if you are doing some kind of mental or physical work, and you need a break, or you just don't want to do it today. What do you do? You take a break. You pause. You might even push it off (and feel guilty). What do you do when you are not yet two years old and can't communicate? Against all the rules, I decided that this would be our plan. I would hold her, comfort her, engage her in a more desired activity, and then quickly re-introduce the programs and do them rapidly. I could not recommend this to Nick, since it was against behavioral theory.

We had a week off for Passover, and when I returned, she seemed to be on a higher level for some reason. Her words were increasing, and her tantrum behavior was far less. I was amazed. So, it was time to try another tact when she refused to work or tantrumed or threw things now that her language was improved. First, I would have to teach her some words to let me know that she did not want something. I decided on, "finished," because she knew that word meant an activity or program would stop. The other word I worked on was, "gimme." If she could comprehend this, then she could request when she desired something and let me know when she did not desire something.

I wrote Nick and asked him to try this as well. I also introduced two signs: one for "shoes" and one for "juice." She had a pair of shoes that she liked to wear and would not allow you to take them off! That was good in any case, as they helped her stop toe walking.

The Center decided that after Passover, she would begin coming there for classes with other children. There were morning and afternoon classes. If she went into a class that conflicted with my time with her, I would lose her. She was doing good at home. I did not want to lose her. Her service coordinator didn't care what I wanted, of course, and she was not at all happy about my intervening. I'm just a taxi driver. Don't mess with dispatch! The paperwork was submitted, and now we have to wait for City's "change of services" approval. The family was going away for ten days. All was on hold until then.

The family returned, and we went back to work. She'd learned something while away: She could say, "No" when I suggested we do something. She was using words to argue with me! This was a whole new level. That being the case, I knew that now the time had come to back off on my practice of hugging her when she refused things. She was getting away with murder. She was so cute, you never wanted to upset her or make her cry, but it was now obvious that she understood everything we were doing and simply refused to do her programs. Programs that I could make fun for her, she was ready to do; but ones she had to learn, that weren't fun, she refused.

I established a strong strategy, particularly for Maria. When she refused to do her work, I folded up my arms, put my chin in my chest, and closed my eyes. She did not know what to make of this. She would tap my arm, or pull on it, and I would say, "No. Go away. You're not my friend." This really irritated her. She'd pull again, and I would look up and say, "Okay, let's do your work." This worked most of the time. It is not the kind of tactic I could suggest to others.

The month of June was a roller coaster. She was certainly not the little girl she had been when we started. Now she comprehended things, engaged with others, and was using some words to request and refuse. She was more like a cute little girl with a speech delay. But that little temper was still there, and the tantruming behavior that went with it.

By mid-June, she decided that she'd had enough of this therapy business. She would run away from me as soon as I walked in the door. She would not come back to our workstation. She threw things in anger. I would lure her into the back room with her favorite fig bars and juice, but once having eaten them, she'd run to the door and bang on it.

I spoke to Dad on one particularly bad day. He told me that she's been like this with everyone all week. I left a long note for Mom and therapists to report whether this was the same with them or was it just with me. The next day, Mom was home, so we had a talk. I was concerned that this would continue; in which case, I would either have to create a completely new program, or I would need to stop the therapy at home, and she would continue at the Center.

The speech therapists suggested that this new behavior was due to teething. Nick suggested, as your average behavior analyst would, that "it's all about reinforcement." It is—with pigeons. It's not with children. I changed some programs, and by the next week, the behavior was gone.

We did well through July and into August. She now understood facial expressions and related to emotion. She still had her outbursts and refused to do things that she didn't like, but she was two years old. There's no cure for being two years old.

It was "status quo" throughout September. On October 9, she began to go to the Center. That meant that the teacher would take over as team leader and write the programs. Her adjustment to the Center was not so smooth. They said that she tantrumed often— good days and bad days. In other words, there was no consistency, and that is not a good sign. She was doing well at home, however, and I did the simple programs they wrote for her. I'm sure they bored her to death, and she and I just kept plugging away at verbal communication.

After Thanksgiving, she was able to speak three-word sentences. She began to call me, "Missa Ben," which meant "Mr. Ben," as that is what her brother called me. Her brother Anthony became a very useful part of our sessions. His "speech disorder" had improved tremendously. In the beginning, I could not understand a word he said. Now, he had perfectly good articulation. I used him for peer interaction, as Maria adored him, and when he came home from school, she'd push the table away and run to him. It was a perfect opportunity for verbal communication and social skills training.

I was contacted by the Center, however, regarding her behavior. They told me that she still tantrumed a lot. I had no doubt it was due to boring programs and inexperienced trainees. The classroom teacher and the supervisor did not know how to improve her attending to tasks and working. I had no advice for them, as they insisted on using discrete trial teaching. I wasn't, but they would have blamed me for her behavior if they knew that.

In December we had three weeks left, so she and I concentrated on answering "wh" questions: where, what, when. These were hard for her. Was it language, or was it cognitive? When things became too hard for her at this point, she would simply ignore me—no more tantrums, no more throwing. She was acting age appropriately now. I had not seen any "stimming" for months. She no longer toe-walked. At the end of December, the family moved to Florida.

Years later, I still get emails and videos from Mom. Both children are in regular education. Seeing them, you would never know that they had developmental disabilities when young. Mom told me that when she told the schools in Florida that Maria had been diagnosed as having autism, they did not believe her.

Brenda

Brenda was one of those unusual success stories. Considering the environment in which she lived, it's a miracle that we were able to help her at all. All the odds were stacked against her. I only knew of her because of her sister, a little girl named Sally, who was in the Center program. You can read her story in the chapter titled, "Different Kinds of Mothers." Brenda's story needs a little background and should be read after reading about Sally.

What comes to mind when one thinks about the famous Coney Island Lunar Park? The boardwalk, the famous "Cyclone" roller coaster, the street performers, the circus side show, the equally famous Nathan's Hot Dog Eating Contest, the Mermaid Parade, and the ocean just beyond the boardwalk. In the summer, it is a major tourist attraction, with thousands of visitors from all over the world coming to this small, isolated little area of Brooklyn. It is also home to the huge Brooklyn Aquarium. It's fun, it's exciting, and you can actually find parking—if you're willing to pay a bit. If not, the local buses go there from anywhere in Brooklyn. It has a record of being a safe environment day and night.

The Lunar Park is only one small area of greater Coney Island. If you were to travel west for another ten minutes, you would see a completely different world. In this world of NYCHA housing, there is little amusement, no excitement, a sense of gloom throughout, and safety, upon entering, is immediately on your mind. One of my great pleasures was to bring friends from the United States to visit the Lunar Park, and then to take them down a few blocks to show them another reality.

The Coney Island Projects are in the West thirties. It may as well be on another planet. It is known for poverty, violence, drugs, truancy, and criminal activity. Oddly enough, just beyond that is an area called Seagate. It is on the ocean at the very tip of the island. It is a gated community of Orthodox Jews who keep to themselves and a low profile. Is this picture fair to all of the regular, normal, hardworking people who also inhabit the projects? Not really. The projects are meant for low-income people with reduced rental fees set by the City of New York and is maintained by the City of New York. One must qualify in order to get an apartment there. And, yes, it is predominantly African American.

The service coordinator at the Center called and asked me if I could take a young girl with FTT ("failure to thrive") as her diagnosis. I told the service coordinator that I had no experience with that nor knew what to do with a child with this diagnosis. She told me that the little girl seemed severely retarded and needed help to eat. I told her to get a feeding specialist. But no, the "team" had decided that she needed behavioral intervention, and that is what her service called for. I was hesitant until they dropped the bomb: It was Sally's younger sister. What?! I reminded her about the problems I had getting to see Sally. I never was able to see her due to her mother's very serious drug problems. Why would it be any different with her sister?

"Oh no, that won't be a problem," I was told. Both Sally and Brenda had been taken from the mother by the New York City Social Services and given to her sister Nikki as custodian. Nikki lived just across the street. It was November 11.

I had heard of FTT but never saw a child that had it. I did some basic research and found that there are two different kinds: endogenous and exogenous. The first is due to internal physical problems, and the latter is due to external problems, such as insufficient caloric intake or neglect.

I was to begin work with a little girl who was terribly underweight, assessed as profoundly retarded (called "cognitively delayed" these days), with no other therapists involved, and I was supposed to help her. Who would help me?

I entered the apartment building past the graffiti, stuffed garbage containers, litter, and cats. Once in the main foyer, I would take the elevator up to the sixth floor. The foyer was full of teenage guys hanging out and discussing the important business of the day in their world. They eyed me suspiciously as I walked between them, but no one said a word—typical reactions I had found in all the hoods I worked in. Each apartment looked exactly the same as the others. On the outside, heavy door with multiple locks and peep-holes. They were all colored brown, spaced like a prison, ten feet away from each other, distanced by grey/yellow bricks.

Nikki let me in. She was a big woman with a beaming, happy face. She was very friendly and helpful, and I suppose I didn't expect that because of preconceived notions of what I would encounter in such a gloomy place. Her husband was also home. Another big person! Vince was also full of smiles and welcoming. They had a fourteen-year-old daughter sitting at a table playing computer games. She, too, was big. Then, waiting for me in a highchair, was a skinny little girl with her left eye barely open. She looked very weak, fragile, like a rag doll. We would work in the cramped living room just off a tiny kitchen.

On our first session, I saw that she was able to repeat words of things she liked. She was easily engaged and quickly learned how to manipulate objects after having observed me do it once. She could open things and push the button to turn on the strobe light. Eye contact was spontaneous. I thought that she'd be able to learn a lot quickly, though I found her to be on approximately a ten-month-old level. I introduced formal programs, which were fairly standard for two-year-old children on the autism spectrum, but after two weeks, I noted that she was not doing well.

This was an important lesson for me. She was not doing well because I had written programs for a child with autism. She did not have autism! It was obvious to me that the problem with "lack of progress" was not due to her—it was due to me! I was guilty of blaming the victim! I threw the program book in the trash and began doing only "functional tasks," i.e., using objects for her to operate, manipulate, explore, and follow directions. This appealed much more to her, and now her sessions became fun.

By early December, her verbal language was increasing, and her social interaction and ability to follow instructions were much better. Vince and Nikki commented on her increase in language use and ability to engage. The one thing I could not get was eye contact when using her name. She simply did not respond to her name, and that bothered me.

On December 23, her mother came to visit. We were in the middle of the session when she knocked on the door. I was taken aback. I had talked to her on the phone but never met her other than the time when she'd run out to rush to the emergency room. She just said, "Hello," and sat in the small living room with us and watched the session. Mom had no questions for me and spoke little. Her presence made me very nervous, though I wasn't sure why. We discussed getting Brenda into the program at the Center. I wanted it for her. I gave Mom a copy of the annual progress report for her and listed all the new skills that she had acquired. The report was hard to believe, as few children made such progress after only a few months.

Right after the December break, my back went out. This would mean a minimum of a week in bed. They sent a replacement for me—a young white woman. The woman walked into the foyer where the young men hung out. She would have to pass through them as they sat on the stairs with the music blasting. I was told that the woman immediately turned and ran out of the building. Uh, so no replacement for Brenda, and she would have to wait two weeks.

When I returned, she had forgotten nothing. We picked up from where we left off. I noticed how much better she looked physically. Her left eye was no longer closed. She had put on weight. By the end of February, she was following instructions, requesting things with words, laughing a lot, and we began doing complicated things like puzzles and other manipulatives that took thought to operate, like dressing a doll and combing her hair. Her mother had made one more visit, and I was surprised to see that Brenda wanted to be with her mother. I was not sure if she even knew her, but she would cry when Mom walked out of the room. I guess there was a lot going on that I was simply unaware of. I had misjudged the mother. She was evidently serious about turning her life around and getting her kids back.

As a result of Brenda's last progress report, the Special Ed offices decided, in their infinite wisdom, to reduce her services. I would henceforth see her twice a week for an hour. They also wanted her to enter a special education program with another agency. That meant our time together would be limited and probably not last much longer. Fortunately, all changes require a lot of paperwork, and that takes a lot of time. I had her until the end of March and then I could no longer work with her, as she would go into a new program with a different agency.

She had made amazing progress between November and March! She had gone from a pathetic-looking abandoned rag doll to a happy, communicating little girl ready for school. How much improvement was due to me and how much was due to her going into a nurturing environment, I can't say. There's no question that moving with Sally to their aunt and uncle's apartment made a huge difference. I never saw Sally all the time I worked with Brenda. I was also very encouraged to see that Brenda wanted to be with her mother and that her mother seemed to be turning her life around. Her aunt and uncle thanked me and said that I had made her into a talking machine. Getting paid for our work is nice, but results like these are the only reason therapists do this kind of work, if they are genuine.

Just a side note. Vince and Nikki went to work every day. The babysitter for the girls was their fourteen-year-old daughter. I asked the girl one day if she ever went to school. She turned away from the computer games she played all day and said, "I don't play dat." Uh, okay. I wondered whether I was mandated to report this. Again, social services were heavily involved, so certainly they must be aware of the situation. I just felt bad for the girl, as she was obviously not on a good path.

Lacy Ann

Lacy Ann is a perfect example of why I never know if the evaluation team of professionals are correct in their assessments. Lacy Ann was exactly two years old when I started with her. Her parents were Latino, not married, so Dad wasn't around much. In fact, I never met him. They lived in a huge, public housing apartment building. Mom worked as a teller in a bank. Mom told me that everyone spoke to Lacy only in English.

Lacy presented as the typical child on the spectrum: no eye contact, no words, just sort of floated around the room looking at everything, attending to nothing. She did not respond to her name and did not seem to understand language. I started working with her on November 28 expecting the usual sorts of responses one would expect with a two-year-old on the spectrum.

Lacy was also very much afraid of anyone unfamiliar. I figured this little girl was going to take a lot of time to get close to. Amazingly, however, one month later she was using words, following directions, engaging in play, and responding to language and people. She just got better and better as the days went by. She had some quirks to be sure. She might bolt out of the chair and refuse to come back. She might suddenly jump up startled if I made a move she was not expecting. In other words, she could work, engage, respond, but she was still cautious around people other than family. Was it our work that "brought her out of it," or had she been misdiagnosed?

She was not doing as well at the Center. There was a lot of tantruming, I was told. At home, she was scoring high on her programs but not at school. This is not atypical. A lot of children are comfortable and relaxed at home but not in a noisy, brightly lit, crowded, and unfamiliar classroom. Her inconsistent scores on programs between home and the Center made it difficult for the teacher to write new programs or to update old ones. I could not follow the program book after about six months at all because she was bored with them at home, as she quickly mastered them. But they had to continue doing them at the school, as her scores were low.

I convinced the teacher and the supervisor to let me write my own programs for her at home and not to try and "generalize" her school programs from the Center environment to the home environment.

A word about "generalization" is needed here. Often, children on the spectrum who learn a skill in one environment will not exhibit that skill in a different environment or with a different person. Generalization was one of the early criticisms of the ABA method. It was claimed that children learned, like animals, to perform "on stage" (in the therapeutic environment) but not at home, or on the street. "Generalization skills" had to be programed. In New York, a child was taught in the school environment, and to make sure that generalization took place, the same programs were used in the home environment. The hope was that the parents would also practice those programs and reinforce newly acquired skills.

Asking the supervisor to allow me not to do the programs at home, not to generalize her learning, was an unusual request. So, I filmed a session at home to show the classroom teacher how Lacy Ann was doing at home. What they saw amazed them. This little girl who refused to work in the Center, who tantrumed often and for long periods, was responding at home like a typically developing child. Obviously, I am not a magician and can only account for the difference in performance by considering that Lacy Ann simply was not used to the classroom, and all the stimulation was just too much for her. What else could it be? I was given permission.

We worked now only on language. Particularly "wh" questions. Where, who, and that particularly hard one, "why?" By May, seven months after we started working together, she was pretty much responding at age level with all but expressive language. Her receptive language was fine. I asked Mom to have her re-evaluated. Mom took my advice, and the new evaluation said that she did not need as many services. Things changed after that. Mom cancelled a lot of sessions, or Lacy Ann was asleep when I got there. I did not get paid for these sessions, and business is business. I was losing a lot of money and really thought that she only needed speech therapy at this point. I asked them to find a replacement for me who could work with her at a later hour in the day, after her nap. My only concern was that a replacement, if not experienced, might try to do the old "discrete trial" teaching with her that bored her to death and caused tantrums. But that was not my concern. My concern was helping children progress.

Lacy Ann went as far as I could take her, and there were plenty more children on waiting lists who needed therapy. Very rarely does a child with her diagnosis progress so rapidly. Was it autism?

Lanny

The question often arises in Autismland, "What do you mean by success in therapy?" Does success mean fully recovered? Does it mean that the child talks now? Does it mean, "He's doing much better!" It's pretty clear what "failure" means. But what does "success" mean?

Thirty some years ago, the man who started the techniques used primarily by ABA people, Professor Ivar Lovaas, claimed a forty-seven percent success rate.[2] By that, he meant the child was indistinguishable from typically developing children. Forty-seven percent? Are you kidding me? The whole autism world said that he was either a bold-faced liar, that he'd completed his studies with children who were very high functioning to begin with, or somehow he'd skewed his numbers. In young children with autism, almost fifty percent of the population is indistinguishable? C'mon!

Ever since then, I've never really been able to answer what "success" means. Lanny is an example. He is a child I would call a success, but to others who met him, they probably would wonder whether my numbers weren't a little skewed as well. He was two years and eight months old when we began. We worked together for eleven months. He was non-verbal when we started, and he was non-verbal when we finished. He did not master any of the goals his teacher wrote for him in his programs. At the Center, he did not progress at all. He was extremely difficult to work with there, tantrumed, cried, self-injured, and would avoid any attempt at eye contact. He did not point, he did not imitate, he did not attend. In the beginning, it was the same with me.

Lanny lived with his mother, father, grandmother, two aunts, and a seven-year-old sister in a big, beautifully furnished attached house on a major street in Brooklyn. His father was a Black, American-born man, and the rest of the family was from "the Islands." Grandma was a nurse. Mom had a successful catering business, and Dad was a fashion designer in Manhattan. This was Mom's first child. The parents were initially cautious with this White Jewish man who would be his therapist, every day, for two hours, over the course of the next year.

Mom or Dad initially sat in every session. They were also a bit nervous because Lanny loved to just sit on the bed, with a pillow or covers over his head. Any attempt to get him off of the bed would most likely lead to tantrums, SIBS, or striking out. Because the only room available to work in was the room where his parents and he slept, the bed was going to be my greatest adversary. I had to be more attractive to him than the comfort and security of his bed and pillow.

We started the last week of September. He was not yet enrolled in the Center program. Our first month was pretty much just trying to get him off the bed and to sit at the table with me. He wasn't very interested. He repeated words occasionally but for his own stimulation, not to communicate with me. Still, I was glad that he could do that! We worked hard on eye contact, but it was definitely not moving. His first day at the Center was a month later in mid-October.

Little by little, we were building a rapport. He really liked rough and tumble play on the bed, so we indulged in that often. It brought eye contact and laughs. He had the cutest laugh I'd ever heard. There was a sweet little boy under all that difficult behavior!

Occasionally, words would pop out: fish, star, triangle, up. He quickly learned how to put pieces in Mr. Potato Head. He could do five-piece puzzles. Occasionally, he would do something, such as looking directly into my eyes and say things like, "triangle," when he picked one up.

At the Center, things were not going well. Not at all. Unfortunately, he had the one teacher who was, in my opinion, in the wrong business. She was a rookie, fresh out of training, and during her training, I was thoroughly unimpressed and then shocked when they actually hired her to be a teacher. But what could I tell Mom—your son's teacher is worthless? Mom was smart enough to quickly learn that for herself, as she saw him crying or screaming in class day after day.

The last thing I wanted was to go to war with the classroom teacher. It's a tragedy, therapy wise, when team members don't get along. The parent is trapped between the teacher and the home therapists, both of which are telling her something different. Who should she believe? Not to mention that this teacher knew I did not like her professionally, and the supervisor who hired her would back her no matter what the problem. It may have been best for me to simply be replaced, but I saw Lanny making progress. I saw great potential. I did not want him to get stuck with such a bad teacher, with silly programs, and a home therapist who would do, without question, whatever the teacher instructed.

I decided to "just do and score the programs," as the teacher wrote them, to keep the teacher and supervisor happy (have to have that data!) and continue to work on what I thought he needed, secretly keeping my own scores.

The teacher continued to write simple, beginner programs, and he scored one hundred across programs at the Center, as all the responses were physically prompted. The teacher was not updating the programs. Not updating programs means that he is being "taught" to do the same things he's already mastered day after day. Boring. Boredom is the biggest enemy of children on the spectrum—or any child, for that matter. But if a child is non-verbal and has no communication skills, the only way that boredom can be communicated to others is through tantruming, crying, and shutting down. That's all he did at the Center. I showed Mom the scores he was getting at school—which indicated that he had mastered them, and they should be updated—She suggested that she should contact the teacher, as the teacher would not read or write in the communication book between us.

By New Years, he was making much better progress. He was able to ID pictures in a field of three. He was verbally labeling some pictures and objects. He quickly learned puzzles up to eight pieces. He was doing imitation with objects, such as feeding baby with bottle and playing piano. He could label the entire alphabet. He would sing along with me the first line of "Old McDonald" and "The Wheels on the Bus." Great! Mom and I were thrilled.

It was obvious now that Lanny understood far more than it appeared. The therapeutic trick with Lanny was that he liked manipulating things. He liked putting things together: Legos, puzzles, magnets. The thing to do was to use this interest and build programing for skills around these activities. He loathed following discrete trial teaching, such as the teacher saying, "Do this," and touching his nose. These kinds of things (called "non-functional) bored him to death, and he tantrumed whenever a therapist tried to "prompt" him to do them.

The problem was that this sort of teaching was all his teacher knew. That's all she had been taught, and so she kept writing these programs, and I was to keep trying to get "correct" responses and write down the scores so she could graph the data. I kept telling the teacher that his continual tantruming at school was due to a program that was not good for him. She insisted, as unfortunately so many do, that if you just "increase the amount of reinforcement," you will get correct, consistent responses to the stimulus. Skinner proved that with pigeons! So why was he tantruming at school? I didn't ask.

By mid-February, he was repeating words more often and had greatly increased joint attention, as he often looked in my eyes either for guidance or to make sure I was enjoying what he was enjoying. He was imitating and able to identify pictures and objects, though he wasn't thrilled with those kinds of activities. One day, he slammed his hand on the table and said, "No!" I was excited! A direct, verbal communication. Good sign. It appeared to me that he understood language far more than his behavior indicated. With non-verbal children, it is often hard to determine why a child won't do something. Does he not understand, or is he simply not interested? He desperately needed a way to communicate. I made him a simple communication board to express his desires. I took pictures of things that he liked and placed them, two at a time, on a board, and he could now point to the one that he wanted.

I sent a note to his teacher that I had begun using a communication board with him and that he had learned rather quickly to point to the picture of the item that he wanted. I explained to her that functional communication was the best way to replace inappropriate behavior. (Anyone with an autism background was familiar with a landmark paper by Carr and Durand called, "Replacing inappropriate behavior with functional communication."[3] It was standard reading for students.) As she had no background other than a special education degree, she was not familiar with the paper or the concept.

I filmed a session with Lanny and me and Mom using the board to show her and the supervisor. The teacher said that they couldn't use it at school! She suggested using a PECS[4] picture exchange communication system) program and promised to begin initiating it soon.

His slow but sure progress at home continued. There was no progress at school. Something had to be done! The teacher was angry because I was not following the programs she wrote for Lanny nor taking data on them. That was why he was not progressing at school according to her. To me, there was no point. He was scoring 100's at home.

The ABA supervisor called requesting a meeting with all the therapists to "get us on the same page." I agreed, though I saw no point, as the teacher, Jane, was a newcomer, ignorant, and a cry-baby. It got heated, as the supervisor was really just a spokesperson for Jane and kept criticizing everything I said. In the end, however, they rewrote some of the programs according to what I suggested. The fact that Mom also did not like this teacher is probably why they acquiesced. Or maybe it's because the teacher was able to swallow some pride and admit that what she was doing simply wasn't working.

Lanny shut down after this meeting to "get us all on the same page." At the Center, he continued to cry, tantrum, and try to "escape," as they say in ABA land. Mom was angry and complained to the supervisor. The supervisor told me that Mom was causing a lot of trouble! She argued with the teacher and complained about the sudden lack of participation by Lanny and his increasing aggression. The other problem our supervisor had with her was that Mom told the other mothers in the waiting room daily that she had the best home therapist, and it was too bad they didn't have him. So, the problem was not boring programs that had no function, it was that his mother complained too much.

I continued trying to work at the table to do his Center-based programs for the sake of peace. He mostly refused and objected by crying or trying to avoid me until it got to a point where I couldn't take it anymore. I could not torture him anymore with discrete trial teaching when it was so obvious that this was not the way to go with him. I decided to follow his programs for the next two weeks until the Passover break just to "get a baseline" of how his program was working, knowing full well that it would show how inappropriate it was. After Passover, I decided that things would change, supervisor or no supervisor.

I had to find something that Lanny really enjoyed, and his mother suggested music. Usually with children on the spectrum, the song, "Barbara Ann" by the Beachboys is a big hit. "Bah Bah Bah, Bababa-rann." It's simple, rhythmic, and consistent. Lanny did not like it. Mom suggested classical music. I had to think of a classical piece that was like that, and one came to me: "Musette" by Bobby McFerrin and Yoyo Ma.[5] I played it, and Lanny was mesmerized by it. He wanted to hear it over and over. His attention to the screen was immovable. It didn't matter to him whether we were sitting on the bed or at the table, as long as the music was on.

The next thing I tried was making things out of magnets. He quickly mastered complicated structures and was also transfixed by this. Another toy he really liked was a drill set—a real electric drill made out of plastic with different colored screws to screw into a board to make shapes, objects, and patterns.

Then a miracle happened. After nineteen years, the supervisor quit! It would take time to find a new one, but in the meantime, I did not have to worry about the teacher whining to the supervisor that, "Ben's not doing the programs." Lanny had until September 1 with me, and I was going to use those last few months to get him to progress doing things he enjoyed and throwing away the program book and the data sheets.

Things were going well. Lanny enjoyed the sessions, and Mom was happy. A new problem emerged, however. Lanny had not been going to school. I got a call from the service coordinator to ask me what was going on with his absences. I had to tell her the truth. Mom was not happy with what she was seeing at the Center. She found no help from talking to either the teacher or the supervisor and so had decided to stop sending him. I had advised Mom to put her complaints in writing so that she would not be later accused of refusing services. The city would never work with her again if they thought that she was "bucking the system."

She put it all in writing. The service coordinator talked to the new supervisor. The new one had a master's in special education and was board certified in ABA, the same as me, though with considerably less experience than myself. I asked her how long one should keep a program if they see that there is no progress? I suggested two weeks, and she said, "That's about right." So, I showed her that Lanny's programs had not been updated for two months!

We had only six weeks left now. The PECS program the teacher had promised never happened. It no longer mattered to me. He was communicating with his board, and more importantly, he was repeating a lot of words. He was now singing along to Barbara Ann. He sang it all the time. We accomplished many goals by working with building objects. He had to request a piece, he had to take turns, he had to put them in by color and shape. He had to find them. "Lanny, where is the red one?" It was behind, under, in back of things. He was laughing, making eye contact, and there was joint attention. In short, he was doing great.

He still had to endure the OT a few times a week. He often tantrumed with her. This was unusual for an OT, as they're basically harmless, but this one had angered him by taking away his iPad one day. I made sure that he had no iPad around on the days I came.

The school year ended, and now, five years later at the time of this writing, his mother still sends me updates via video. He is talking, enjoying his new school, and participating in programs. Mom is thrilled. When I left him, he was still scoring very low on professional evaluations, did not use speech to communicate, and was still very much in his own little world, but I considered him a success because of the progress and change in personality.

His mother continues to work very hard on his language skills, and I expect he will do great things in the future.

CHAPTER TWO

A Few More Successes

Elan

I worked with Elan for exactly two months—April 17, 2005, to June 17, 2005. Taking a case in April is not a good sign. Children usually start their programs in September. The Center's service coordinator inquired if I could see him once a week. I always said "no" to such requests because if I take a child for one day a week, that means that my usual five-day-a-week child has to give up one day. Worse, if another child is offered to me to work with, I won't be able to do a regular five-day week because of this one-hour interfering with the schedule. That means I would have to give up a five-day program for a one-hour-a-week program. That would mean losing almost a week's pay for one child, and it just wasn't economically feasible.

I said, "Sorry. Can't do it." The service coordinator was very insistent, and when she told me that he only lived two blocks away from me and I could see him on Sunday, I accepted. One hour Sunday morning, in the summer, when the kid is only two blocks away, was not going to interrupt anything. Yet, what can you do with a child, supposedly on the spectrum, one hour a week? Why did he need that anyway? Strange.

The service coordinator told me that the parents were very demanding, and what they wanted was someone to do make-up sessions. Evidently, the people who were doing his regular program were not showing up consistently, and they had seen no progress in the child. His behavior while in therapy and when not in session was out of control. Mom was a medical doctor, and Dad was some kind of researcher. It seemed to me that Dad had what they used to refer to as "Asperger's syndrome," and Mom was a bit weird. They were Orthodox Jews, like me. I was supposed to work with him until September.

During our first session, the parents hovered around almost the entire session trying to help. "C'mon, Elan, you can do that! Say 'ball,' Elan," as if their encouragement was all he needed to succeed. I found him to be a beautiful child and very bright. He knew colors; numbers; the alphabet; how to imitate; and how to draw lines vertically, horizontally, and in circles. He had good receptive language and occasionally made spontaneous verbal requests. His mother told me that he has "sensory issues," such as sound sensitivity, skin sensitivity (he won't sit on a plastic chair unless clothed), won't wear shorts, covers his ears a lot, and toe walks.

Our first session went well, despite his parents interfering. He enjoyed it and had fun. It was apparent from the notes left by previous therapists that the child was not getting quality services. There was no program book! No programs? So, what were they doing with him all this time? How did different therapists know what and how to teach? Where was the data collection? What was the speech teacher working on? How did therapists communicate with each other in order to incorporate each other's goals into their programs? Where was the supervisor? Very strange. This blew me away. They had wasted two years of this child's time!

After a few weeks of my working with Elan, Mom called to ask if I could replace the other therapist or could "make up your hours."

I didn't know what she meant by the latter. In any case, I felt so bad for this boy that I returned the call to say that I could work on Friday's and Monday's as well as our arranged Sundays. I could do this because he had so many make-ups to fill.

The first thing I did was write a program book for him and explained to the parents how an ABA program is supposed to work. Specific skills are targeted, and data is taken on successful achievement or lack thereof of those goals. If successful, the teacher would update or write new programs. If unsuccessful, they would determine whether he was capable or not. If not, it was not an appropriate program for him.

Next, I made a communication book for all therapists to read and write in. I had a page for their names, telephone numbers, days, and hours of service. Without that, therapists have a million excuses, such as, "Well, I usually don't work that day." Or "The other therapist is coming during my sessions." When you write everyone's hours down in the book, there are no excuses! The parents were impressed. I told them that they shouldn't be, as programs, data, and communication are standard parts of any good ABA program.

Elan had some strange behaviors—at least they would be in the typical world but are actually pretty common in Autismland. He was a toe walker. He covered his ears often. He would not sit on plastic surfaces if he did not have pants on (that is, when wearing only a diaper). He would not wear short pants. He ate only pizza, and it had to be cut into small pieces and hand fed to him. These things are very familiar to parents who have children on the spectrum and to experienced therapists. But it was new to these parents. They made the mistake of asking the OT about these things. They got the standard OT answer: "He has sensory issues." No kidding. The mother said that because of his "sensory issues," he could wind up an alcoholic or in jail. She was serious. I told her that he was going to go to cheder (Jewish day school), grow up normally, go to college, and work for NASA.

After a long talk with the parents, I was able to convince them that all the OT nonsense was just that. But I wanted to prove it. I slowly raised his long pants to knee level and showed his mother that he could tolerate short pants. She said, "Well, sure, when he's distracted."

I explained that it's not a "sensory issue," or he'd be screaming. He simply doesn't like it, and I don't like wearing shorts either. He also began to wear t-shirts, which he'd never tolerated before. I just engaged him in a favorite activity, and if he wanted to continue, he had to wear shorts and a t-shirt. As far as having to cut his pizza and hand feed it to him, I asked Mom to just leave a slice on the table. Sure enough, he grabbed it and fed himself with no problem. As far as covering his ears and running out of the room, I taught him to say, "Noisy," and ignore it.

The covering of the ears, I had learned from reading, *The Siege: The first eight years of an autistic child*, by Clara Claiborne Park,[6] that her daughter Jesse used to cover her ears when she heard something she liked. "Too good," she would say with a big smile but still, covered her ears. I experimented with Elan and found that such was the case with him as well. He covered them when he heard something that he liked and something that he didn't like. I did not see this as a problem.

Another "sensory issue" that he overcame was gross motor activity. Initially very much afraid of being lifted, swung around, tickled, or anything remotely similar, he came to love these things. That was the end of his "sensory issues."

Mom was doing much better with daily behaviors and teaching him things like getting dressed, eating, brushing his teeth, speaking instead of whining, etc. After two months, he was a different child. I asked Mom what she attributed his unusual progress and good behavior to. She said that she was getting firmer with him. I told her that was correct and that I saw very little wrong with this kid, if anything. I told Dad as well that, in my opinion, he's fine, and I would not call what I do with him "therapy." More like play.

On paper, I was still just doing make-up sessions. Once they were completed, I could not continue to work with him. He had until September, and Mom wanted me to continue. "Maybe you can replace the other therapist?" I couldn't, of course, because I had other children and did not have the hours. Perhaps I could have convinced the service coordinators to make the switch, as per the mother's request. Mom could simply fire the other guy. But I told her the truth instead, which was that from what I saw, Elan was a pretty normal child. He was certainly more intelligent than most kids his age, his communication skills were now age appropriate, and "I simply don't know what else I could do for him." That was my last day. I knew I was going to miss this remarkable child.

Elan Noam

This is hardly a success story, as I was only with him one month, from mid-December to mid-January, and didn't do much. Unlike most of my kids, Elan lived in a very wealthy, White neighborhood. As a rule, I did not like taking cases in such environments. I found working in the hoods much more enjoyable, and the parents there were usually very trusting and grateful. I seldom found that to be the case in wealthy homes. (My apologies to my rich families who were grateful!)

It was a bizarre case where I was his main therapist, but I did not write the programs nor make any therapeutic decisions. A woman named Helga was in charge. Helga was a very experienced, highly qualified professional. She also had an adult brother with severe autism. He had been placed years ago in a home for people with his condition. I was there simply to implement the plans she wrote.

The other strange thing was that she had been working with him, hands on, and had to stop for some reason, so I was to work with him three hours a day! I never worked with any child more than two. If the child is "low functioning" (again, I hate that expression), then it gets quite boring after a half hour. If he's "high functioning," three hours is a long time to spend with a child who does not need a lot of service.

Elan Noam was really not a "high functioning" autistic—he was pretty much typically developing. How he received a diagnosis of autism, I'll never know. But then, that was a problem with the PDD/NOS diagnosis. You could make anybody fit in, including your cat.

Mom really had only one problem. Her little blue-eyed, blond-haired angel was spoiled rotten. This is a very unprofessional concept to say! We are supposed to say, "Child exhibits escape behavior when presented with undesirable requests." We are supposed to say, "Child's symptomatic rigidity of routine prevents flexibility in daily living skills." "Due to lack of communication skills, child exhibits tantrum behavior." Sure. But this kid was spoiled.

Mom expressed concern about the discrete trial teaching format. It is rigid, highly structured, and unless you know how to work with children, boring and aggravating for a child—especially children who don't need it. It was obvious to me that Elan Noam definitely did not need it. As I was not running this program, it was not up to me what or how to teach, but I told Mom that after I got a feel for him, I'd see about switching the method. I never did do discrete trials with him.

Mom's two main concerns were his tantruming and his eating habits, or lack thereof. He would not (could not?) feed himself. Elan Noam was a second child. The first was a girl who was typically developing. It seemed to me that Elan Noam, being the first son, was simply pampered, and his unruly behavior was not due to "autism" or "sensory issues," as the OT had claimed to Mom, but just bad parenting.

Mid-December is not a good time to start working with a child. There was usually a week, or longer, break until after New Year's. Establishing a good rapport is the first thing a therapist must do with a child. If the child does not like you, forget it. He won't learn, he won't listen, he won't pay attention to you at all. If it took a month to establish that relationship, without doing any work other than playing, so be it. But ABA people like to see data. It's hard to take data on, "rapport establishment." There was not much point in trying to establish a rapport only to lose it over the break and have to start from scratch after the break. Fortunately, it was quick and easy to build a rapport with Elan Noam.

Mom was nervous about a new therapist. She hovered around a lot. I had different times of day I could work with him. On the third day, I worked with him from five to seven p.m. It was a disaster. His sister was home and wanted to "play" with us. Mom was unable to get her to leave. Mom said that I was "too lenient" with him, and he would, "walk all over me" unless I was more strict with him. I bit my lips, as that is exactly what I wanted to tell her. The reason he behaved like he did—shouting to get what he wanted, tantruming, throwing, etc.—is because those things worked for him! Mom "reinforced those behaviors" due to "negative reinforcement." Negative reinforcement is often confused with "punishment." Punishment decreases behaviors; negative reinforcement increases behaviors. If you take something away from the child and he screams to get it back, and you give in to him, he learns that screaming gets you to leave him alone. Mom learns that it's easier just to give it to him and stop the screaming. Mom is "negatively reinforced" by having the screaming stop. That's what they call "spoiling" in the real world. I would begin to work on this. Here was the plan:

I would take things from him, and when he began to scream, I would say, "No screaming," and, sure enough, he stopped. Simple enough to stop the behavior, but he needed a "replacement behavior," which was to ask, using words, for what he wanted. He was verbal and readily did this. I taught him to say, "stop it" when I did something that he didn't like. It surprised me how easily these things went!

Whenever Mom had to leave the house, she told me he would tantrum, and I should be ready for it. The next morning, as she left to take his sister to school, sure enough, as soon as he saw them putting their coats on, he began to whimper. By the time they got to and out of the door, he was screaming, "No, Mommy, don't leave."

I took him to the door they had just walked out of, pulled back the curtain, and said, "Look, Mommy is going, and then she will come back. Now let's go play." He stopped! No crying, no tantrum, nothing. He was ready to go to work. I had a nice talk with the maid, who was also a primary caretaker. She said that she marveled at the improvements and how much more he related to her and how much easier her job was now. Amazing—nobody's done anything yet! Money for nothing.

The second biggest problem was his not eating by himself. I asked the caretaker to leave his food for me to feed him. It took no time to show him how to eat, and that if he didn't eat by himself, he'd get pretty hungry. "Learned helplessness" is when you do something for a person that he can do himself but "learns" that others can do it for him. That's what was going on here. Fact was, he could do anything that he should be doing at his age level.

I was supposed to work with him until September, but I could not see spending so much time with him. What would we work on? His programs were simply the kinds of things typically developing children would learn. Meanwhile, the service coordinator who assigned therapists to children was pressuring me to work with other children. I couldn't take any more cases because of all the time I had to spend on a child who didn't need it.

After a month, I was pretty much at the end of my patience. Elan Noam simply did not need therapy. His mother did. Well, not therapy, but parent training, as Elan Noam was a pretty normal kid who had, by age two, become the boss in his house. How do you tell a parent that the problem is not the child, it's you? Why hadn't Helga seen this?

On January 9, Mom asked me if I could add an hour! I thought, *Add an hour?* I wanted to drop this case and take two new children who needed it. I really loved working in the poor neighborhoods with difficult children who were a challenge. I was bored and really tired of coming into a rich house and spending hours with a spoiled child who simply did not need it.

I bit my lip and stayed until January 27, and then a miracle happened. My back went out. That meant a minimum of two weeks in bed. I called Helga and told her the "bad" news. She said that she would have to replace me. I told her, "Gee, that's a shame."

Luke

I called him Luki. He was born Christmas Eve, and I started working with him on December 6, just before he turned two. He was very dark skinned and small, like a fourteen-month-old child. He was very cute. He should be in the "very cute" chapter, but his incredible progress makes me put him in this chapter. The formation of his legs appeared to be affected by scurvy. They were pretty bowed. The family doctor said they would straighten out eventually. He could walk, but his gait was very slow. He could not manage on thick carpet or step over anything, no matter how small, to get past it. He did not seem to have much strength in the rest of his body either.

Our start was fairly unsettling to me, as the family—Luke, his ten-year-old brother, and the parents—was essentially homeless. They were staying at the mother's sister's house, who was seldom home, as she attended college full time. The sister lived in a tight, one bedroom apartment with two full grown Dobermans. They had to be locked up when I came. They barked. A lot. Neighbors complained often. The house reeked of the smell of dogs and poop. When I left the apartment, I was covered in dog hair.

Mom said that they were actively looking for an apartment. Dad was a barber, Mom stayed home. However, there were many days when it was me and Dad. Both parents were very friendly and accommodating. Dad was a small Black man, and Mom was a skinny lady almost a head taller than him.

During our first session, Luki and I and the parents all crammed into the tiny living room and sat on the floor. Luki was readily engaged, and while he avoided eye contact, he was able to point to things and manipulate simple toys appropriately. He laughed a lot. He was really like a baby in size and ability, but his nature made him a pleasure to work with. That was fortunate because he had not begun going to the Center yet, and he had no programs to follow. I was not going to write them, as his teacher would be responsible for that when he began school. Until then, I would just probe whatever skills he might have, such as receptive language, imitation, and cognitive ability. I was to see him two hours a day, even after he started school. That's a lot of therapy, but it was clear that he needed it. In spite of that, I thought that he might be gifted, as he was able to draw in straight lines and patterns according to model.

From December tenth until the fourteenth, they canceled. Not a good start and not a good sign! The service coordinator, or SC as we called them, told me that she had not been able to get ahold of Mom. Dad did not answer his phone. Mom also did not respond to my phone calls. Previous experience taught me to run from cases like this. Instability in the home, cancelled sessions, SC unable to make contact, etc., were all indicative of a case going nowhere. But on the fifteenth, when I went to see if they were home they were, so I decided to give them another try. It was a strange day because as we worked, as usual, the dogs were barking continually in a back room and someone was pounding madly on the door. I was home alone with Luki now because his mother had gone to the local grocery store.

Being alone with a child often happens, even though it's illegal. I often found that when working with lower socio/economic families, I often had to also be a babysitter. Moms—especially Moms in the hoods—had other children, no car, and no way to leave a child to go shopping. Often, I was asked if it was okay, "if I run out." Yes, it was illegal. And yes, had I been some kind of pervert, the child could have been in real danger. Fortunately, I was just a working stiff who loved his job and understood how hard life was for these mothers. Something as simple as getting to the store for diapers and milk was often a great challenge. I always let the mother go and never reported it.

But this day, I was startled by the banging on the door. I had to leave Luki on the floor (remember, he couldn't move much) and went down to answer the door. One policeman and one police-woman met me. Their uniforms were not New York City black and white. They were green with big brass badges on them that said something like, "Animal control unit." They had come about a report of abuse of the dogs. I did not know what to do.

I told them that this was not my house, and I couldn't let them in. As they turned to go, they handed me some paperwork to give to the owner and let her know that they would be back to take the dogs. "Uh, okay…." (I hoped they would!)

Luki started school the next week. I saw him a few more times before Christmas break. The dogs were still there. I hated going into that house, but on the break over Christmas, I got my nice Jewish boy's Christmas present: the parents found an apartment! I would see him from now on in their new apartment. It was much bigger, closer to where I lived, and no dogs, thank goodness. They did have a very cute little black and orange snake, but he lived in a terrarium and was very quiet.

Luki and I had a huge room with a lot of windows on the second floor to work in. After Mom got to know me well, she stopped join-ing our sessions. Truth is, two-hour sessions with a two-year-old can be pretty boring, even for parents. Mom spent her time in the living room watching TV, very often on the phone with her mom.

Luki now had a program book from school. He learned quickly, and the teacher, who had twenty other children to write programs for, did not update as quickly as Luke needed. Because he had nowhere near two hours of work program-wise, I started working on his walking. He had a PT who worked with him, but I was not overly impressed, as he brought out the standard equipment—cones to walk between and steps to go up and down. Luke was nowhere ready for that intensive stuff; he could barely walk, and the living room where they worked had thick carpet, making it impossible for Luke.

I took him and Mom to our work room, which had hardwood flooring. We played a game, wherein Luki would run from me to her and back. We would play games with balloons, which he loved. We hit them, or I'd blow them up and let them fly, which he found hysterical. He would run to get them. Then, we transitioned to the living room on the carpet. That was hard. He had to hang on to furniture to walk.

One day, the mother told me that Luke was afraid to go into the kitchen. "Something in there scares him, and he cries when I try to get him to come in." I doubted it. I carried him into the kitchen, and there was no response. Nothing. Mom came in to see his reaction, and it was clear that he had no fear. "Well, that's weird," she said, "he'll never come in for me." I looked at the floor and saw the problem. The living room had thick carpet, and the kitchen floor met the living room floor at a divider that jutted up about a half inch over the door jamb that separated the rooms.

I sat him on the living room floor, pulled a balloon out of my pocket, and then sat down on the kitchen floor. I blew it up and offered it to him. With great effort, he tried to get over that ledge. Mom saw the problem immediately. He simply could not make the step up to the kitchen, and when she tried to coax him, it made him cry. He was non-verbal! This sort of thing happens very often in Autismland. We try to read psychological fictions into physical inabilities or what look like emotive behaviors. He simply had no way to communicate that he needed help getting over the terrain. He was not afraid; he was frustrated.

We did not work the last week in December, and another week was missed in the first half of January and almost another in the latter half. A lot of these absences were due to either my being sick or someone in the family being sick. In either case, Luke was missing a lot of therapy. I inquired if I should continue with this case, as there were absences and inadequate communication between parents and the SC. I really liked this little boy, so I wanted to continue. I saw a lot of potential and did not want to trust his therapy to a rookie replacement. We began from scratch in February.

By the second week in February, he had mastered walking on different textures. I would work with Mom on feeding because he would only drink milk and refused all food. I was surprised that the Center did not offer assistance with this. This was very unusual, as the service coordinators were usually on top of things like this. I knew the SC for this case, Bessy, and she was one that I could always depend on for efficiency and dependability. I don't know how food refusal was missed here. It could be that Mom never mentioned it during the evaluations. I was also not happy with his programs. They were way too easy for him. They took ten minutes, and I had two hours a day with him. There was no communication book between teacher and therapists.

By the middle of March, there had been some significant progress. First, he began filling in the word, "hey" in the song, "Jingle Bells." Next, he began to repeat words, spontaneously. As I had no contact with the speech teacher at the Center, and there were no programs for "verbal imitation" or "oral motor imitation," I just wrote my own, kept my own data, and let those at the Center do whatever they were doing. Of course, this is a disaster for children on the spectrum, as all therapists need to be "generalizing" his progress from environment to environment. What could I do? The teacher did not respond, the Center's supervisor was the teacher's good friend, and if I reported anything, I knew it would go nowhere.

At the end of March, we had a team meeting with the Center staff and the parents. It's never a good idea to get into a confrontation with the teacher in front of the parents, so, unusual for me, I kept quiet the whole meeting. What could I say? "He's doing great at home and terrible at the Center?" Or "He's beginning to use words at home and at the Center he is still showing no verbal skills?" I said nothing, but after the meeting, I asked the teacher why his programs were still on a basic level and why there were no updates. She said that he was not scoring well at the Center, and she suggested that the reason was due to lack of attendance.

What? They hadn't been sending him to school? That explains why the data sheets were not filled in. I was astonished. "You mean, they have not been sending him to school, at all?" She answered, "Rarely."

That answered a lot of questions for me. I saw him for two hours every day in his home. We had a strong rapport. I understood him very well. At the Center, assistants work with the children, and they switch children a lot in order to ensure that the child generalizes across instructors. Luke was, no doubt, simply ignoring this new stranger every day and would not attend or respond.

The next day, I called the SC. "Did you know that Luke has not been coming to school?" Bessy replied, "What? No! How long has this been going on?" I told her that I don't know because the teacher does not read or write in the communication book, and it was she that should have informed the SC a long time ago. I was furious. This is not how to run a quality autism program. The teacher and I had small wars about the communication book in front of the supervisor. There is no question that it is hard for a teacher to read and write in twenty communication books. For that reason, most therapists don't write much unless they have a question about the programs. Most therapists also just followed the programs with no questions. They let the data do the talking. But in this case, there was no data, as he wasn't going to school! I should have been informed after three days. I made sure that both the teacher and the SC knew I was angry about this.

Now I had to do the one thing I hated most: confronting the parents. It is hard to confront parents who are in a lower social economic status. Such parents have their hands full. They don't have money to send their child by taxi if they miss the bus. They can't just "hop in the car" and drive them because there is no car. Often, there is no father, making the burden on the mother impossible. I don't know how they do it! In Luki's case, I simply did not know that he was not going to school.

I asked Mom, "What's up with Luki not going to school?" She said, "He goes!"

I showed her the attendance sheets from school. "Close to fifty percent absence."

I told her that I couldn't promise Luke would make any progress if he didn't go to school every day. She vowed to be more consistent. Fortunately, she was, and his learning began to reflect that. By June, he was spontaneously using words to name pictures and objects. He repeated words that he heard for fun. It was obvious that he understood language completely but still had problem saying words. The programs at the Center were a waste of time. I wrote as much to the teacher, who updated with programs that were also below his level.

I was happy now. Luke was moving, his speech was getting a bit better, and I essentially just ignored his program book. He no longer required programs for discrete trial teaching, which is the normal fare for children in such programs. At home we did NET, or natural environment training. Whatever interested him, that's what we did. We included his mother a lot. Balloons, bubbles, running after each other (on carpet), etc. He was really flourishing.

Toward the end of July, Mom was not home much, and neither was Luke! I would show up, and no one would answer the door. I didn't ask. I figured that his mother saw that whatever this "autism" stuff was all about, it's not about that anymore.

In the middle of July, I got a call from the teacher. "How come Luke has not been coming to school?" Yeah. Sure. I was not going to discuss this with Mom again. The SC said that Mom never answers the phone, never returns calls, and so she was also not going to put any more effort into trying to contact her. Usually, a child would be removed from the Center for this, but fortunately, they kept him, and I continued with him. There was probably too much paperwork involved to drop a kid. We didn't have much time left, as he would age out at the end of the next month.

On August 8, with three weeks left in his program, the SC said that they'd found him a speech teacher. Now? He'd been without all this time, and in spite of that, he was making good progress with speech. He was asking and answering questions with one-word sentences. We had spent the last three weeks running around the house and playing games. He had to use words to play, and to watch him now was pure joy. His parents were thrilled. Then, he turned three, and we parted.

A side note: I used to sleep in my car between children. I never had any time for breaks during the day. One child might be in Coney Island, south Brooklyn, and the next, in north Brooklyn, so there was travel time as well as session time. If I was lucky, I could eat lunch or catch a short nap on any given day. One day, a few years after I had finished with Luke, I was passed out somewhere in Brooklyn (I don't remember where now). Suddenly, there was a loud banging on the hood. I jumped up to see a small Black man with a beard banging on my hood. *Okay, what's this?* I thought. I jumped out of the car, and the man gave me a big bear hug. It was Luke's father.

"Ben, you have to come and see Luke. You won't believe it. You HAVE to come!"

I said, "Uh, well…"

He went on excitedly. "All he does is read! He's the smartest kid in his class!"

I took down the new address and told him that, for sure, I'd stop by. I meant it, but it never happened, as life got in the way. In any case, I was not surprised at all that Luke was a genius…

Hank

Hank was a cute little guy. Very little. Short and sweet, as they say. He had light skin and deep, dark eyes. Beautiful smile. He was a very busy, very happy little boy and the first child for Mom and

Dad. They lived in a beautiful old apartment on New York Avenue on the second floor. Well, Mom lived on the second floor with her sisters and a man friend of one of the sisters and a teenaged brother. Dad lived upstairs with his mother. Downstairs were other relatives. They had the whole building.

The parents were young. Dad worked for UPS working nights and sleeping days while Mom stayed home with Hank. I thought it a bit strange for Mom to live on one floor and Dad on the other, but they weren't married, and I was not sure what exactly their relationship was. It was none of my business. They were a Black family from "the Islands," and everybody there treated me like a member of the family.

We began in November in 2008. On our first session, Hank made no eye contact. In fact, he was gaze avoidant (would purposefully avoid eye contact if you tried to make it). He walked on his toes and seemed not to understand language, as he didn't respond to questions or instructions. In short, typical symptoms of autism.

Mom was with us the entire session, with Dad passing in and out of the room. Hank did respond to balloon and bubble play and would do some simple, one step instructions, such as, "Give this to Mommy." I also saw at that first session that he was hyperlexic. Here is how that discovery was made. As I was getting to know him and getting info from Mom on his history, she told me that if she took him into the kitchen, where the ABCs were on a page on the fridge, and she pointed to a letter, he'd say what it was in response to the question, "What letter is that?" It was not just a rote repeating of them, such as singing along to the ABC song; he knew them all in isolation. He would not do this anywhere else in the house. In other words, if you were in the living room with a book and pointed to a letter and asked him what letter it was, he would not respond. So that told me something: He had "rigidity of routine." That meant he'd do something in one room, one way, but nowhere else. I had an idea. I took the page into the living room and held it up on a wall. Then I asked him what letter I was pointing to, and he correctly responded every time. Mom sat in a little chair next to us as we did this. I got another idea. I drew a circle, a triangle, a square, and other shapes on a piece of paper, held it up to the wall, and asked him, "What shape is this?" Again, correct every time. Mom jumped up out of her chair and screamed! He had never said anything but letters before. We did it with numbers as well, no problem. I had a feeling that he was going to learn to use phonics to put letters into words soon, though I'd never had a child so young do that before.

Mom worked with us when she was home. She sat right at the table, and after I did a program with him, she would do it—the way it's supposed to be. He performed for her just as well as with me. Occasionally we had to work upstairs by Dad and Grandma. We had just a tiny piece of floor to work on there. Dad was usually asleep but did join us sometimes. Grandma never did. She never watched and never said a word to me. I had to assume that she was one of those, "Ain't nuthin' wrong with that boy," grandmas. No matter, as she didn't interfere.

One of Mom's concerns was his tantruming. Hank, like any two-year-old, did not like it when someone took something away from him or did not allow him to do something that he wanted to do. Doing that was a big mistake a lot of therapists made. Once in a while, I'd also forget and just grab something from him. Naturally, he would start to scream. Hank's first real tantrum with me was upstairs with Grandma when I made that mistake, and I was afraid that she would be upset. She didn't say anything. That also made me nervous.

Things were going well, but his little temper would flair occasionally. As he lived in a house full of adoring adults who always came running to hug him or give him a cookie when he cried, it was easy to reinforce his crying behavior.

I came up with a plan that I hoped Mom and others would use to turn tantrums into requesting. It consisted of working on getting him to give me things that he did not want to give up without tantruming. He did well with it.

Things were going great. This kid was very cute and very autistic. He ran around the room wildly flapping his hands while emitting a high-pitched shriek. While he could name many objects by now, the thought never entered his mind that if he asked somebody for something, verbally, the person would give it to him. Was this a "communication" problem or a "theory of mind" problem? I'd let the researchers worry about that. We would all work on getting him to verbally request things.

Through December, he continued making progress, and our sessions that included Mom were a lot of fun. He even did programs with us that he did not like, such as "block building." This is a higher-level imitation program wherein the therapist takes a number of blocks and makes a formation, and the child is supposed to make the same formation with other blocks. He did not like this and refused to do it at the Center. He didn't like it at home either, but he did it. I filmed it so I could show it to them at the Center, as they did not believe me.

He was doing well with the speech teacher at home as well. She got him to use a lot of words. The OT, however, was another story. Hank would not sit for the OT at all. This was unusual because OTs usually do fun, interesting things, despite the fact that there is not a bit of research to verify any kind of efficacy with children on the spectrum.

Mom did not want to continue with the OT, as Hank would cry when he made any attempt to work with him. On one particular day when I arrived, Mom was nervous, as the OT told her that Hank wasn't sitting and working with him because of "sensory issues." Aha. Another OT, another "sensory issues" fabrication. I told the mother that the next time he says this, ask him, "Which sense, and what's the issue?" She said that she would.

I explained to her that if a movie is boring, no one sits for it. If Hank isn't interacting with the OT, there can only be one reason: The OT is boring him. Don't blame the victim.

Hank continued to improve until the third week of December. Then, there was a two week break at Mom's request. All of her initial fears were dissipating, as she saw so much improvement in so little time. It was obvious to me that he was doing so well at home because Mom took such an active role in his therapy and put into practice the advice on how to get Hank to use words instead of tantrums. But it still frustrated me how this guy was doing so well yet continued to refuse to make eye contact. It's not so much that he refused; it was more like he simply did not understand why he should. I'd just have to keep working on. I didn't want to do drills because then his EC would only be rote responding and have nothing to do with social or communication skills.

After the break, I came back to see that he had forgotten nothing. We picked up right where we left off. He was also asking for things verbally much more often. The programs they were writing for him were way too easy. They bored him but they demand data, so I would quickly run through his programs, write down his scores (always 100 every program), and then work on eye contact and verbal skills at the table and away from it.

Truth is, I wanted to leave this case because it was blatantly obvious to me that while Hank was definitely "on the spectrum," I just didn't see any need for so much therapy. He was in a program at school for three hours a day, plus two hours of ABA at home, speech, and OT. He clearly did not need all that. He was approaching age level with all but speech. We were getting bored with each other. And, as usual, they kept begging me at the Center to take other cases. The only way I could do that was to put a hole in my schedule.

Hank no longer needed an experienced therapist. He was capable of working with anyone if all they did was run the programs. They told me of a child who was much lower functioning and in need of an experienced therapist. That kind of work was more challenging and a lot less boring.

The teacher never wrote in the communication book, so I had no idea what they were doing with him at the Center other than the boring programs written in his book. As far as I knew he was still in the beginner's class doing discrete trial teaching. I thought that this was a terrible waste of his time. I did not want to call the teacher because it was always so hard to get a teacher to answer the Center phone. If it was just a matter of "well call me if you don't understand something," and I could easily get her on the phone, I would do it. But what I usually got was, "One moment, please," and then she was paged to go out of the classroom and find a phone. Most of the time, teachers just didn't do it! This particular teacher seldom answered if I tried to call her on her cell phone.

"Phone was in my purse in the other room." But this had to be addressed. He didn't need me; I didn't know why he was still in the beginner's class, and I wanted to work with a different child who really needed it. This time, I got lucky. The teacher answered her phone and told me that Hank had been bumped up to the intermediate class!

"So why are you still sending programs?" I asked her.

"He still needs one-on-one instruction. He's kind of a not-here-not-there kind of kid," she told me.

This was unusual, but okay, he'd do both. I just could not see continuing with his boring programs at home. I told them that I was not going to do the programs at home. I would work only on what he had problems with, like communication and eye contact, and take my own data. I did not think this would fly with the supervisor, but she agreed.

I brought new toys for him that he loved. One was a little stairway that pushed up little penguins who would then roll down a slide and come back to go up the steps. The noise it made was maddening, but he liked it. The other thing he loved to do, more like an autistic child, was take it out of the box, set it up, take it down, put it back in the box, and repeat the process endlessly. I used that preference to increase his speech by saying, "Okay, which piece do you want now?" and "Where is it?" My "Where is it" program incorporated putting the pieces under things, behind things, next to things, etc.

Another favorite toy was a collection of plastic vegetables and a plastic knife. He could cut the veggies, peal the banana, remove pits, take off leaves. He had to request each vegetable and tell me what he had to do." For instance, "Take out the pit. Peel it."

By the end of April, I simply did not know what else to do with him. He still preferred using echolalia to saying "yes," and he was still gaze avoidant, but those were not things to worry about. When he wanted to look, he'd look. Echolalia may be a problem for a child that is on a lower cognitive level, but I knew he'd drop it the more time he spent in regular ed classes, which I was sure he was eventually going to go into.

In April, he was evaluated for his next school. They said that he was not PDD, but they'd keep the label so he could get services, and they recommended a program that was not so intensive.

Through May and June, he continued to improve. Mom did not participate so much anymore, as she had so many other things to do and did not feel required to be at the sessions.

Hank was now "functioning" like a normal child. I experimented with some higher-level skills called RFFC, or Responding by Function, Feature, and Class. "Give me something you drink with. Show me something that has a handle. Where is some furniture? What animals are on a farm?" This was a little bit harder for him, and I expected he would space out or cry. He didn't like doing it, but he did it. This was a good time to introduce using, "I don't know," but I was afraid because many times once someone learns that response, they'd use it all the time, even when they *did* know, because it's quick and easy.

Our last day was to be August 31, and then he would start his new school. If it weren't for the gaze avoidance and occasional echolalia, no one would know that he'd had an autism diagnosis. He was incredibly smart but was happy to be completely alone. For our last few weeks, we more or less just played.

A Young Black Jewish Girl

I don't remember her name. It was many years ago, and I was only there a few times before I was fired. You know the old expression, "The truth hurts?" It did in this case.

I had a full schedule and certainly was not looking for any work. The service coordinator called and asked if I could see a little girl a few times a week for an hour. I told her, "No. I'm booked." A few times a week is not sufficient for any child, and I would lose money if I had to terminate a five-day-a-week case for a few-day-a-week case." Thanks anyway."

Ayelet, the woman responsible for finding therapists for cases, had heard all this numerous times before, and it was difficult to believe that she didn't know better than to offer me such a case. She switched to plan B. "Aw, c'mon, Ben, you can find a few hours a week to squeeze in! This is an unusual case, and the director wants to make sure someone good goes there," she said.

"Gee. Thanks for the compliment, but all cases are 'unusual.' That's the nature of autism, isn't it?"

"No," she began. "This one is really unusual. It's not clear if this girl has autism, but she was diagnosed PDD (the catch-all diagnosis in those day applied when a child did not meet all the symptomatic criteria).

"What do ya mean, not clear? What do her assessments say?"

She filled me in on the unusual circumstances. This little girl was three years old, Black, and adopted by a Lubavitcher family. Lubavitchers are descendants of Chassidic Jews from Russia—otherwise known as "Ashkenazim," which usually means, White, Yiddish speaking, and followers of their Rebbi. It was extremely unusual that such a family would adopt a Black, gentile girl. I asked why they had done so and was told by the service coordinator that the family had an older girl, about twelve years old, and were medically unable to have any more children. Evidently, it was too difficult to find a Jewish baby to adopt, so they adopted this little girl. None of my business, but what bothered me was that they told me they weren't sure she had autism.

"So, what does she have? What's the problem?"

The coordinator explained that evidently, she "exhibited" extreme tantrum behavior, aggression toward her sister and others, and was unable to socialize as a result. Ah. Great.

I told her, "Send them someone who specializes in behavior disorders. I hate that kind of work!"

Behavior disorder specialists are expected by school boards and parents to come up with a magical plan that will completely change their child's behavior within a week. You even hear such claims made on the radio: "Turn your kid around in one week. Call us!" Or you read research papers: "Adult exhibiting violent aggression. We undertook a functional analysis and determined that lack of communication skills prompted aggression when hungry. We made a communication board with choices for snacks. Client ceased all negative behavior upon implementation." I read tons of such papers. They reminded me of the TV show, "Leave It To Beaver" whereby wise old Dad had all the answers and solved Beaver's tremendous problems with a puff of the pipe and a simple analysis. Sure.

"No thanks."

Not to be put off, she said, "Ben, the director told me that he wants you to take this case." Grr. I owed the director favors to be sure, so I settled.

"Okay. I'll do it." What a pain! This would cut into my gym time.

They lived on Ocean Boulevard. Strange, as most Lubavitchers lived in the Crown Heights section of Brooklyn near the Rebbi's house. It seemed even stranger when I met the family. The parents and older girl were exactly as I expected—typical Orthodox Jewish attire, East European appearance, typical home set up with lots of books around a dining room table used for meals on the Sabbath. The little girl would have fit right in the picture except for the fact that she was Black.

I sat at the table with the family and asked all the usual questions: What's the problem? When does it usually occur? With whom? What have you tried to do about it until this point? Can you pinpoint specific triggers? Describe in detail what the behavior looks like.

They described the behavior as "tantrums," screaming, rolling on the floor, hitting others, biting others, but they had no idea about triggers. It happened with everybody, and they usually just ignored it or said, "Stop that!"

Not sure where to start with her, I took the two girls into another room, and we set up a game that required rolling dice in turns and then moving objects on a gameboard. It appeared that this little girl did not like taking turns. Taking turns meant having to wait more than three seconds, and she did not like waiting. Or so it seemed. When someone rolled the dice, she would immediately reach out and snatch them regardless of whose turn it was. When she grabbed like that, I told her, "It's not your turn" and withheld all access to the pieces.

The first time I did that, she seemed stunned. She looked at me, and I asked her, "Do you know when your turn is?" Maybe she didn't understand what taking turns meant.

I explained that first her sister rolled, and then I rolled, and then it was her turn. We helped her by saying whose turn it was before each roll. When we did that, she had no problem waiting her turn. Hm, well, that was easy. She participated fully and happily! Was it simply a matter of her not understanding? Did I assume that because she had a diagnosis, her behavior was "inappropriate?" Or did she understand and simply refused to wait? I had to think about it.

The next session there, I tried an experiment hoping to give me a better idea of the problem behaviors as reported. I explained to the parents that I really needed to see the behaviors they'd described as, so far, I hadn't seen them. Here is how the experiment went:

I had the parents, sister, myself, and the little girl sit at the dining room table. I asked the mother to give her some ice cream in a bowl. So far, so good. I then told the older sister to simply pick up the bowl of ice cream, carry it into the kitchen, and put it into the freezer. As she carried it into the kitchen, the little girl followed her into the kitchen and out of our sight. Suddenly, we heard a loud howl. The older sister had been bitten on the arm hard enough to draw blood. Then, the little girl was back at the table, calmly eating her ice cream as her sister howled in the other room. I waited for the parent's response. They looked at each other as the older sister came into the room crying.

I looked at the parents. "What just happened?"

"She bit her!" Mom said in shock.

"Yes, I see that," I replied. "Then what happened?"

They stared at me. I told them that, in my opinion, the reason she'd bit her is because biting gets her what she wants. "She bit her sister, and she got her ice cream back. It seems that she has learned that when she bites someone, or hits them, she can get what she wants. She is smart enough to learn that there are other ways, appropriate ways, to get what she wants."

It seemed to me that she was never given either instruction or discipline. In other words, the parents simply were not doing their jobs as parents, but I couldn't say that. "Discipline" has become a dirty word.

I didn't know the little girl's history. Maybe she had been in an orphanage where these things went on all the time. It just seemed to me that she was smart enough to learn appropriate communication and social skills and did not need a therapist for this. It would be a hard job for the parents, but with some training, I was sure everything would change for the better. That's what I told them after my second visit. The next day, I got a phone call from the Center.

"Uh, the family doesn't want you to come back." Fair enough.

CHAPTER THREE

The Ones I Couldn't Help

When I was in graduate school, one of the professors told our class that there would be some children in our careers whom we would not be able to help. The unreachable star, as it were. I was fairly new at the game and very idealistic and remember thinking, "No way! What a terrible thing to say to us! You can always get through, somehow, with something. We can maybe touch their souls if nothing else."

Thirty years later, I have to admit two things: One, that he was right, and the other that it would have saved all of us a lot of pain and frustration had we believed this coming in. Trouble is, when you take on a case with a young child who has an autism diagnosis, you never know "what's in there." The child may be a genius for all you know. Over half the game is trying to figure out how to tap into any potential the child has, as each child is different. It's a living, breathing, beautiful child, and you just cannot accept that there is nothing you can do to get through to him or her.

While visiting my parents in Florida, still new to the business, I saw an ad for a special education teacher in a school in Plantation, Florida. I'd never heard of the place but hopped in the car and drove for two hours to an interview. The manager was a man in his late thirties—a very nice guy, as I recall. He was smiling, upbeat, and positive. He showed me around, and it was clear that he was all set to hand me a contract. Trouble was, it was more of a clinic than a school, and all of the students, of various ages, were quadriplegic, unconscious, or simply sitting strapped into wheelchairs. I asked the manager what I was supposed to teach them. He said, "You don't teach them really. They're just vegetables that you water twice a day." He gave me a wry smile and told me about changing feeding tubes and diapers and operating oxygen equipment. I've no doubt that he had seen the look of shock on my face many times before on the faces of others he'd interviewed. This was my first lesson in reality. Some children, you cannot help. But that's not the case in early intervention children with autism. When you see an eighteen-month-old child with an ASD diagnosis, you see potential. Each child is like a lump of clay, and you are the sculptor. If you have good clay to work with (children on a higher cognitive level), you can work well. If, however, the clay is poorer quality, you will have to adapt and try to work around the poor quality of clay.

You soon learn that reading the child's evaluations probably won't help. Child evals are famous for things like "the child cannot do this, the child cannot do that." They use fancy jargon, and it all looks so scientific and iron clad. It does not take long working in the field to understand that the evaluations are not predictors of progress and are in no way indicative of what this child might be capable of. The one thing the evaluations do accomplish is giving the parents despair.

This chapter will be about all of the children that I could not assist. Children that I was unable to establish a rapport with him. I could not get a smile out of or a one-second glance into my eye. Children that responded to nothing. Or children that screamed and cried non-stop whether I was there or not. Children whose parents had to tell me that it is not working out, sorry, and they would try someone else. Those hurt the most. The cases I will be discussing in this chapter were such that I had full access, support, time, good team members to work with, and helpful parents. Despite all of that, these children were simply beyond reach. At least, my reach. I suppose this chapter will be the "first of its kind" in the autism library for the simple reason that it does not have a happy ending. There was no child "hidden inside" and our miraculous team "got him out." This chapter is one where nothing helped. There may be other books like this out there, but I don't recall seeing any except, *When Snow Turns to Rain* by Craig Schulze.[7] I didn't read it. I was afraid to.

JD

The Marlboro Houses in Brooklyn, New York are much like all of the other NYCHA (called "Nitcha" colloquially) houses. The buildings look like huge monoliths that sprang spontaneously out of Coney Island a bit farther to the west and south. The area where they ominously loom, however, is not a crowd attraction, like its famous Coney Island neighbor. The area is called "Gravesend," and it is most fitting for the huge buildings that sit like massive sepulchers at the end of a long-abandoned path. The area was once very fashionable. Here is a brief description of the houses from *Bklyner Magazine* in 2013. The title is "List of City's Worst Housing Projects, Marlboro Houses list 41st out of 349."[8]

"The Marlboro Houses at 2740 86th Street ranks as the 41st most neglected development under the New York City Housing Authorities' management, with some residents waiting years for repairs for leaking pipes, crumbling walls, and peeling paint, according to a new 'Hall of Shame' list produced by Public Advocate Ben de Blasio. Crumbling ceilings and walls, broken floorboards, and damaged doorways account for just over a quarter of complaints with six hundred and thirty-three on file. The agency has ignored these requests for as long as four years, and an average of two hundred and thirty-one days. But they ignore vermin even longer. Residents have had to live with mice, roaches, and other pests for more than two years."

Funny they say "mice" when far worse, there are scores of rats and rats' nests all around the buildings. The chipped paint is often eaten by children, which no doubt accounts for the reason that our Center serviced a lot of children with lead poisoning. The houses were often in the news, and when they were, it was not for anything meritorious: drugs, murder, violence, gang members, alcohol, graffiti. One had to qualify to live there: that is, you had to be poor or unable to sustain yourself without assistance. Just another one of the "hoods" in NYC.

Small wonder that it was hard to place therapists at the Marlboro Houses. I had been asked to take this case for the same reason I had been asked to take most of my cases in NYCHA houses. No one wanted to go into them. Certainly, no females, unless she was Black, and there weren't very many male therapists.

I received a call from Ayelet, our placement coordinator. "Ben, we have a new case."

"Okay, what's with this kid? Where does he live?"

She was very cagey. "He lives on eighty-sixth street."

Most of eighty-sixth street was White, middle class, blue collar, and near a very busy part of town leading into Coney Island. It sounded like I could fit him into my schedule. I had visions of a nice little house just off of eighty-sixth. It would be tight, but hey, I could use the extra money, and I hate saying no.

If one drove on the busy eighty-sixth street past the stores and coffee shops, one probably wouldn't even notice the Marlboro Houses, as they are set far back from the street.

I had trouble finding them because there was no address that I could see. It wasn't until I was scratching my head wondering at the eighty-sixth street gas station that I looked across the street and back into the distance toward the ocean and saw a bunch of housing apartments. "Oh. That must be it." Parking, as usual, would be a problem.

I found the right set of apartments after passing from "house" to house. Each house was actually a big building, a unit, containing many apartments, seven floors high. All of the entrances had a steel door with thick glass windows on the side to let some light into a dingy lobby. To gain entrance to the building, you had to ring the doorbell and wait for someone on the inside to press the buzzer. That wasn't a problem here, however, as the glass had been broken out, and all one had to do to enter was reach through the pane and push the button on the inside of the lobby. The elevators were immediately on the left. Riding up to the fourth floor, I noticed that there was no lightbulb in the elevator, and the fan in the roof did not work. The apartment being on the fourth floor could have been a curse, but in this building, fortunately, the elevator always worked.

JD was young, twenty-three months, but he looked younger, like a big baby. He ate the same thing every day: SpaghettiOs.[9] These were little circles of pasta in a sauce that came ready-made in a can. You just heat them up. There was another reason for his lack of growth in my opinion. He sat all day, every day, in a highchair facing a video player with cartoons. He ate in that chair, napped in that chair, and that's the only place I ever saw him. The chair was in the living room in a small, two-bedroom apartment. There was no furniture save for a dining table in the living room. The room was squalid and dark.

JD was attended by his fifteen-year-old sister, Shawna. I saw JD at four in the afternoon. Shawna was home from school attending both JD and his four-year-old brother, Jake. Jake had a diagnosis of ADHD, and he literally swung on the chandeliers. The chandeliers were actually overhead lights with cords hanging down, and Jake would swing on them until Shawna screamed at him; or he'd be running around the room trying desperately to get some attention. It was heartbreaking. Mom worked, leaving Shawna to feed the boys, change JD, do her homework, and babysit. The burden on this little girl was tremendous, and yet, she had good grades and took her studies very seriously. She was a petite girl with a broad smile, though I rarely saw it. I had met Mom on the first day, and after that, I rarely saw her, as she worked. They informed me that there was an uncle that resided in the house, but if so, I never saw him.

JD was a ghost child. His eyes glued to the video; he never made a sound. When we began to "work" together, he was always in his highchair. I would turn off the video to begin, but as soon as I turned it off, his eyes went down to the tray of the highchair or up into the corner of the ceiling, and that's where they would remain the entire hour. I could get his attention with nothing. The electric, musical tops stirred nothing in him. The windup toys drew no attention, not even a glimpse in their direction. Even candy, placed on the table in front of him, sat unexamined.

He was in the morning program at the Center, and I asked them how he was doing there. His teacher told me it was exactly the same story there. He would sit in his chair silent, unreachable, attending to nothing. Even in the big playroom that was full of small bicycles, balls, slides, all kinds of rolling things and bouncy things, he did nothing. If you placed him in the tub of plastic balls, he would sit or lay there and not stir a muscle. It was heartbreaking.

At this point, nothing worked to get his attention. I had to break some of my own rules! Don't strap a child in a highchair. Don't use food as a reinforcer. Don't use video as an attention grabber. There was no other way. If I tried to work on the floor with him, JD would sit like a rag doll on the floor, unresponsive, or meander aimlessly. There was nothing in the room to draw his attention other than the video. Out of the chair, I was just a ghost he could not see.

I hated to, but I had to keep him in the chair hoping to get some kind of "stimulus control." After a few weeks, Mom was home, and she sat with us the whole session. She usually slept when she was home and never attended a session. Another therapist from a different agency had started with him, and I was afraid that she told

Mom that I wasn't very good. Could be—there certainly wasn't any progress. He'd just sit there staring at nothing. I felt like this boy was drowning, and I couldn't reach him.

He caught a cold at the end of October, and he remained sick for over two weeks. It was warm in the house, but he'd caught a cold somewhere. Trying to get his attention under these conditions made a difficult job, much harder.

After two months, his "progress" was small. He could not follow one step instructions. Words seemed to mean nothing to him. He did not imitate. He would point only if you prompted him to do so. In short, nothing. Was it me? Maybe another therapist would do better? He had two ABA therapists now, and those at the Center, yet no improvement. His programs were at basic level, and there had never been any updates, as he never mastered any skills. His doctor said at this time that JD was ten pounds underweight. Yet, no one seemed to be alarmed by this. He looked like walking death to me, but Mom insisted that he was fine. He was, "just not talking." I asked her if he ever made eye contact. She said, no, and that he doesn't respond to his name. How could no one see how dangerous this situation was?

What should I do? I wasn't helping him at all. He did not respond to me, my toys, anything. Only the video grabbed his attention, and once that was on, there was no diverting his attention. Sometimes, he'd be asleep whenever I got there. It was not possible to awaken him.

I felt that I had to leave this team. I told Mom that I felt that I could not continue. It was professionally unethical. She said that it's "the weather." I asked about a time change for sessions so maybe he'd, at least, be awake when I got there. She said that wasn't possible.

One day, late in November, he had a big bandage on his arm. In New York, old steam radiators warmed the homes. Steam pipes run through the houses inside of the rooms. In fact, in New York today, they still call heat "steam." As in "turn up the steam." These pipes are boiling hot! Countless children get burned on these pipes. The alternative to getting burned is going to a hardware store and buying insulation sleeves that fit over the pipes. No big deal for people who have money and can simply hop in their car and go buy them. But if you're poor, and you have no car, and you don't understand that the man at the hardware store will ask you, "which size pipe?" it's not easy. There were many times, when I took on a new child, especially if the parents were from places like Bangladesh, that the first thing I did was buy insulation for their pipes. They had no idea. That is, until one of their children got burned.

I did see some kind of change just before the December break. JD was always aloof. He never seemed to care if he was strapped in a chair or not. But lately, he had been fighting it. Lately, as his sister tried to put him in the highchair, he would kick his feet and make vocal noises of disapproval. I saw this as a good sign. I also found an activity that he enjoyed, which was putting in the pieces on Mr. Potato Head. He was showing some temper occasionally now, but I could not determine what caused it. Maybe it was because he seemed to always be sick: runny nose, cough, tired, like a rag doll. He seemed to be angry about being stuffed in a chair all day. I couldn't tell. It was getting close to the December break, and I just could not continue facing a little boy that I was doing nothing for. Nothing. And lately, Mom began to cancel a lot, or I'd show up and there was no answer at the door, which did not mean that no one was home necessarily.

I called the service coordinator and the ABA supervisor to let them know that I was wasting this child's time. I was not helping him. I had used up all of my tricks and simply did not know what else to do. Maybe someone else would have more luck with him. As the coordination office was always looking to find therapists for new cases, they made the rare exception and allowed me to quit the case so I could take other cases somewhere else. They would, hopefully, find someone to replace me, though it would not be easy in the Marlboro Houses.

On my last day there, the mother was home. I told her that they were looking for a replacement for me. She said only one word, "Okay." No questions, no comments, no concern apparent at all.

JD remained in the Center-based program, and I was happy to hear months later that he was starting to respond a little. They also told me that his fifteen-year-old sister, Shawna, was in a facility for observation after a failed suicide attempt.

Jacky

It sounds cruel to say this, but Jacky was a little boy that should never have been born. I keep notes on all my children, but for some reason, I have no personal notes on Jacky. I had also forgotten his name as I sat to write this and had to concentrate very hard to recall it. No surprise, as it was a case that I wanted to forget.

I remember only a few things because this child's very existence was so bizarre. His parents were White people in their fifties. This was a second marriage for both parents. Mom was too old to have children and had never had any. The father also had never had children and really wanted a child. So, they used his sperm and impregnated another woman. This is not so uncommon today, but it was back then. I got no sense of any maternal feeling emanating from Mom. Of course, I could not have known how she felt. Did she really want this child, or was she just trying to please her husband?

The father was an electrician for General Electric. They told me that he used to be a professional musician and played with John Lennon. There was a private photo of Lennon and Yoko with an inscription to them hanging on a wall in the back room where Mom spent most of her time doing something or other on the computer. Mom was an x-ray tech who used to work in an office in Manhattan. She worked in a private, "high end" office and serviced stars such as Mick Jagger. They had an upper middle-income home in an Italian section of Brooklyn.

A few things about this case I remember clearly. One was that I did not like this mother. At all. It seemed to me that she really did not care about "her son" and had very little patience for a disabled child. Because Jacky was on the very low end of the spectrum, he was extremely difficult to reach.

One day, he was tantruming for an unknown reason—as is often the case with non-verbal, cognitively-delayed children—and she slapped him in the face. I was taken aback, but, hey, it's her kid. She often screamed at him to "stop it." He did not understand a word. She did not sit in on sessions, did not engage in instruction, and did not ask any questions. I felt that this whole "autism thing" was just a damned nuisance to her.

The father adored the child! As soon as he got home from work, he would pick him up and hug and kiss and talk to him. He did not see anything wrong with his boy. He was perfect.

Another thing that I remember was how frustrated I was trying to get Jacky to do anything. There was nothing—no imitation, no joint attention, he did not understand a word. Other therapists also expressed frustration. Jacky often tantrumed, unstoppable, for hours. He might calm down if he sat in his mother's lap on those rare occasions when she came out of the back room to sit in the dining room with her computer or phone and gaze over at us in the living room. Aside from tantruming, he bit. He struck out or bit anyone who tried to invade his private, happy world of sitting contentedly doing nothing. Mom used cookies a lot to calm him down. This was a big mistake, of course, but she just wanted some peace, and cookies restored it.

I really wanted to help this boy, as it was evident that he would need it. And so I continued until the end of the case despite the fact that there was no progress. When he turned three, I was glad that I would not have to go back to that house. I felt very bad for the father and was relieved to be away from the mother. Jacky would go on to his next Center, and I thought that he was fortunate in that he would most likely never comprehend how or why he came into the world.

Kathy

It was love at first sight! Kathy was such a pretty little girl. Her skin was very dark. The dark Black skin made a beautiful frame around big dark eyes and shining white teeth. Her hair was always braided. She was two years old when I was assigned to her case. She floated about like a little angel. She was happy, smiling, engaged by everything, and attending to nothing.

She lived in NYCHA housing on the Queens border, which was a slightly higher caliber than the bigger projects in the Center of Brooklyn. This "hood" had a gate you could not drive through unless you signed in, and you could not sign in if you were not on the list of residents or guests. You were also not allowed to walk into the compound without signing in.

The fact that it was on the Queens border meant that I had to drive over a half hour to arrive there from my previous child, and it would take another half hour to get back to the middle of Brooklyn, where most of my kids were. They asked me to work with her for one hour a day. I told the placement coordinator that I had to work with her at least two hours a day, or it wasn't worth my trip out there. She begged me to start and was sure that Kathy would get an increase to two hours a day.

When I was assigned to her, I had hoped that she'd do well; otherwise, two hours a day, five days a week with an unresponsive child is very monotonous. You feel more like a babysitter than a therapist.

I never read her evaluations for the same reason I rarely read any child's "evals." All the evals told me was what the child couldn't do. I was interested in what the child could do.

There was an eleven-year-old sister, Keturah, who I would see when she got home from school. She went to a Catholic girl's school and was a very bright, courteous young lady. Mom was a big lady who had a very bright, happy, optimistic personality. She was always smiling, always pleasant. She worked as a security cop in a local high school. She wore the police uniform with all the radios and other gear that hangs from their belts. As she worked every day, I did not see her much.

The main caretaker was the father. Nice guy. Quiet guy. He was very tall and thin, with a bit of a funny gait when he walked. I would walk into the living room, take Kathy by the hand into her bedroom while Dad stayed in the living room, usually napping. He was not Keturah's biological father, but he was good to her. He was the father of Kathy, and he adored her.

Kathy was also attending the Center. She was assigned to Lacy's class. I was happy about that because Lacy had many years of experience and was well versed in both special education and autism. Between the Center and home, Kathy was getting a lot of therapy—all morning in the Center and an hour a day at home, plus speech, OT, and PT.

Kathy was two years and one month old when we started with her. She was obviously on the spectrum, with all of the usual symptoms. She was quite distant, but I was hopeful that with all the therapy and Lacy running the program, Kathy would make great strides. From day one, Kathy and I had a good rapport, which surprised her mother, as Mom said that Kathy either avoided or ignored strangers.

We started the first of February. She immediately sat at the small table I set up for us. She could be engaged with my toys, liked deep pressure such as squeezing her hands or fingers, and tickles. When she became bored, she would start to cry. That meant I had to keep her happy, or I'd lose her. She missed a few days of school her first week. I would soon find that her not getting to school would be a continual problem.

During one session in the second week, I wanted to see if she could repeat anything. With her parents present, I instructed her to say, "help me," and to my and the parents' amazement, she said, "Help me quick." It would be a long, long time until I heard another word.

Our first two weeks together, we worked on establishing a rapport. Lacy had not yet written programs for her, so I brought my "floor bubble." It is a large bowl that children can lie in as I spin it. All children like vestibular stimulation, like swings, so I attempted it with her. She was hesitant to get in, but once lying in it comfortably, I spun it, and she was transfixed by the feeling. I put on children's music, and she was as if in a trance. When it stopped, I got eye contact. I tried to get her to say, "Go," but, not yet. Still, it was a good start! Maybe too good, as she screamed when I had to go, and Mom tried to get her out of the bubble.

At the end of two weeks, Lacy had written programs for her. Lacy was known for writing more difficult programs for kids, and one of them was NVI-O, or non-verbal imitation with an object. In this program, I was to model scribbling with a crayon, and she was to imitate that action. I usually waited many months before trying such a program. Kathy did not like it. She would not touch the crayon, and if I put it in her hand, it would go sailing.

The other program was "block building." This was simply putting one block on top of another up to three high. For a two-year-old, this should be simple. Kathy would throw the blocks. As Lacy was writing the programs, and the team leader, I did not have much say in the programs. I usually never start a child with block building or NVI-O, as those are hard programs. A child needs to be able to follow instructions and demonstrate imitation skills before starting such a task. I assumed that her evals suggested that she was on a higher level, so Lacy wrote more difficult tasks.

The other problem with such programs is that that are not "functional." "Functional" means that there is a purpose to doing the task. If I want to teach, for instance, "push," I would use a toy that when you pushed a button, something will pop up or play music. The pushing had a function. Stacking blocks may be useful for TD (typically developing) children, but not autistic children. Imitation with an object might be functional if the action is something like turning a crank on a music box. If I found that she would tantrum or throw the objects, I would write a zero for her score and attempt to convince the teacher to back up a bit.

By the end of February, she was settled down and loved to come to the table and "work" with me. She was doing better on programs and often repeated words! She had a rough start at school, but there, too, she settled down and performed better. She was echolalic. She would repeat things that you said (called, "immediate echolalia"). If I asked her to, "clap your hands," she would say, "clap your hands," but not do it. If I said, "Look at me," she'd repeat it without looking. Echolalia is a common feature of autism. There are major arguments amongst professionals about what it means, if it means anything, and what to do about it. Encourage it? Extinguish it? Because most of my kids were non-verbal, I was thrilled that she said anything at all. It had to be a good sign.

She also exhibited "delayed echolalia." That's when someone repeats something they have heard in the past. Kathy would say, "Peek a boo—I see you" many times, even though there seemed to be no context for it, and she was not looking at me.

By the end of March, she was doing better at home and at school, but she had begun crying when she did not want to do something. Her father asked me one day if Kathy was "regressing." I asked him why he thought that, and he told me that she almost never cries, but now he hears her crying in our session. I told him the truth. "That's a good sign. It's the ones who sit and stare off into space that I worry about."

One of Kathy's problems in the beginning was constant drooling, and the other was her "spacing out." Spacing out meant attending to nothing or staring off at a particular angle when there was nothing there to see. March came and went with on again, off again crying.

There would be great days and days I could do nothing with her. The drooling had stopped by now, but the spacing out continued. She might be working fine one second and in a trance the next. This scared me because I was afraid it might be focal seizures. At this point, I did not want to alarm the parents with my suspicions. I was not qualified in any case to diagnose seizures, but I would monitor it and record her instances of staring off into nowhere.

A good session was when she worked well and didn't want to stop. She would repeat everything I said practically. Object manipulation remained a tough program, but it was getting easier to prompt her through it. The parents wanted a three-week break until April third.

She was ill when I returned and cried as soon as I entered the room. She was not as easy to work with as before the break. She cried a lot more, but she would work when instructed. It was hard to determine why so many tears now. Was it due to her cold? The erratic schedule? Or was she simply bored with all this? Just before the Passover break, we had a staff meeting with the parents. It was noted that the drooling had ceased, she no longer threw items, and she could work well if motivated.

The third week in May, her sleeping patterns seemed to be off, as she was falling asleep in session often. She also began a new behavior that was not like her. She was usually a sweet child, and even when not willing to work, she did not become aggressive. Now she was scratching or hitting when presented with something she did not want to do. Strange. Maybe it was due to the increased difficulties of her programs, or maybe because new programs were being added. Lacy added a sorting program. This is simply putting little red or blue objects into the same color bowl. It should have been easy for her, but she did not seem to get it. Matching simple objects also should have been easy, but no. It seemed that any program having to do with visual discrimination, she could not do. Color blind? She was certainly smart enough to do these things. What was the problem?

Another new problem started to make things even worse. She simply was not getting to school. I was unaware of that. Usually, I would review the scores she made at school every day and compare them to mine. Mine were usually higher, as the assistants were in training and did not really know how to work with a girl like Kathy. There hadn't been any scores from school. I called the teacher. "Oh, she hasn't been coming." What?! It's a big problem when there is no communication between the teacher and home therapists. It's vital, but all the teachers, except one, at the Center, refused to read or write in the communication book. "We don't have time. Call me." Sure, as if calling were so easy. It was very difficult to get a hold of a teacher at the Center.

I was hoping that this new aggressive behavior would stop without having to incorporate any kind of intervention. Because she could talk, I tried to get her to say "no" or "finished" if she didn't want to do something. But she didn't get it. Then, another bizarre behavior began—forced laughing that she would not stop. I assumed it was escape behavior. She also returned to throwing and hitting, but when I increased the reinforcement schedule and decreased the demands, she was fine.

In the month of June, I began to worry. She had been doing well but seemed to have peaked. She repeated words a lot but could not seem to do the simplest programs. She fell asleep a lot. She spaced out a lot. The inappropriate laughing increased. (I had read in a book written by someone with autism that explained the reason he laughed for apparently no reason: "I thought of something funny!".) The aggression stopped but not the spacing out. I suggested to Mom that the hour we met every day, 5 p.m., was not good. I convinced her to let me come when Kathy got home from the Center at 2 p.m. She would have had time to eat and go right to work with me. This strategy seemed to work. She was more attentive and not battling fatigue.

July was the same as June. There was no progress, and she was yawning a lot, or spacing or laughing. Mom told me that she would get up around 3 a.m. and fool around until 8. I asked Mom to keep a sleeping record to see what her patterns were. We had to figure out a regular sleeping schedule and try to get her to keep it. After a few weeks, I asked Mom for the records, and she told me that she'd lost it! I'm assuming that she never did it to begin with, but what can you say? I had to try something else.

Throughout August, she continued to miss a lot of school. I called Mom and told her that it's a waste of time if she is not consistent in school, and Mom promised to get her there every day. Over the next few months, she would still miss school fairly often, and I just gave up talking about it. Lacy had been replaced by Tina, who was also a very good, competent teacher. Kathy was "on and off" with accurate responding until the end of the year. She was still working well with many programs but unable to do others that should have been easy for her. She sang a lot, all the time, and she could answer "yes/no" questions. While there was speech now, there was no language. I worked on things like, "Open" for the door or "Give me," and she would say them if I modeled it for her, but she never asked without a prompt.

Our two-hour sessions began the third week of November. Two hours is a long time for a girl on Kathy's level. She would fade in and out, and I had to give more breaks to keep her alert. On days that she did not go to school, she would be fast asleep when I got there. The erratic sleeping habits were interfering with her attendance at school and affecting our sessions.

The last week in December, Kathy had a very bad cold. I suggested that they take her to the doctor. They didn't. Every day that I came, she was so sick, yet she sat in the chair with me at the table. By January 2, I was ready to scream, as Kathy was still sick and hadn't been to the doctor. Going to the doctor is not so easy when you don't have a car and live on the border of Queens and Brooklyn and Mom works all day. On January 3, she seemed to be over the cold, and we started over. Unfortunately, my back went out, and we had to stop for two weeks. I felt terrible about that, as Kathy could not afford to miss sessions.

While I was out, the speech teacher had decided to do a PECS [4] program with her. It worked like this: Hand me a picture of a cookie, and I'll give you a cookie. What is the purpose of using an alternative communication system when she was capable of speaking? I was not a team leader, so I had no idea, but usually it is a team decision to use alternative methods, not individual speech teachers. This was not a little girl who would patiently walk over to a communication board, select a picture, and hand it to someone. Mom was not going to use PECS in any case. It took training, time, and a lot of patience to learn how to use. When would that happen? In any case, Kathy could speak! Why use pictures?

They introduced PECS while I was out for two weeks, but as I surmised, she just didn't get it. Usually, the ability to speak is indicative of some level of intelligence, but while Kathy could speak, she could not do a lot of simple tasks. I had begun a "give me X" program, wherein I would show her something and see if she reached out for it: juice, for instance. If she did, I would prompt her to say, "Give me juice." She did well with this, but when I tried to reinforce spontaneous requesting, that is, just leaving the juice, out of reach on the table, she never did do it.

Her peculiar behaviors continued. She would "space out," which always consisted of her right hand going to her right temple and leaning her head slightly to one side and staring off into a corner of the ceiling. This could last for a few seconds, or up to a minute. Whenever I saw it, I did nothing. I wanted to see how long these spells would last or if anything in particular set them off. Was it "just a behavior," or was it some kind of seizure? She would laugh uncontrollably sometimes for a minute or longer. Again, what prompted this? Maybe it was as simple as thinking of something funny. Could it be no more than that?

In the last week of January, she became ill again. This one was bad. Mom did not take her to the doctor until February 2. The doctor said that it was an ear infection. That last week of January and the first week of February, all I tried to do was to get her to relax and drink. Her parents could not get her to drink anything, and she was dehydrating. I used a simple trick that, evidently, her parents hadn't thought of—a straw!

An ear infection. I wondered. So many times, when I worked with children and they became ill, they always came back with the same diagnosis: ear infection. Fluid buildup in the ears was supposedly common in children with autism. I have no idea why children on the spectrum would have more fluid in their ears than a typically developing child. Many of the children I worked with had tubes put in their ears. Did it make a difference in the amount of time they became ill in the future? It did not seem that way to me. I did not look to see if there was any research on the incidence of fluid in the ears for children with autism. It didn't matter.

After two weeks, she returned to her normal self. She had an increase in language but not much. I made a noise like a duck, and she said, "Duck." I taught her to say, "Open the window," and she then would say it often, though I am not sure if it was a request or echolalia. She finished a sucker, handed it to me, and said, "All done." I had not taught her that. Maybe her parents had or at the Center they had.

February and March, she continued to work well with occasional crying. One day, she would come into the room and work happily, the next, tantrum to not go in. Moody? Did it all depend on her irregular sleeping patterns? I was certain of one thing: I had no "stimulus control." She had me stumped. What could I do for her? Sometimes, she acted as if she were drunk—really drunk. On those occasions, I tried two approaches to get her to settle down and concentrate: extinction (ignoring the behavior and just carrying on teaching) and increased reinforcer and/or breaks. Nothing worked, though the latter did for a while. I felt that something other than autism was going on here.

I called Tina at the Center, but she reported nothing unusual. I showed the parents the behavior, but they could not think of any reason she was acting like this. She'd recently added ear covering and other odd behaviors. I was afraid that she was getting worse, as if there was some organic brain disorder. Well, sure she had a "brain disorder," as her diagnosis was autism, but why would these typical sorts of autistic behaviors start now, after we'd been together a year and a half? She had never covered her ears before or tensed when excited or disturbed. Now she could not recall the names of objects she definitely knew. Or she could but wouldn't say them.

Worse, she now began having what looked to me like "mini seizures" that lasted for a few seconds. There was wild shaking and eye movement. She was forgetting the names for things that she'd learned. I was getting nervous. What was going on in her brain? Was there some kind of organic decay? Was it just typically strange but common autistic behavior? I had not seen these "late onset" behaviors in a child before. Could it be sound sensitivity?

Twice in one day, she fell from her chair into my lap for comfort while covering her ears—once when Mom screamed at her sister and once when a loud truck drove by. On sound sensitivity, there was a lot of research, but how would I check?

Late April was the Passover break. I did not see her for almost two weeks. The school was also closed, so she had not been to school for a long time. I returned to find her quite ill with a bad cough, runny nose, and lethargy. She also has large patch of ringworm on her stomach. On my next trip to see her, I brought bandages to cover it and some Vicks for her chest and neck. When she felt better, I introduced a new program called "joint attention," which I should have begun a long time ago. Joint attention is where you look at something, point it out to someone else, and they look at the same thing, with you. Like when you're driving and your child points excitedly outside: "Mommy, look at the cows!" This is a very important skill that is required for any child to learn. It was not going well. She did like to look at books as you turned the pages, so we began with that.

It was Dad's responsibility to get her on the bus every day, as Mom was working and her sister was already gone to school. Unfortunately, I did not have much of a rapport with Dad, as he didn't talk much. One day I came to find that she hadn't been to school, and I asked Mom why not. She told me that he couldn't send her because her socks did not match! Unreal. She was "stimming" a lot and making a lot of autistic faces. I was sure that she was regressing and should have a 24-hour EEG. Not being a neurologist, it wasn't for me to say. Yet, I felt that I should say something. We were working on things she should have understood. Things like, "get down" off the bed, "go sit down" in the chair when it was five feet away. "Come here" and other simple, one step commands. She wasn't getting it. I felt that I had to say something so I suggested to Mom that, "In my humble opinion, I think she needs a reevaluation and possibly an EEG because I fear she's getting worse."

At the end of May, I saw hand biting for the first time. While "wrist biting" is not uncommon in the autism world, she had never exhibited SIBS (self-injurious behavior) before. There is a lot in the literature about SIBs. Supposedly, they are "learned behaviors." That means that the behavior serves some kind of function for the child. That's what the behavioral literature says anyway. I was skeptical. They recommend using, "Differential reinforcement of alternative behavior." They make it sound so easy in ABA classes: "Just do a 'functional analysis' and find out what the behavior is for—escape, access to something, internal stimulation (feels good), and replace that inappropriate behavior with an appropriate one that serves the same function." Easy. It's not. Especially not with SIBS because if it is an "internal stimulation," how do you figure that out? How can you tell how she feels on the inside and why she does this? And where did she "learn" this behavior? Learned means reinforced. Who was reinforcing her SIBS?

At the end of the first week in June, I was completely despondent. She was gone! Far worse than when we started. I definitely did not want to, but I felt that I had to tell her parents my opinion. Something far more sinister than autism was going on. I asked Mom if she would mind if I wrote letters requesting new testing. She agreed.

There was one other possibility for a child losing skills. It's the one possibility that is rarely considered: therapist ineptitude. Maybe I was simply boring her to death? While she had speech, she had no communication skills, and maybe the fact that she did not talk to me and others was simply that she did not know how to. Maybe this was causing her to space out, laugh, or maybe even bite herself. Could that be? Maybe she wasn't performing well now because she'd had it with this whole discrete trial teaching technique, i.e., sitting in a chair facing the teacher and doing tasks that were boring. Was it me? I decided to test this theory.

I backed off on the amount of work, increased reinforcement, let her up a lot more for longer breaks, and played a lot of music. This seemed to help! She was more compliant when in the chair and worked well without the behaviors. It's a sad case, but it is often the case, that ABA therapists do not seem to understand that there is more to working with children than "reinforcement." You see it in every book on ABA: If the child is noncompliant, "increase reinforcement schedule." That might work. But reinforcement is not the only consideration. If you don't want to mow the lawn for ten dollars, you probably won't do it for twenty either. Check yourself, not the child. Are you boring? Is the task boring or nonfunctional? Are there "competing contingencies?" In other words, the child would rather do something else. As Kathy spent most of her days simply flitting around the living room, attending to nothing, the competing contingency would be to just run around. I had to be more exciting than running around, and evidently, I wasn't.

The entire month of June, I was out with a bad back. I was afraid that I would be replaced, but they found someone just to fill in until

I got back. This was good, as I really wanted to see how Kathy would do with someone else. If I came back to find that she was doing better then I would know for sure that I was the problem. Actually, that's what I hoped, so then Kathy could get the help she needed so desperately. I'd happily eat my pride.

When I returned July 1, nothing had changed, and she was back to zero. I worked with her until the end of August, when she aged out by turning three. Though not yet three, she would start a new program in September. The last month she did seem to work better, and maybe I was the problem! That is, what I was doing with her (following the programs) in discrete trials was boring, and I did not sufficiently adjust the reinforcement schedule nor make the programs more fun. I blamed myself for her increase in crying and whining, but there was also a deterioration in skills, as if she lost everything she had learned, and that was not my fault. They should have noticed as well at the Center, but nothing was ever said. There was an increase in autistic-like behaviors of stimming, staring off into space, laughing for no apparent reason, tantrums, SIBS.

When out of the chair, she was completely wild. She would not come when called by me or family. She just flitted from the curtains to the couch and back to the curtains. There were no activities for her out of the chair when I wasn't there. I left her feeling like I had not accomplished anything. I had not given her anything that would help her in her next learning environment. I left her with a heavy heart. I couldn't help her.

I want to record an incident that happened while I worked with her that was very important and was a big lesson for me. One day while at the Center, I was reviewing tapes of my "work" with her. I did it in the parents' lounge because that is where the video machine was. There were three other mothers in the lounge at the time. All three mothers had children in Kathy's class. There was a feeling that we were all one big team—parents, teachers, and therapists helping and supporting each other. Or so I thought.

As I reviewed the tapes, one of the mothers remarked, "Wow. Look how happy she is. I've never seen her smile before!" She loved to dance, and our dancing consisted of holding both hands and usually moving in a circle, stop, move, stop. She would laugh aloud whenever I said, "Stop!" She really enjoyed this activity. I was hoping she'd learn words like "stop," "go," and "dance." The other mothers took glances at the tape as it ran. They did not seem at all interested. Then I got a phone call. The director of the Center called to say that a complaint had been registered against me for "inappropriate" behavior with a child.

I said, "Uh, what?" He asked me if I had watched a video of one of the kids in the parents' lounge.

"Sure. So?"

"Well, first of all, that's a breach of confidentiality," he said.

I replied, "What confidentiality? We all know each other, we all know each other's children, we're all in the same situation together. Where's the breach?"

He said, "Well, don't do it again."

"Okay."

He then told me that one of the mothers said that I was inappropriate, and the other mothers agreed. I doubted that the other mothers agreed, but okay, that was the charge. He asked me what I had been doing, and I told him, "No problem, you can watch the tape yourself."

He declined and just told me that "the matter" would not go any further and not to review tapes in front of others again. Later, I talked to the teacher and asked her about it. She told me, "The mothers said that you were, 'inappropriate.'"

I asked her how. She said, "Well, for one thing, you were dancing with her."

I told her, "I've got a little secret to tell you. I dance with all my children and have been for twenty years—boy or girls. And here's another secret: You all dance in the classroom, don't you? Is that inappropriate?"

She looked down and said, "Okay, but that's what the mothers said."

I was furious. I called Kathy's mother and asked her when she would be home next, as I wanted to show her something. She was home that week. I informed her that I had a tape of one of our sessions and wanted her to understand how it was going. That was all I said to her. We watched the 90-minute video together, and Mom was crying at the conclusion. She thanked me so much for assisting her little girl and was so happy to see some progress.

Then I asked her, "Did you see anything you would consider inappropriate?"

Her head flew back, her eyes widened, and she said, "What?" I told her that some mothers in the Center were watching the tape as I reviewed it, and they reported my dancing with Kathy as inappropriate. Mom leaped out of her chair. She was wild!

"Who? Who said that? Let me get ahold of her…"

I told her that maybe I shouldn't have watched it in front of them, to which Mom replied, "We ain't got no secrets! Who was it?"

I didn't tell her who the mothers were, but I informed her that no charges were being brought, and I could continue to work with Kathy. I related the conversation with Mom to both the teacher and the director. Later, at my insistence, these mothers had a meeting with the director and were told that what I was doing was appropriate, that it was standard procedure to do activities that children enjoyed in order to facilitate communication and that "Ben" was one of our senior therapists and had years of experience with no history of accusations of any kind. In other words, they were put in their place. They were also informed that the mother of the child was aware of their accusations and was very angry about it. This taught me a valuable lesson.

I always thought that "where there's smoke, there's fire." If someone accused a teacher or therapist of being inappropriate, unprofessional, or abusive, there's got to be something there or there would have been no such allegations. Guilty until proven innocent. I learned that sometimes, allegations are false—completely false. The accusations against parents made supposedly by children on the spectrum via the use of Facilitated Communication [10] is a blaring example of this truth.

One other time, later in my career, I would be accused of "child abuse" by another mother. You can read about it in the chapter called, "Some Difficult Mothers."

Just a side note. I went one day to visit a clinic near my house. The supervisor was someone I had worked with in the past, and I just wanted to visit another place and see how it was run, communication techniques, method, etc. As I walked through, there were a lot of children sitting on a mat on the floor with a therapist and a few aides. One of the aides was one of the mothers who had reported me. When I walked into the room and saw this mother on the floor, I debated whether to talk to her supervisor and warn her about false accusations and to not let this lady be around other children. I decided not to. The lady looked up at me with a look of trepidation on her face. I glared back just for a second to let her know that I remembered her and then looked away.

One other side note on the comical side, sort of. I once asked the father why he didn't work. He told me that he was "lucky" and did not have to.

"Why not?"

I knew he wasn't independently wealthy if he lived in a NYCHA house. He told me that he gets social security because he was shot in both knees. The other thing I noticed was that the doorbell rang a lot, and whenever someone was at the door, Dad would step out with the person instead of inviting him in. I figured he had a side job: pharmaceutical entrepreneur.

Tuvia

These cases are all hard to write about. I wish that they all ended like most of the books you read about children with autism. You know, we did this unusual thing, and the child was cured. Sorry, I mean, "recovered." "They knocked off the gluten, and we all lived happily ever after." "Had him listen to AIT, and is good as new," or "Yes, we did an intensive ABA program and now, look, he's indistinguishable from his peers." Or even the ones where the child did not "recover," but progress was great, and he's making great strides. He's special, and he's neurodivergent, and the world has to learn how to accept him.

Sure, it would be nice if the world were more accommodating to people with special needs. Itzhak Perlman will not play in any venue that does not have wheelchair access. Newscasts are including sign language. Fashion magazines are including models in wheelchairs these days. That's all great. But it gets tiresome for some of us who are in the trenches with parents who simply cannot adjust their lives to one that includes a disabled child. Do you blame them? Don't. As the old saying goes, "Walk in their shoes."

Tuvia was one child who was "given up." He was a first-born son to a young couple who looked forward to a pleasant life. The father was just starting a practice as a dentist. Mom was a rare beauty who was thrilled with her new life. They both grew up on Ocean Blvd. The Ocean Blvd. in Brooklyn is home to very wealthy Syrian Jews. They have their own little world there: Syrian synagogues, Arabic, Hebrew and English schools, shops. Two generations away from poverty and anti-Semitism, they made it to New York and prospered. Tuvia was born to a young couple whose whole life was mapped out to live happily ever after. When they had him, there were great celebrations.

Unfortunately, Tuvia was not developing properly. At age two, he could not respond to his name. He made no eye contact with his mother or anybody else. He was silent. He could not feed himself, dress himself, and was not toilet trained. When he got excited, he would wildly flap his hands. Other than hand flapping, Tuvia did not engage in any kind of physical behavior. He had no interest in the usual toys for children his age—no interest in anything. His mother felt like a nurse and was simply not prepared for this. His father was a busy man starting his new practice.

I would be on a team, once again, with Lacy—an experienced therapist who had seen hundreds of children like this. She would write his programs, and I would be one of the therapists hoping to get him to respond, learn, and progress. I never saw Mom smile while working in her house day after day. I only saw anxiety and desperation. There was not much talk between us. I let Lacy answer her questions.

It was obvious from the start that Tuvia was going to be a challenge to work with. He sat in the chair in front of the table easily enough. Tuvia didn't seem to care where he was: in a chair, on the floor—it was all the same to him. Lacy had written a lot of beginner programs for him, but I got no responses. The data sheets showed that no one else had either. What he did do a lot was cry and simply turn off the therapist facing him whenever in session. I knew that to make any kind of connection with a child such as Tuvia, I would have to spend a lot of time just trying to figure out what got his attention, if anything. In ABA-land, doing that is called a "reinforcer assessment." I called it, "trying to reach this unreachable star."

I was lucky. He reacted wildly to my first item: tops. They don't teach you in ABA much about autism itself. At least, they didn't when I was certified back in 2003. They taught you all the fancy jargon, like three-term contingency, reinforcement ratios, and differential reinforcement. But unless you read a lot about autism, particularly books about raising children on the spectrum written by parents, you would not know where to start. I read that children on the spectrum like consistency. They like things that spin. They like to spin in circles. A top spins and has a consistent motion. Time after time, it spins.

What can you teach by spinning a top? You can teach a lot of stuff with a top. "Go," "Stop," "Show me what you want," "Look at the top," "Give me the green top," and "Give me the big top." Tuvia did not learn any of these things. When I spun them, he would wildly flap his hands, his eyes grew wide, and he got very excited. Every spin, every time, every day. The best thing about tops for him was that he could sit happily at the table for hours, and I could prompt him through his other programs.

Everything with Tuvia was at "prompt level." We worked in his bedroom, and Mom would pop in to look once in a while. She was always hoping for a scene like in *The Miracle Worker*. You know, the water scene where Hellen first understands what water is and that there's a word for it. Unfortunately, there would be no miracles for Tuvia. His cognitive level was just very low and limited. The only difference between me and the other therapists was that Tuvia and I had fun together. I made no more progress than they had, but at least he would sit happily with me.

I must admit, I was getting tired of Mom asking all the time, "Anything new? How'd he do today?" It's my job to be reassuring, yet I couldn't lie. My thought was that Tuvia was just not going to be able to progress much, if at all. It probably showed in my face when asked by Mom how he was doing. He was such a sweet boy, and there was simply not much we could do for him. I had hoped that Mom had caught on to that by now—if not from me, at least from the other therapists. But apparently not. I felt like a plumber who was taking too long to get the leak fixed when I knew that all the pipes needed replacement. I couldn't lie to her, and I couldn't hide my sadness. Naturally, Mom was not thrilled with me.

One day I came to work with Tuvia, and he had weights on his wrists. I saw in the communication book that Mom was distressed by Tuvia's hand flapping. Someone, no doubt the OT, had bought into the "sensory integration" nonsense and used one of their tricks to stop the flapping. I thought, *Okay, I'll do it just because I'm not team leader, and it's required.*

What I found was, indeed, Tuvia did not flap his wrists! But then, he didn't lift his hands off the table either. I took them off. Mom came in and asked me why I wasn't using the wrist weights. I told her that there is no research to validate that they decrease hand flapping.

She said, "The other therapists are using them."

I am not the most patient person in the world and did not want to have this conversation with Mom.

I replied, "Putting weights on his hands is just torture, and I'm not going to have any part of that."

Then I asked her what the big deal was about hand flapping. She looked at me in utter amazement.

"Well, what if we're on a bus?" she asked.

"Uh, yeah, okay, you're on a bus, then what?"

She is astounded. "And what if he starts flapping his hands?"

"Yeah, okay, now he's flapping his hands. Then what?"

"Well, people are going to stare at us."

I saw where she was going. "Okay, people are staring. Then what?"

She became outraged. "Then they'll think there's something wrong with him!"

I should have stopped here, but it made me angry, too.

"Okay, now people on the bus think there's something wrong with him. Then what?"

She left the room, slamming the door behind her.

A few days later, Lacy and I spoke on the phone, and I told her that I was just not going to use the weights. She said that she had been taking data and found that the use of the weights had actually increased his hand flapping when not wearing them. I told her that if Mom was embarrassed to take him on the bus, I'd be happy to take him for her. Lacy felt that I was being unprofessional. She was right.

I remained working with the team but after a few months it was pretty obvious that Mom did not want me on the team anymore, and so, I was replaced. A while later, I had heard that Mom had a baby girl and had given Tuvia up to the State. That was probably the best thing for him. The girl was typically developing.

Chapter Four

A Few More I Couldn't Help

Renny

Renny was a little girl who lived in a cluttered, second floor two-bedroom apartment. Her family was from Bangladesh, like most of the families in that building. I am not sure how they managed to sleep, as there were a lot of people in that apartment. In one bedroom there was a big bed, where Renny jumped all day. I assumed she slept there with her parents. In the other bedroom was a strange little man who spoke no English and seemed to be some kind of Patriarch. I didn't understand his language, but I understood his tone. He argued angrily a lot with everyone else in the house.

There seemed to be two other women who lived there. Then, there were cousins in and out. Fortunately for me, one of them was a young lady in college who spoke English. Mom's English was understandable but difficult. Renny also had a seven-year-old brother who spoke only English. He understood Bangladeshi, of course, but he always responded to his parents in English. He was a cute kid who always wanted to "play" with me and Renny. It was hard keeping him out of the room. I had to lock it from the inside, which did not please the parents. He was trapped and bored in this apartment. It was sad. The boy had also been diagnosed as autistic but now was completely age typical. There was no stimulation for him or Renny. Nothing but a TV that was in the grouch grandpa's room. The boy was starving for affection and attention. I bought him a pack of small cars, and he was over the moon!

Renny wanted to do two things in life: bounce on the bed, endlessly, and suck her thumb or shirt sleeve. Sucking on shirt sleeves is very common in Autismland. Hers was always dripping with saliva. Her thumb sucking had caused her palette to rise into a high arch in her mouth and pulled her teeth up along with them. The only time that her thumb was not in her mouth was when she was bouncing on the bed.

I was the team leader, and my job was to get her to sit at a table and do programs. These included physical imitation, oral imitation, matching objects and pictures, pointing to desired objects, identifying objects and pictures, following one step instructions, and sorting by FFC (Function, i.e., something you drink with; Feature, i.e., something that is round; and Class, i.e., furniture, animals, clothes, etc.).

I saw on day one that this was going to be difficult. Sitting at a table was a foreign idea to her. Joint attention, where two people concentrate on the same thing together, was clearly not going to be easy. She had no language—receptive or expressive—so following instructions was going to be another incredible challenge.

The apartment was very cluttered. The building was in bad need of repair. Cracked paint was seemingly endogenous to the environment. It was probably lead-based, as most of them were in the city when they built them years ago. Cockroaches scurried about in every room, with long trails of ants marching in lockstep across the floors and walls. Then, there were the mice. Out of the closet, across the floor, through a crack, and out of sight. The overhead light fixture was just a wire with a bulb on the end. Water used to seep through it and drip onto the bed. I had become immune to such things over the years working in Brooklyn, but the water in the electric outlet scared me, and I told Mom I would not come back until that was fixed. It was fixed the next day.

Another problem was that Renny received 20 hours a week of home services, just for ABA, not counting speech therapy, occupational therapy, and physical therapy. I was in charge of writing her programs and accumulating the data from the other ABA therapists who were supposed to be following the programs I wrote. If they had any questions or suggestions, there was a communication book for us and Mom to write in. The speech therapist was also supposed to look at the communication book and keep us informed of what she was working on and how we could incorporate the skills she was working on into our programs. That's the way it's supposed to work in a good ABA program. Unfortunately, it did not work that way.

The other two ABA therapists were both men. One was named Harvey, who I had never met, and the other, Mic, who unfortunately I had worked with before. What do you need to work with children on the spectrum in New York City? A master's degree in special education, psychology, or social work. Do you have to be ABA certified? No. Do you need a background in autism? No. Maybe experience or training in working with children on the spectrum? No. Just a masters in a non-related field was all you needed to go to work.

Did Harvey have any experience? I had no idea. He was from another agency. Mic was in it for the money. It paid really well in New York, where they seem to believe if you pay a lot for something, it's worth something. Money cures everything. His scoring of programs was not dependable. He showed up when he felt like it and had a million excuses for when he did not show up.

With another child we had worked with, he used to meet with the speech teacher, and they took the kid to the park every day and told me that they were working "in tandem." This is, of course, illegal, as the City is paying for individualized therapy. But in those days, there was no way to verify what the therapists were doing. The only evidence was what they wrote on their session notes. They wrote what they did, supposedly, and the mother signed it. Mothers never read what is on the note—especially if English is not their language. Just, "Sign here, please," and she would sign. Or a babysitter who could care less would sign. Mothers never looked at the times or dates. If you skipped a session and would lose that hour of pay, no problem. Next time, just write two session notes—one for today and one for the day you didn't show up, and Mom would sign them, no questions asked.

Nowadays, sessions, scores, times, and signatures are all done electronically on your phone so you can't cheat, but before this, people like Mic were making tons of money by falsifying times and having Mom sign for days they were not there.

One scandalous case that made the *New York Times* was of a speech therapist who went to the Caribbean for two weeks and had Mom sign all her session notes as if she had worked. The speech therapist was paid for the supposed sessions she gave while sitting on the beach in St. John. Fortunately, she was caught. She lost her whole career for that vacation!

Another woman I knew used to show up exactly on time and leave exactly an hour later. Every child, every session. What was wrong with that? Children were to get an hour session. That means a full sixty minutes of therapy. If you arrive at three and leave at four, that means the therapist wrote out her session notes on the child's time. It took at least five minutes to write a session note and longer if she was one of those rare therapists who wrote in the communication book. It also means that she was more concerned with squeezing in an extra hour a day of pay because it was impossible to be on time like that every day. Sometimes, the children are tired, or tantruming, or have a cold. In such cases, your sessions took longer if you really cared about the child and making sure he/she got a good session every day.

I was notoriously late for every child, but if I came fifteen minutes late, I stayed fifteen minutes longer. (Then, of course, I was late for my next kid!) This lady eventually got fired for cheating on her billing. Electronic billing cured a lot of dishonest therapists. Too bad because she was good.

Renny and I began our work in November. It was obvious from the first day that I was probably not going to be able to help her much. She was gaze avoidant and sat passively in the chair like a rag doll. If a toy interested her, she would manipulate it, but if not, her thumb went right to her mouth. The skin on that thumb was raw. The "behavior reduction techniques" for thumb sucking never did work for me with children. Maybe I did them wrong. I could see her thumb was going to be my greatest adversary. That, and her complete aloofness. I wasn't sure what was wrong with this little girl with the big dark eyes, but I was sure that autism was the least of her problems. She was dirty. She always had food all over her face and the pajamas that never seemed to get changed. Her hands were dirty from hanging on the one dusty windowsill that looked down to a market and train station below. If she wasn't bouncing on the bed, she was at that window looking down at the market below with stores on either side of the local train running through. Her hair was very greasy. It was unkempt and continually fell in front of her eyes such that I often could not see them.

The other thing was that she absolutely did not want her hands touched. This was a problem because often I would have to prompt her to do an action or form a point to show me what she wanted, but she would immediately draw her hand away if I tried to touch it. It would take a long time to gain enough trust for her to allow me to touch her hands. Yet, she did not mind if I picked her up and we bounced on the bed.

I brought a "first learner" book of pictures of various things. She liked looking at this very much. I would point to a picture, say its name, and then try to prompt her to point to the picture with her left hand, the one that was always in her mouth. Like so many children on the spectrum, she would take my finger and use it to point to something. She did this with Mom, me, and all others. I showed her mother how to replace that by taking her finger, hand over hand, and making her point.

One of the pictures was labeled "pasta." She would laugh hysterically whenever I said the word. She would immediately repeat "pasta" and break out into gales of laughter. (It reminded me of a little girl I worked with in Israel. With her, I would use sets of plastic screws and bolts, and we made things. The word for "screw" in Hebrew is, "boreg." She found that word very funny, and, like Renny, would repeat it and burst out in laughter.)

We used that book for all sorts of different programs: picture ID, verbal imitation, joint attention, pointing, "wh" questions (Where is the seashell? What color is it?), and one step instructions (Open the book. Give me the book). I wrote a lot of programs all based on using the one thing that captivated her interest.

The other therapists were not doing the programs. I had no idea what they were doing for twelve hours a week. They did not read or write in the communication book. By the end of December, it was obvious that the other therapists were "not on the same page" with me.

I didn't think that they were on any "pages," as there was no data being taken and no communication in the book—no questions, no suggestions, no comments. Nothing. Because the therapists had been sent from another agency, there was no supervisor to complain to.

And so it went, through New Year's. The thumb sucking had to stop. It was destroying her palette and misshaping her teeth. It also interfered with her responding. She would not be able to follow simple commands like, "clap your hands," or "do your puzzle," or "hold a book and turn the pages." She acted like a one-armed child. The OT, as usual, suggested that it was "sensory issues." Thanks, no kidding. What isn't? The speech teacher tried massages with "Nuk brushes," or flavored foam rubber tips and things to stimulate the mouth. Of course, these things had no effect because stimulation was not the problem. Nor was "sensory issues," whatever that meant. She did it for the same reason all kids do it. They like it! It becomes habit, and habit becomes nature. It was as simple as that.

Mom tried the home-style techniques: hot pepper sauce on the thumb. She'd rub it off. Gloves. Off they came. Band aids. No good. Finally, she bought a plastic thumb guard. It fit over the entire thumb and was strapped to her wrist. This annoyed her terribly. It had two effects: She bit through the plastic straps or would scream instead of sleep because sleeping meant, thumb in mouth.

Okay, I'm a behavior analyst. I thought I should try a typical behavioral approach. One was to give her a lot of "reinforcement" any time the thumb was not in her mouth. I would use a timer and reward her for doing nothing other than keeping her thumb out of her mouth.

I would reinforce her whenever she worked on something that required either two hands or made her work with her left, as she had no interest in sucking on her right thumb. Sounds easy in the textbooks. Always works in the research articles.

February was the beginning of our fourth month together. I felt defeated. She could and would point now, but that was our only accomplishment in four months. Children like Renny are very humbling. As I worked with so many children and often saw good to excellent progress, I started to think, *I'm something special. A miracle worker!* Little girls like Renny reminded me that I'm not something special. She made me feel inept, and I began to wonder whether I was in the right profession. Then there were all those other professionals who always laugh at such things and try to convince others that if only… "If only you did Floortime or Verbal Behavior, or TEACCH, or some of the other methods, well, you'd get responses. You would have seen progress. The problem is ABA." Such talk reminded me of something I had learned from Dr. Temple Grandin, the most famous living person with autism today.

At an autism conference in Jerusalem, I spent three days clinging to her side. Temple really wanted to see the exhibit on dolphin therapy that is popular in Israel.

I told her, "Temple, I can't believe you want to see that! Do you believe in such things?" She told me, "It's not the method, it's the therapist."

I painfully recalled that now, as I felt like I was not getting through to this child. I tried other approaches. I began a VB (verbal behavior) protocol source using their "bible" the VB MAPP[11] both verbally and an attempt with sign language. Nothing—just thumb sucking and stares. I tried NET (natural environment training), where you let the child follow her own desires, and you use what she is most interested in. She loved to jump on the bed, so I used that to get her to say, "jump" or "stop" or "go" or "pillow" (she loved to throw and thought it was funny if I threw it at her). Nothing—blank stares, or if I did not respond or prompt fast enough, she'd simply turn away from me and jump.

I tried the window that she loved to look out down below to the busy cobblestone street lined with shops, people, birds, dogs, and under it, visible through a dome, a train. She liked it when I opened the window. I tried to prompt her to say "open" or "window." Never once. If it was raining, she loved to put her hand out and feel the rain. Prompting, "open" or "open window," or "rain." Nothing. Yet she could repeat "pasta."

In the meantime, I was still getting no correspondence from Harvey, and Mic was writing high scores and notes to the effect, "She's doing so well!" One day, I decided to watch a session of his. This meant canceling one of my sessions with another child to be there, but if this guy was working miracles, I wanted to know how he was accomplishing it. I sat in the for the entire session and told him to ignore me and just concentrate on doing his usual session. She did sit at the table for most of the session but did not do one program—not even one trial of one program. She sat there with her thumb in her mouth staring at the ceiling.

"Uh, Mic, I see she's sitting well, but I don't see any responding."

He told me, "Yeah, well, she's not responding so well today. You know, some days are better than others."

Yes, sure.

The new kid on the block in autism therapy was called, "The VB Method." This was verbal behavior based entirely on the work of Skinner, who believed that "verbal behavior" was no different than physical or nonverbal behavior. If that's true, then a therapist should be able to "operantly condition" that behavior. I, like all the other therapists in the world, started taking course after course in "Verbal Behavior." We had to read the book, written by Skinner, called, you guessed it, *Verbal Behavior*.[12] It's possible that a more boring book has been written, but if so, I would not be real interested in reading it.

I bought the hot new VB Assessment, along with it's manual, on how to test verbal operants (manding, tacting, intraverbals, echoics, etc.) This was fancy jargon for things we were already doing. "Manding" just means "requesting." "Tacting" just means identifying things. After one completes the assessment, the therapist simply begins to work on each particular "operant." Simple. The other change was that VB leaned heavily on getting away from discrete trial teaching and working in the natural environment. Nothing new there either. They insisted, no matter what the assessment results were, to start with "manding." Makes sense. Something that someone wants, something "reinforcing," should be easy to teach. Yet, I always found that the children far more enjoyed "tacting," or naming things, usually the ABCs, shapes, colors, than requesting things. But okay, Skinner is the boss.

I "worked" with her until the third week in August. In all that time, my notes were pretty much the same as they had been in the beginning months. The only difference was that she started saying words spontaneously. One day, I handed her a small stick, and she said, "See-saw." She might occasionally say, "up" or "pillow," or some word I never imagined she knew, such as "window," once, and then, never again. She loved bubbles, so I tried to get her to say, "blow" or "bubbles," but if I waited more than five seconds after the prompt, she would just turn away and jump on the bed.

She liked to do a finger puzzle that I had. One had to put in the fingers and palms and then we would count them. She also loved to put letters in the ABC puzzle. But I could not get her to repeat names. She knew them. Once we did the ABC puzzle and the letter R was missing. I spilled out some letters from a different set, and she immediately picked up the R and put it in our puzzle. So, Dr. Skinner, if verbal language is "operant," like physical behavior, why doesn't she "operantly respond" when I try to elicit the behavior? So much for VB.

It is long, hard, and boring to work with a child who never responds. The other two therapists simply stopped coming on a regular basis. The "make-up" sessions piled up.

I assumed that they were either getting Mom to sign them off and collecting pay for no services or just not coming. I wrote in the communication book to them that one possible reason for lack of progress may be due to inconsistency in therapy. They did not reply.

The months rolled by. Nothing. She was still gazing off to nowhere, still madly sucking her thumb. She could be prompted to simple programs and would sit happily as I turned the pages in a book, but she never said a word except for "pasta." I tried a simple three-piece puzzle, but it only made her angry as I tried to prompt her to do it.

In late July, the speech therapist called me in exasperation to ask what I could recommend, as she was getting nowhere with her. I had to tell her the truth: I was also getting nowhere with her and did not know what to suggest.

Mom cancelled a week in July, and when I came back, Mom gave her to me a total mess. Her face was covered in chocolate and dirt. Her beautiful jet-black hair was extremely greasy. And she was thirsty! I cleaned her up, put up her hair, and brought her a small bottle of water. She drank half of it right down. Dad was also home this day, but he had no questions for me. It was a different atmosphere in the house now. Mom no longer said hello or goodbye. She would sign the paper and ignore me. I thought it was me, but a week later, Mom told me that Renny had been using more words lately. She began to name things in her favorite picture book, such as, "see-saw," "butterfly," numbers, shapes, and a few other words. Maybe the mood in the house was not due to us at all. It was obvious that this family had a lot of problems.

August 21 was our last day, as she was turning three and aging out of the program. I brought her a helium balloon, which fascinated her. We played. I left the house feeling that day as if I were a complete failure. She could say words, but I couldn't get her to. She seemed to be able to do a lot of things that I just was not able to get her to do. I felt that maybe the others might be right: maybe it was the wrong approach, or the right approach but the wrong therapist.

Davy

He was such a beautiful child. Sweet, quiet, aloof. In his own world. But then, that's why I was seeing him, wasn't it? He lived on the second floor of a brick house in a nice Black neighborhood. Mostly people from the Islands. I don't remember which island his family was from, but it was one of the English-speaking ones, fortunately for me.

He lived with his mother, Lucy, his aunt, and their mother. The aunt was in college and worked and was seldom home. Mom also worked, nights, so I saw her often. Grandma was always around. Grandma was a big-time Christian, so the TV was continually on a Christian station in the kitchen. I don't think Grandma had ever seen a Jew in her life.

Immediately out of the kitchen was a dining room, and then a living room, and then a back room, which overlooked the street below. The apartment was very nicely furnished, with a huge chandelier in the dining room. I was afraid the TV would be a distraction, but I was soon to find that very little distracted Davy. He had only one passion in his little life according to Mom: a large rubber ball, half as big as him, that he would bounce, forever! He was interested in nothing else, she informed me.

Mom worked the night shift in the post office, and she tried to stay with me and Davy for every session. It is very rare that a mother will sit through a whole boring session, day after day. A mother's direct involvement is always the best chance for improvement. Davy was her first and only child. I had no idea who or where Dad was. It was none of my business. Mom would often watch as we worked in the living room while she sat at the dining room table if she couldn't be down on the floor with us. She very often fell asleep at that table. She was exhausted and trying her best to stay with us. It broke my heart to see such devotion and love for a child who was so distant. Otherwise, it was me and Grandma, who was not at all impressed with this whole therapy thing. She was always polite, however.

Our first session, October 31, surprised both Lucy and me. I had expected no response at all. He was clinging to Mom's side, as I laid out all my toys on the table. None of my beginner toys attracted him, but when I broke out the bubbles, that got his rapt attention. Then I blew on the harmonica, and he quickly learned how to do it. He was fascinated with it. Now he was laughing and making eye contact. I wanted to try my next trick, which is vestibular stimulation: holding him, spinning in circles, and singing, "The Wheels on the Bus." Mom said that he lets no one pick him up. He let me and was thrilled with the feeling of spinning in circles. He learned to push the buttons on the tape player. I left that day feeling very hopeful for his progress. So was Mom.

He was to start a school program this first week. He had a rookie teacher, and the teacher needed a lot of direction to work with a non-responsive child. She wrote typical beginner programs for him all at the "prompt level." He was passive as you "prompted" him through these programs. I suggested to his teacher that they work on only functional activities in the Center, as at home, he was able to turn a crank on a small music box, push the lever to let cars roll down a ramp, and bend a wrapper snapper upon my modeling it for him.

Mom and I felt like we were seeing progress at this early stage. Unfortunately, over the next two weeks, either I was sick or Davy was sick, so I didn't see him again until December 13. The next two days we reviewed what he had learned until this point. Unfortunately, he did not respond well.

By mid-December, it was obvious, to me at least, that typical discrete trial programs that were being written at the Center were not going to help. I wrote a letter to his teacher suggesting that we do different kinds of activities instead of matching, or imitation, or the other usual non-functional kinds of programs. I doubted that she'd be willing to switch. She wasn't.

I asked for a meeting with the teacher and the supervisor and Mom. I was able to convince them to switch from a Center-based program to a complete home program. There I would only work on functional things—at least until I started to see some language comprehension. We would submit the paperwork to the City for approval. In the meantime, I would have to follow the teacher's programs. Mom solved that problem. She quit sending him to school. He seemed to do better at home, where we could be out of the chair and use his favorite ball to work with. Slowly, I was able to get him to sit for up to ten minutes at the table.

I was soon to realize that Davy might learn something one day, do it perfectly for both me and Mom, and the next day, it would appear as if he'd never learned the skill. My notes were consistent. One day, great responding. The next day, no responding. When he did not respond, he would, like other children I had worked with, find a favorite spot on the ceiling to stare at. Angels that only he could see. Other than his big red ball, there was nothing I could attract him with. I used his ball to try and get "mands" or requests either verbally or with sign language. "Throw it. Push it. Bounce it. Go. Stop." No luck. Either he had it and bounced it like mad, or he did not have it, in which case, he would lose attention.

While I was pleased that we were now doing a home program, there was one big problem. It meant that he would be getting twenty hours of ABA, of which I could only do ten hours. Two hours a day. The service coordinator would have to find other therapists to fill in the other ten hours—either someone to work with him two hours a day or two therapists to work one hour a day each. This would not be easy to find so late in the year. Very few therapists that worked in early intervention knew anything other than discrete trial teaching. NET and PRT are difficult to implement, and I was afraid that they wouldn't find someone competent. They didn't. Two others were tried, and Mom fired them both, as Davy simply cried when they came. When I came, Davy would meet me at the door, take my hand, and lead me into the other room. Grandma was amazed at this. I was not. I felt a strong connection with Davy for some reason.

Mom had one other big concern: Davy was a "selective eater." Worse, there was food refusal. Mom could only feed him Pediasure in a bottle. You could touch his lips with neither spoon nor finger. In March, when he was two-and-a-half years old, he was taken for evaluations for his next school to begin at age three. In the course of the evaluations, they saw that he would not eat anything from a spoon and decided that a "feeding plan" must be implemented immediately. I had no objection, as I had observed it frequently in children with Down syndrome and occasionally with children with ASD.

Who and how would she run the program? The usual course of action was to bring in a "feeding specialist." If one was unavailable, either the speech teacher or the OT would "run the program." Whenever this situation came up, there was always an argument between the ABA teachers, the speech teachers, and the OTs. To the OTs, food refusal, like every other problem a child has, was due to "sensory issues." Which sense? What's the issue? The OTs never had a definitive explanation of what the "issue" was. But they did have the best example ever of an "explanatory fiction." They said that the child has, "sensory integration disorder (SID). If one were to point out that there is no research to verify "sensory integration" as a diagnosis, they would ignore you.

Everything to an OT is due to "sensory issues." Helen Keller had sensory issues. Which sense? Sight and hearing. What was the issue? Scarlet fever had made her blind and deaf. Specificity is required before dealing with any kind of malady. "Issues" is not specific. SID was a concoction made up by Dr. A. Jean Ayres.

"Ayres and her followers have portrayed sensory integration concepts as rooted in well-established scientific models of neurological structure and function. However, its basic concepts are unsubstantiated, and some have been refuted by research. In 2005, experts at the University of Rochester Medical Center concluded that there had been no adequate controlled studies either supporting the existence of SID as a distinct and definable entity or clearly demonstrating that SIT is more effective than no treatment at all."[13] The old saying applies when referring to OTs who diagnose "sensory issues": When all you have is a hammer, everything looks like a nail.

Most often, the speech teacher is assigned the job of coming up with a plan for food refusal. Why the speech therapist? Are they trained in such things? Not to my knowledge. Davy's speech therapist did not impress me much. For instance, she recommended to Mom that she write down the names of household objects—chairs, windows, tables, TV—on cards and tape them to all the items in the house. This would help Davy acquire language supposedly. Brilliant. If a child can read, it may indeed help. Davy could not read, of course. He was two years old! I showed the mother how crazy this idea was by doing the following.

I wrote the names of objects in Hebrew on cards and placed them on various objects. Then I asked Mom to look at the cards and name the objects. "But it's in Hebrew! I can't read Hebrew." I told her, "Davy can't read English! Don't waste your time with this technique."

I had no faith that this speech teacher would know where to begin with a feeding program. Another problem is that speech therapists usually meet with a child for a half hour three times a week. That gives them precious little time to work on speech acquisition and feeding.

I also had no training on food refusal. Oh sure, I'd read tons of ABA research papers on it and passed the tests to get credit and put the fancy little diploma on the wall, but reading about it and doing it are two entirely different things. It all seems so easy in the research papers. They're all the same: Child won't eat. We did this. He went from 0% to 100%, like most of the behavioral research papers that you read regardless of the problem.

On March 9, we began a full, twenty-hour-a-week home program. This was easier for Mom, as she wouldn't have to worry about getting him on buses and going to team meetings at the Center. His responding had improved a bit just before we started his home program. It was the last week in March when it was decided that I would be the one to work on feeding problems. I had no training and little experience with it. All I had were studies on the Premack Principle,[14] which states that the more probable or desired behaviors will reinforce less probable or undesirable behaviors. Your grandma taught you same thing: If you want ice cream, you must eat your peas.

We had to put him in his highchair for the feeding program, and he did not like that chair at all! I tried putting some banana pudding on the tip of his Pediasure bottle. It shocked him, but he ate it. I tried chocolate, and he rejected that. I tried to get a spoon to his lips and was able to touch his cheeks with it only. After a few weeks, I could touch his lips with a dry spoon but not a wet one. I used a spoon with his favorite juice, but he just went berserk when I tried to put it in his mouth.

In mid-April, he let me put it a glass to his lips, and so I then dunked it in his juice and put it to his lips. Surprisingly, he took the glass and drink independently! But it did not work with any other substance—pudding or water. Very small steps, but progress.

Then we went on Spring break for a week. When I returned, Mom had some exciting news for me. She told me that she and Grandma got Davy to eat from a spoon. Half a yogurt, one bite, break, bite, break. There was great celebration. A few days later, Mom told me that he would now eat while in the highchair. He also took a cheese doodle by himself and ate it. Finally, some optimism! It's a big thing when any child starts eating normal food. For one thing, no more Pediasure. That stuff is expensive, and even when the City subsidizes it, that's just a lot more paperwork and having to go to the pharmacy to get it. The best part was that it was not the OT, or the speech teacher, or me, the ABA teacher, who had successfully gotten him over that hurdle.

By May 2, he was eating all kinds of textures. He ate fried potatoes with ketchup even! That was the end of our "feeding program." In five weeks, he went from only Pediasure bottles to eating anything. So much for "sensory issues."

His progress in other areas, unfortunately, were not as good. We plugged along. On May 10, he finally got another ABA (supposedly) therapist to do an hour a day with him. His name was Alex. He was Russian, and I had not worked with him before. I was just glad that Davy would be getting more hours now. Hopefully, his responding would improve.

Alex was friendly and assured me that he had a lot of experience. "Don't worry, it'll be good." For Davy's sake, I was hoping he was right. Davy was a difficult child to work with: nonresponsive, evasive, prone to simply checking out and staring at his angel.

Two days after Alex began, I popped in early to watch a session. Davy was howling when I got there. Mom and Granny sat watching. I had brought a small new table and chair for him hoping I could get him to work at it. The plan was to ease him in and find enjoyable things for him to do there, such that he'd want to come to the table. Alex commented to me while Davy screamed, "This is good. You can trap his legs under the table!" Great.

One of the strongest complaints against ABA is that it was advised, for many years, that the therapist "trap" his legs under the table and thereby, "prevent escape." You can see it on old training videos and still find this "advice" in older books. Today, you will not find such suggestions, but for many years it was standard procedure.

Davy got used to working at the table with me, as I always made sure to have fascinating things on it ready for him. If he became bored, we took a break from the table and did other things away from the table.

After a few weeks of having introduced the table and chair, it was going well. Because there was no communication book, I had no way of knowing what the other two therapists were doing with him or how it was going unless his mother told me. Mom told me that Davy had been crying or screaming with Alex fairly often. My fear with that was making the table and chair aversive to him. If sitting at the table meant being bored for an hour, and Davy had no way to communicate that, naturally he would scream or cry. It would affect our work together as well. I told Alex that Davy must not cry during sessions. I suggested that, for now, just play with him. Soon, Mom told me that he did not cry but that Alex did not prompt or reinforce correct responses. I knew then that Alex had no such experience. Mom knew what "prompting" was and what "reinforcement" meant, as she had worked with me from the beginning. She did not see Alex prompting. When she asked him why he didn't prompt he told her that Davy must learn to do things for himself. Davy was becoming resistant to any work at the table. My biggest fear having being realized, I took a week vacation at the end of May. When I returned Davy smiled when he heard me at the door. I brought him to the chair to begin work, but he did not want to sit in the chair this day. Mom said that she'd Alex fired while I was gone because Davy cried too much. Maybe that's why he wouldn't sit at the table. Alex had indeed made it aversive for him to sit there.

One day, I brought a big—as in, a child can sit in it big—red bowl. He loved to sit in it and spin. We often did his programs while he sat in the bowl. He would rock or spin and laugh. He would have to learn to sit at a table, but for now, if this is what he wanted, this is what we would use.

On June 6, a new ABA therapist started with him. She was a Black woman named Connie, and I was told that she had a lot of experience and was good with kids. They told me this at the Center because I was upset that they'd sent me this guy who was destroying our program. It was better we didn't have another therapist than to have someone like that, even though the Center would be, "out of compliance." Fortunately, Connie was all they said she was.

July was a good month for Davy, for Connie, and for me. He sat well, attended better, responded better, and his affect was good: smiles, hand holding, eye contact. But his rate of learning was not improving. He would sign for something but only if prompted. His programs were still at the beginner level. He still stared off into space often.

We had a month left together. He'd certainly improved since we'd started, but he just wasn't learning. There was no increase in anything verbal. Nothing. In the course of our work, Davy learned a few signs, such as ball, drink, and spin (when sitting in the bowl). He had to be prompted to use them. He never used signs spontaneously, suggesting to me that it was not communication, just a rote response.

He managed to learn a few simple imitation behaviors and a few one step instructions but little more than that. He was good at Mr. Potato Head and the ABC puzzle, turning a crank on a music machine, and some other simple, functional activities. This was fairly typical, as often kids in special education do well on "performance" tasks and poorly on "verbal tasks." I used the performance tasks that he enjoyed to teach language but was not successful.

From our time together, October 2010 to August of 2011, I could not say that we accomplished much. There was little progress. He aged out on August 31st. I left them feeling like I had let him and Mom down.

A few side notes for a couple of interesting incidents that happened while I worked with him. One incident that was particularly sad firstly comes to mind. Mom was very private. There was never any talk of Davy's father, her personal life, or small talk. All I knew was that she worked nights at the post office. Mom usually worked with us by day. She was very involved in his program and very hands-on during therapy. She would watch me do a particular task with Davy and then she would do it—the way it's supposed to be in ABA but rarely is. If she was not right at the table or on the floor with us, she would watch from the dining room table, under the big chandelier. More often than not, she would fall asleep at the table. The therapy was routine, boring, and there was little progress to get excited about. It was hard to stay awake also because she worked nights, and Davy and I worked late in the afternoon.

There were about ten days when Mom was not home. This was unusual. I thought that maybe she had taken a mini-vacation or some kind of break. When she came back, just for the sake of conversation I asked her, "Where were you? Take a break? Have a good time?" She just said, "No." I could see that she was not interested in pursuing this conversation. About a week later, when she wasn't home, Grandma confided in me that Lucy had fallen asleep at the wheel while driving home from work and crashed into a tree. She had been in the hospital and insisted that Grandma not tell me.

I was very moved by the sacrifices she made for her son. She never complained. She did everything she could to provide for her confusing little boy and the rest of the family. She was evidently embarrassed about the crash and never mentioned it.

Another incident that was a bit more comical was that one day, as she fell asleep at the table under the big chandelier, suddenly, the house jumped, and the chandelier began wildly rocking from side to side. I was afraid that it would fall on her and jumped up from the floor toward her while she, also jarred by this, jumped up as well. Our eyes met. "Earthquake?"

I had never heard of an earthquake in New York, but sure enough that's what the news reported immediately on the radio.

Another (mildly annoying) event was the time Grandma interfered with our session. Davy loved to be tickled. I was able to get eye contact with it, worked on either saying or signing, "stop," and to strengthen our relationship, which was no easy task with Davy. Suddenly, Grandma shouts from the kitchen in her thick Caribbean accent, "Stop tickling that boy!"

She was angry. I asked why, and she told me that in her country people knew that tickling caused stuttering. I told her, "I'm sorry, but that isn't true." She said that everybody in her country knew it, so I'd better stop. Uh, okay. I stopped (when she was around).

One other memory that stands out is that a few houses down from Davy's—in this middle income, well-kept area—parking was usually not a big problem, but everywhere in New York is a problem when it comes to parking. Especially with their insane "alternate side parking" policy, which limited which side you could park on during certain times in order to facilitate street cleaning. One day, I came and found a large area of the street and an entire house roped off. This limited the already sparse parking. There was a sign on the front door that said, "Do not enter by order of New York City Police Department." I asked Lucy what happened there, and she said, quite matter-of-factly, "Oh, someone got shot to death."

Over the years in New York, I would hear this a few times. Where I grew up in Wisconsin, when you heard that someone got shot, you knew it was a deer hunting accident. I never got used to a lot of the "facts on the ground" living in New York.

Charley

Charley was a Black child who I saw every day, for a total of three months, in a daycare Center owned and operated by Orthodox Jews. They had an entire pre-school population of local Black children in the Crown Heights section of Brooklyn. The teachers and assistants were Black, and the administrative staff was mixed, Black and Orthodox Jews. The school staff reflected the neighborhood of Crown Heights: Primarily Black with an island of "Lubavitchers" in the middle. Lubavitch is the name of a group of Chassidic Jews who came from a city of the same name in Russia a few generations ago and settled there. It was a well-run school primarily utilized by working mothers in the "Crown Heights hood."

Charley had a funny last name. It was the name of a famous old Irish city that I cannot name due to confidentiality laws. His mother was, uh, something else. To me, she was always very friendly and concerned about her son, but she was a strange lady. To the service coordinators, she was an enigma. She never answered her phone, she never called them back when they left a message, and she refused social work services or team meetings. She was supposed to send lunch and diapers and bottles of juice every day, but often, her son came with an empty bag.

She did not answer the phone for me either. She would come the next day, and I would ask her, "What happened, Anna?" There was always some excuse: "Had to go shopping." "Went to the doctor." "Gee, I don't know, I sent it." "Maybe one of the other kids took it!" The school staff wanted her out but had no legal means for denying her service. The service coordinators at the Center were always calling me to ask how to get ahold of her. "She has paperwork due from the doctor!" He would lose services if they didn't have that paperwork. I told them that all I could do is ask her if and when I saw her.

Charley had a home program, meaning, at the daycare. He did not attend the Center, and all of his twenty hours a week of services were at the daycare. That was four hours a day of ABA. I could only do one. The service coordinators looked for someone else, or two others, to fill the other three hours. They were not successful. Crown Heights was not a neighborhood that people wanted to work in. So, aside from not attending the autism Center, he was missing three hours a day of therapy.

The daycare Center was run like a regular education preschool. Charley could not participate in classroom activities, follow instructions, socialize with peers, or follow any kind of schedule. I set up a little workspace for us in the basement. His teacher told me how relieved she was that one hour a day when I took him out of her classroom. She had to continually monitor and check him, and this took up a lot of time from her assistant.

His nose ran continually during our entire time together. At our first session in mid-October, I saw that he was very autistic: heavy hand flapping, little eye contact, and it seemed like he was completely deaf. He did not turn to look at noises or follow with his ears or eyes anything I tried to attract him with.

Our little set up was actually in the hall. They had a small classroom in the basement, but Charley would run to all the toys and posters, and it was impossible to get him to concentrate. The hall was better—no distractions. Unfortunately, the principal came down one day to tell me that we could not sit in the hall due to fire department regulations. So, we went into the classroom, and I partitioned it so he couldn't see past our "stall."

Charley did not attend to me much no matter what the setting: this room, that room, in a chair, out of a chair, other kids present, no kids present, this toy, that toy. He was going to be a challenge. I tried everything with Charley—ABA, NET, PRT, all the "best practices," and even a TEACCH program. Nothing. He either just giggled, rocked, or did nothing. He was very, very low functioning, as they say.

I also had another problem on this case. A new service coordinator had been hired and assigned to his case. She was Russian. Like many service coordinators, she did not know anything about autism or child development. Their job was to find required services for the children. Autistic, Down syndrome, brain damaged—it was all the same to them. Most of the other service coordinators had worked with me often over the years. They knew that if there was a difficult child needing an ABA therapist, I was the one to send. They also knew that I was one of the few who had no qualms about working in the hoods. They also knew how I felt about the "field" of occupational therapy and that I did not lie to parents. This often got me in trouble. Charley's case was a typical example. Mom asked me if I could change my schedule to open a spot for an OT.

I said, "No."

The new service coordinator called me, and she was angry! "Did you tell the mother that OT isn't important?"

"Uh, yes."

She said that the OT tried to call me repeatedly to arrange a time to work with Charley and that I had blocked his phone number. I laughed because at that time, I had just purchased my first smart phone and had no idea how to block phone calls. In any case, the service coordinator said that I could not tell mothers that OT was not important. I told her that I could not lie and wouldn't. She got hot. Finally, I told her, "I've got a schedule with this kid, and I'm not changing it for an OT, period."

As expected, I soon got a call from the director. "You can't tell mothers that OT is a waste of time!" I chuckled. The director felt exactly like me about OT, but what was he to do? The State, like the entire world, believes it does do something for children, regardless of the serious lack of evidence, and it was required that the Center provide these services. Okay, I got that! They could provide, but not on my time. I would not rearrange my schedule to make room for that nonsense. Fortunately for me, the service coordinator found another OT with available hours.

Three weeks after I started working with him, the Center informed me that they could not find another therapist. They said that I must add an hour with Charley and wanted me to add two hours. Three hours, every day, with a non-responsive child? We'd both be bored to death! That's pretty expensive babysitting. New

York City tax dollars at work! His mother didn't care because she said that he was already so much better! He wasn't. Not a bit.

One thing he loved was when I put him in a plastic tub with a rope and pulled him across the floor. He loved this and other physical interactions, like twirling in my arms or swinging. As this was the only thing he was excited about, I tried to get him to use these activities to communicate simple concepts like go, stop, run, and come. It didn't help. As soon as I stopped, he was back in his little world.

He had a few favorite toys, but I could not get him to name them or point to the one he wanted or use sign language. The speech teacher reported the same. The PT said that it was difficult to get Charley to follow instructions, verbal or otherwise. It was going to be a long year.

I met the father once. He seemed like a very nice guy and obviously loved his son. I was touched by how the father and mother loved him and simply were not concerned about his disability. He was who he was. He will be who he will be.

Charley missed a lot of therapy. He just didn't come. Getting Mom on the phone was impossible, as I said. When he did come, he was often sick, or had no food, or was sent snack foods that often he wouldn't touch. Instead of trying to rectify the food problem with Mom, I just handled it myself. Charley loved meat pies. He would seldom eat anything else. If Mom sent something else, forget it. I had him for two hours every day, and I decided that every day, I'd buy him meat pies from across the street, and juice if he didn't have any.

I would not tell Mom or anyone else. I suppose it was one of the things that a "mandatory reporter" should report, but I knew Mom had enough problems. As long as I had him, I would make sure that he ate and drank enough. I did tell the service coordinator in my Center, but she told me that it was impossible to get ahold of Mom, that Mom did not want social services, and there was nothing to be done. I can't imagine what would have been if I hadn't fed him every day. There just was no point in talking to Mom, and I did not want to hound her. She had terrible relations with my Center and with the staff at this day school. I wanted to be someone she could trust and feel secure with—someone who showed support instead of continually hounding her and telling her that she was negligent in this and negligent in that.

I went to work every day and "tried again" to somehow reach him. There had to be "something in there!" But no. I did not reach this unreachable star. He would age out at the end of December. When our time together was up, I was relieved because I felt helpless and hopeless and frustrated by his complete lack of progress. As they say in England, "You love 'em and leave 'em."

Nate

His name was Nate. I called him, Natie. He was so cute—so small, like a big baby. He had skin the color of fresh caramel and dark eyes that never looked at me. He lived with his mother, her brother, and their mother in an upper two-story apartment right off the very busy Flatbush Avenue. That meant that there would be no parking unless I paid the meter. The meter cost twenty-five cents for fifteen minutes. The ticket for over parking was something like thirty-five dollars. I had Natie for two hours every day, so that was two bucks a day parking for just one of my kids. He was worth it—another sweet baby who was nothing but innocent.

They were from Jamaica. Gotta love that accent. Mom was a very sweet lady who did not understand what was wrong with her only son. Grandma was always smiling. Uncle went to work most of the time, so I didn't see him much, but when he was home, he also had a very quiet, serene nature about him. Mom also worked, and often it was just me and Grandma. I didn't know anything about Nate's father. The subject was never brought up.

I worked with him on Sundays instead of Fridays, and Mom was always home then. The apartment was compact, with two bedrooms, a tiny living room, and a small kitchen. We were together for ten months, and there is not a lot to tell. Natie responded to nothing. He sat with his sweet smile and did not look at me or others, or anything I presented to him to try and get his attention. Even deep pressure did not bring eye contact. This was very unusual, even for kids on the spectrum. He went to the Center and had programs, but they remained at basic level the whole time. No updates, as he did not "achieve mastery" with any of them. There just was no helping him, and it broke my heart.

Between our time together and his work at the Center, he was receiving a lot of therapy—speech, OT, ABA, PT—and none if it had any effect on him at all. He remained on a ten- to twelve-month-old level until the end. It happens. It's a spectrum disorder: some kids will do great; some won't do anything. Natie was one of the latter.

There's not much more to relate about his lack of progress, but there are a few things I'll never forget about this case. The first is that his social worker was a well-intentioned, concerned woman who wanted to help. She was as touched by this scenario as I was. But she made a very serious mistake. I came one day to work with Natie, and I saw tons of bottles of pills on the table. I asked Mom, "What are all these pills?" She told me that the social worker brought him vitamins, fish oil, magnesium, and other nutrients. Once upon a time, it was thought that Vitamin B6 and magnesium would "cure" autism.

In any case, I asked Mom, who had little money, why she'd bought all of them. She told me that the social worker had paid for and brought them and told her that if Natie took all of this stuff, eventually, he'd become normal! My eyes grew wide.

"What?" I couldn't believe it. "She told you what?"

With her eyes full of hope and relief, she told me, "Yes, she told me that it's all a matter of diet."

Sure. Imagine if that were all there was to it. Change your diet, add vitamins, knock off gluten and casein, and viola: no more autism. After all, wasn't that what they said on Oprah? If you can't trust Oprah…. Unfortunately, all of the miracle cures that pop up in autism every few years never deliver. Maybe it works for some kids. Good. Great. Maybe those children had food allergies or maybe some other problem that resolved their autistic-like behaviors. Could be that removing milk from some kids relieved their symptoms? I'm happy for such families. But they never seem to work for more than a few. When these new miracle cures are reported, parents are aroused and research is demanded. In response, there will be launched clinical study after study, and well, that method just did not seem to work for others. That's why it is so important for professionals to be current in the literature. This social worker wasn't, and now I had a happy, hopeful mother to whom I had to tell the truth. Who's a mother to believe? This professional? That professional? This study that says the MMR causes autism, or that study that says the MMR does not cause autism? This mother swears by diets, that one swears by vitamins.

I told Mom that she must not give him anything until she first checks with her family doctor. Is the child allergic to anything? How about fish? A lot of people are allergic to fish, and this idiot social worker had given Mom fish oil! Astounding. I also told Mom that I had to report this. She begged me not to. She liked her social worker and did not want her to get in trouble. I told her I was sorry, that I had no choice. And so, I reported it to the Center and let them decide what to do about it.

The next day, I got an angry phone call. "Did you report me for giving vitamins to Nate?"

I told her that I had indeed. She was furious.

I stopped her screaming with a simple question: "Is Nate allergic to fish?"

She said, "What?"

I repeated the question.

She said, "I don't know."

I asked her how she could give fish oil to someone without knowing whether they're allergic to fish. The child could literally die! She changed the subject.

"What right do you have reporting me, and how could you do such a thing?"

I stayed on topic. "How could you give food supplements to a mother without a team meeting beforehand?"

There's an important concept in any therapy about, "independent variables." That means, if we are going to see progress, we have to be able to determine what caused it. Which variable? The therapy, or the food supplements? You have to take baseline data and then see the results to be able to determine what had the effect. Everybody on the team has to be aware of what is going on. It is irresponsible, if not downright dangerous, to independently give any kind of supplement to a mother unless all are advised. This did not deter the social worker from screaming that I was an idiot and not trustworthy and a few other names.

I told her, "Look, don't ever do that again!"

The Center decided that since no harm had been done, as the child hadn't taken anything yet, and Mom was going to get the doctor's approval, they would leave the matter and let her off with a warning. Mom asked the doctor about the supplements.

He told her, "They won't hurt, but they won't help."

Another thing I remember was that one day I had come to work, and Mom told me that she had fired the speech therapist. I was surprised. It is hard to find speech therapists in New York, especially late in the year. I asked her why. She told me that the therapist had told her and Grandma that I was incompetent, and they should replace me. I have no idea what brought this on. Maybe she'd wanted to try PECS, or maybe sign language, and I did not agree. Especially not PECS, with a completely non-responsive child. In any case, when she said this to Mom, evidently both she and Grandma ran into the living room where she and Nate worked and told her to "Get out!"

Wow. This was a perfect example of what happens when there is no communication between therapists or team meetings.

Now for the saddest part. Mom was about thirty, I guess. She worked, came home, and lived a life of "quiet desperation." It seemed to me she was very lonely. On top of that, her child, like many on the spectrum, did not seem to notice her. She occasionally said things to me that made me very uncomfortable.

"Ben, would you marry a Black woman?"

Uh, uh… I told her the truth—that I am an Orthodox Jew and can marry only an Orthodox Jewish woman. Color was not the issue. If I met a Black Orthodox Jewish woman that I liked, for sure I would marry her. The question was, of course, leading, and it hurt to hear it. One day she asked me if I would take Natie fishing.

"Uh, well, not sure I can do that professionally." As if this little boy would have the first idea what fishing was about. It was just her idea of an outing for "us," and, of course, there could be no "us." Then she asked a question that really threw me.

"Ben, if anything happened to me, would you take Nate?"

I don't recall my answer. I only recall the question and the stabbing I felt in my chest.

Nate never made any progress from beginning to end. Not with me, not at the Center, not with the other therapists. At the end of ten months, he remained inactive and that was the end of our relationship. However, whenever I passed the street they lived on, and I did often as Flatbush is a main street in Brooklyn, my heart always skipped a few beats. I really wanted to stop in and check on them, but I was aware that Mom would likely read that the wrong way.

There was one consolation. There is a school in Manhattan which has, or at least, then had, the reputation as being the best school for autism around. They took very difficult children. It was a private, very expensive school, but if you qualified, the State would pay for it. Trouble was that the demand was so high, the intake director never answered the phone, or her secretary said that she was on another line, and they would call back. They never did. As in, never. While I still had some time left with Nate, I pushed Mom every day to contact them to see if he could get in. Every day she told me that she couldn't get through. I had had this problem once before with them with another child. One day I came, and it was the same story after weeks of trying. So, I called them and got the secretary for the intake director.

I told her that I would like to talk to the intake director. As expected, she told me that the director was on another line, and please give me your number and we'll get back to you.

I asked her, "Do you have an intake director?"

"Yes, but she's on another line…"

I replied, "I don't believe you! I don't believe you have an intake director!"

Taken aback, she said, "What?"

"You don't really have one. Why should I believe you? After months of trying, I've never talked to her. After repeated promises to call back, she never has. I don't believe that you really have one. If you do, I want to talk to her, now, right now."

"Uh, I'm sorry, sir, all I can do is take a message, and—"

I cut her off. "Don't lie to me! You don't have an intake director!"

"Look, sir, as I said, she is very busy and—"

I raised my voice. "Busy? Busy doing what? She's so busy she can't return phone calls? She can't answer the phone? I want to talk to the director."

Her voice was shaking, and she said, "I'm sorry, try again later." She hung up. I also had the service coordinator at our Center call them and complain. Amazingly, I found out that this secretary had been fired shortly thereafter, and Nate was accepted into the program. The service coordinator at our Center called to tell me the good news, and then she laughed and said, "They also said that the secretary was crying, and you are never to call there again."

They should thank me. I had just made them another forty thousand dollars a year.

Queeny

I didn't have time to help this little girl. There was only one visit. She lived with her family in a basement apartment. They were Latino. Evidently, the parents were not happy with any of the previous therapists, so the Center sent me to try. The whole family—Mom, Dad, and kids—watched our first session as I engaged her with toys. She responded well. The parents sat silently watching. I was sure that they were encouraged, as she was doing great! That night I got a phone call: The family doesn't want you back because you work in your t-shirt.

Chapter Five

Twins

I had seven pairs of twins in my nineteen years in Brooklyn. Only one set of them were identical, and three of them were boy/girl. The identical pair was girl/girl. In each of them, there was one other similarity: One child was always far more impaired than the other—except for in the first case, which I will discuss. In that case, one of the boys started out as a genius, and the other was very impaired. By the time we finished, the genius had a seizure and lost everything.

Saul and Den

My first set of twins were two blond-haired, blue-eyed, beautiful little boys born into a wealthy family. They lived in a spacious apartment in Park Slope with a large deck and garden behind their house. Park Slope is considered the "Greenwich Village" of Brooklyn. Houses are all built together like row houses, but you couldn't exactly call these row houses. The monthly rent there was way beyond the means of your average Brooklyn dweller.

The father was finishing his Ph.D. in mathematics. He was from France. The mother had a master's degree in social work and counseling. The mother's parents were very wealthy people. Her father ran his own law firm, and her mother was private secretary to one of the wealthiest men in America. The couple had a live-in nanny from the Caribbean. Unfortunately, autism isn't very impressed with money.

Mom was tall, with long brown hair and an outgoing, very pleasant personality. She had quit her job to stay home with her babies. Dad was quite aloof. None of the therapists ever saw much of him. When he was present, he did not talk much, though his English was perfect. It used to be believed that children with autism descended from highly intelligent parents.

I used to believe that until experience taught me otherwise, but in this family, it seemed to fit the belief of the time. Mom's parents were around often. Although they were very wealthy, they were very down to earth, friendly people who were a pleasure to have around. These were their first grandchildren, and having the diagnosis "autism" was very frightening for them.

Mom spent time researching autism on the web. Usually that's a good thing, but it can also be very dangerous researching on the web. There are a lot of well-meaning people out there who swear that certain techniques, or foods, or medications will "cure" autism—or, at least, greatly improve the child's abilities. Mom bought into the GFCF diet—gluten free/casein free. No wheat or dairy products of any kind are to be eaten by the children.

Tales of miracle cures by the GFCF diet still abound today thanks to Oprah. In my thirty-five odd years in the business, I've seen this diet tried often. I've never seen it help anybody. At all. However, when parents ask me about trying it, I tell them what the research says, and if they still want to try it, go ahead. It's expensive, difficult, and often offers tasteless food. I also recommend they consult with their doctor and/or a nutritionist. I stress to parents that if autism was all about diet, we wouldn't have autistic kids running around. We haven't found a *Lorenzo's Oil*[15] for autism. Mom also bought

Mozart for Babies[16] and all the other videos that promised that if your child watched them, their IQ's would soar.

The boys had just turned two when our team started. They had a complete home program: two special educators, speech, occupational, and physical therapists. Mom's house was invaded by therapists coming and going for this boy and then that one. It was non-stop from 8 a.m. to after four. It was a good team as well. I've been on a lot of teams that were not good. This one was. It was under the direction of a very dedicated, knowledgeable, and experienced woman. There had been a few on the team before I entered the scene, but Mom had fired them. I replaced one of the special educators.

The boys were named Saul and Den. Apparently, no one knew whether they were identical or not. It would have been interesting to know just from a professional angle. Bottom line was it didn't matter. Each child presents with his own skills, abilities, strengths, and limitations. Saul was the genius—the proverbial, "Little Einstein." Before age two, he could name shapes, objects, colors, numbers, letters, and read words way beyond his years. He did not communicate verbally; he just named things in response to the question, "What is it?"

He could do puzzles, shape sorters, and manipulate objects. He made eye contact, he laughed, and he learned. We thought that he was probably "hyperlexic," which means beyond his years in reading ability. I've seen it written that often children that are hyperlexic present with "autistic traits." I've always thought it was the opposite: many kids with autism seem to have hyperlexic abilities. In any case, Saul was fun to work with because he learned so quickly, responded to verbal instructions with the correct action or verbal response, and was a happy, good-natured child. We all joked that Saul would eventually go to Harvard.

Den, on the other hand, was unresponsive. He understood nothing. He did not imitate. He made no eye contact. He could sit and stare off into space for hours. If you sat before him trying to prompt a simple response, you quickly became frustrated because, to him, you simply did not exist. It was hard, and I wondered how his parents felt knowing that he was so disabled. Mom said that Den was her "sweet baby." He was that. Like a little blond-haired, blue-eyed angel floating up in the Heavens indifferent to life below.

Saul's program book grew rapidly. He had imitation programs, verbal imitation programs, picture/object identification, matching by association (pictures of shoe with socks, etc.), one step instruction, sorting by color/class, and function (What do you drink with? What do you ride on?).

Den's program book remained at simplistic levels. Truth is, there was not much data to be taken on the programs he had. He reminded me, once again, of one of my professors when I was in grad school who had said, "With some children, no matter what you do, you will not be able to help them." I remember that I was enraged by that. As I said before, in my naive, young view, I believed that you could at least touch a soul and bring some sort of light into the darkness. Children like Den brought me down to Earth.

And so, we worked. We did our daily programs and had our monthly team meetings with all the staff and Mom. Naturally, we were all very excited about Saul's great progress even though we realized that it wasn't because we were such great therapists. It was because Saul had an extraordinary brain.

For Den, we would review progress, or lack thereof, and make suggestions about what else to try. It went like this for about six months, when all the therapists got that horrible phone call. "Saul has had a seizure and is in the hospital. Please don't come until further notice."

Saul had had a history of seizures, but they were minor. Evidently, this one would not prove to be. When we all returned a week later, we were sure that even though Saul was not responding well, he'd be back to his old self soon. He did not recover. He was now functioning at the same level as his brother. The light was gone from his eyes. It was heartbreaking.

We all finished the year except for one other ABA therapist that Mom had fired. Saul never regained what he lost, and Den never improved. The last time I heard about the boys, they were about ten years old and still wearing diapers. They could not speak and had no other communication system that was effective. Mom and Dad eventually divorced.

Davy and Jimmy

These two were from a completely different world than Saul and Den. They lived in Sunset Park. Sunset Park is not far away from Park Slope physically, but it's another planet ethnically and economically. Sunset Park is half Spanish and half Chinese. On one street, all the stores have Chinese letters; on the next, they are all Spanish. Davy and Jim lived in the heart of the Spanish section. Dad was an MTA (mass transit authority) cop who worked bridges and tunnels, and Mom was stay-at-home trying to deal with autistic twins in a small two-bedroom apartment.

These boys were obviously not identical because one was light and blondish, and the other was dark with jet black eyes and hair. They looked nothing alike. I was working with both of them in the beginning. After about a month, it became apparent to me that Jimmy was not "on the spectrum." He struck me as just language delayed, and with stimulation, I was sure that he would catch up. I requested a reevaluation, and sure enough, he was reevaluated a short time later and was not given further services except for speech. Before too long, he was like any typically developing kid his age and was quite a character. I remember mostly that he was very funny and good-natured. They did manage to pin an ADHD tag on him, however.

His brother Davy was exactly the opposite. He had classic "Kanner syndrome" autism. Right out of the textbooks. He was low functioning. That is PC for no language skills. He had no language, receptive or expressive, no imitation, no eye contact, and no tolerance for any therapists. He wanted to watch videos over and over. If he couldn't do that, he was usually screaming or tantruming. Needless to say, for sanity's sake, Mom let him watch them most of the time. When the therapists showed up, and he had to leave the room where he and his brother were watching a video, there would be a major tantrum that could go on forever.

In the early days of discrete trial teaching, it was thought that the only way to work with a child was to sit him in a chair in a secluded room with no distractions. The child would sit in a chair facing both the worktable and the therapist, who sat across from him. I bought into this belief as well, though I did not sit in a chair. I always sat on a cushion on the floor so that I could be at eye level with the child. The other change I made was that the table would be at a forty-five-degree angle between us, so just a corner would stick out between us. I did this because sometimes the child needs to face the therapist, and sometimes he needs to face the table depending on what task you're working on. The forty-five-degree angle prevented having to continually turn his chair. In a developmental Center, it's not a problem to turn the chair, but in the home, working in a carpeted room made maneuverability very difficult.

When I put Davy in the chair and sat across from him and began our sessions, the tantruming started immediately. I would break out the toys that most kids were transfixed by in the hopes of getting his attention. Davy was unmoved. There was nothing that I could entice him with—not food, not toys, nothing. The only thing that he liked, other than videos, was gross motor activity, such as bouncing on a bed.

Davy was one of my first teachers who instructed me to work "out of chair." I took Davy every day into the bedroom where we jumped and rolled and tickled and threw pillows. He had to make eye contact to get a pillow thrown at him. He had to follow one step instructions like, "jump," "pick it up," and "give me," just as we would have done at the table. In short, all programs written for

Davy by his teacher, we did, but in the environment which he most enjoyed instead of forced into a chair.

Davy did not learn a lot, unfortunately. I thought that for sure he'd never progress much because in a more structured, that is, restricted setting, like school, he mostly screamed and or cried. I ran into his mother a few years later, and she told me that he was now able to talk and was much calmer, though he still had "behavior problems." Patience and perseverance paid off evidently.

I am sure that whoever worked with him after me had to have a lot of patience and really cared about Davy's progressing. And they must have a had a lot of experience.

Ronnie and Paula

I did not work with Ronnie. He didn't need me. Ronnie did not need anybody. He was an absolute genius—definitely hyperlexic, and he had an incredible memory. He also asked questions that were way beyond his years about everything he saw. His vocabulary would put a high school kid to shame. Yet, Ronnie was "normal." He walked, he talked, he dressed himself, fed himself, and amused himself. His twin sister Paula, however, was another classic Kanner syndrome child. She had big, blue eyes, strawberry blond hair, and a smile from the Tundra mornings.

They lived with Mom and Dad in a White, working-class part of Brooklyn known for nothing in particular. Well, except for Italians. The biggest challenge in this case was Mom. Mom did not trust anybody—certainly not the schools or the City's Early Intervention teams. She did not trust the evaluators, the doctors, the therapists, or the team. She challenged everything anyone suggested for Paula and rarely agreed to suggestions. She had a major distrust of Hellen, who ran the program. This was a big mistake. Of all the professionals I've ever worked with, Hellen, who had an autistic brother, was probably the best. We had worked with Saul and Den together. Today, she runs a top-notch school for autism in Brooklyn.

For some reason, Mom liked me. She seemed to have some bizarre attraction to Orthodox Jews and repeatedly told me about all her Orthodox friends and relatives who had married Jews. She listened to me, and this was fortunate because often I could suggest things to her without the expected dismissal. The father—a big, strong Italian man—was like a passive kitty in front of his wife. What she said went. His opinion was worth nothing. He was simply his wife's cheerleader.

Paula was able to learn. She actually picked up a lot of skills and could attend well, but she was in her own little world, and it was not easy to penetrate it. Occasionally, some "delayed echolalia" would escape. "Echolalia" is the term for repeating words, or songs, or sounds that one has just heard. Delayed echolalia is repeating things one has heard in the past with no relevance to the present environment or activity. One man wrote of his son who constantly repeated things like "purple schnauzer," or "there are no blue traffic lights."

After I had worked with her for a while, it was obvious that I was not going to be able to get her to use words to ask for things. She would not repeat sounds or words. It seemed that she was incapable of speech altogether. One day, I held her as she stood on the windowsill looking out. I was pointing out trees, cars, people, bikes, buses, hoping she'd repeat one. It was a bright day with big, white fluffy clouds in the sky. Suddenly, she looked up and said in a chant, "Oh, look at the beautiful clouds." I was stunned. Had she been fooling me? I immediately tried to capitalize on this by asking, "Where, Paula? Where are the clouds?"

She ignored me. I was hoping for a display of "joint attention." If Paula could answer my question, it would suggest that she had joint attention, which means that if she was not learning well, it was because I was not able to get her to focus on what I wanted her to focus on. But, no, all she had done was simply repeat something she'd heard before. Delayed echolalia. Where had she heard it? Probably someone had read a book to her once, or she'd seen it in a cartoon on TV. She was not communicating with or to me. She was not asking me to share a vision with her. She was simply repeating something she had heard in reference to clouds. It did not matter to her if I heard it, or if anyone heard it.

So, why did she say it out loud? Why didn't she just see the clouds and think to herself, *Oh, look at the beautiful clouds*? I don't know. According to the Verbal Behavior people, all "verbal behavior" has a function. What would the function of, "Oh, look at the beautiful clouds" be? They would call it, "internal stimulation." Fine, but that's not communication, that's not even "language." It's simply repeated words in relation to something undeterminable.

I can only guess how many other phrases she had memorized and never repeated. Were the clouds "beautiful" to her? Does a two-year-old child, autistic or not, understand the concept of "beauty?" I doubt it. But even if she did understand that these clouds were beautiful, the fact that she'd said it out loud, in the presence of a listener, still did not constitute communication.

A common mistake made by people working in the autism world is thinking that something one of their kids has been taught to say, constitutes communication. A typical example can be found in the book, *Without Reason*,[17] by Charles Hart, who wrote about his son, Ted, and Charles' brother, both of whom were autistic. Ted's father received an excited call from his son's school when he was in his early teens. They had taught him how to answer the phone. Or so they thought.

Here's how they did it: Ted was in a room with a phone and an aide. The teacher was in another room watching through a two-way mirror. She made a call to Ted's room. Ted was instructed to lift the receiver and say, "Hello?"

Then the teacher, behind the mirror, would ask, "Is Jane there?" and Ted was instructed to hand it to the aide (Jane) and say, "It's for you." So, they brought Ted's father to the school in order to show him the amazing new communication skill Ted had learned. Ted's dad was in the other room, behind the one-way mirror. He called, and Ted picked up the phone and answered, "Hello?"

But Ted's father did not ask, "Is Jane there?"

He said, "Hello, Ted, this is Daddy. How are you?"

Ted handed the phone to Jane and said, "It's for you." This was an "operant" response. He'd been taught to answer, "Hello," listen to words, and then respond, "It's for you."

I was assuming that Paula's, "Oh, look at the beautiful clouds," was also just a response she'd learned to make upon seeing clouds. Simple stimulus-response.

By some miracle, the team lasted out a tumultuous year. Paula was acquiring skills, but she did not learn to communicate, to use words appropriately, to ask for help, problem solve, or much else, unfortunately. Mom blamed the team. Mom also believed that her daughter was "regular-ed" and enrolled her in a school that was probably not going to be able to handle her. Our sessions ended soon after a very unfortunate incident happened.

Someone had left a tissue with blood on it in the little trash can in Paula's room. Mom saw the tissue and went absolutely wild. She immediately took her kids to be tested for bloodborne pathogens such as AIDS and demanded to know who had left the tissue. Naturally, no one was about to take the blame because it would probably mean facing some kind of charges, disciplinary action, a lawsuit, or who knows what with this mother. Truth is that my memory is pretty bad, and it may have been me. I strained my brain to remember whether I'd had a bloody nose that day, as I get them occasionally at various times of the year. It probably was me, but I just couldn't remember. We never did find out who it was.

That is where I left the twins: an angry mother, a little girl who hadn't learned much and was on her way to a school not intended for autism, and a relieved team just happy to be out of there.

About a year later, I ran into Mom, Dad, and Paula at the supermarket. Paula was standing up in the cart. She was looking and labeling all the things she saw. "Bananas, apples…" to no one. I asked how it was working out at the new school.

She said, "They're a bunch of idiots."

Annie and Ruth

The girls were identical twins—short, with jet black hair and eyes. Beautiful smiles. Like little dolls. I first saw them in the integrated classroom. "Integrated" here doesn't mean what is usually meant by that term in special ed. Integrated usually means typically developing children in the same classroom with children who were non-typically developing but higher functioning, like Down syndrome, speech delayed, or mild mental retardation (today, called "cognitively delayed"). In Annie and Ruth's case, integrated meant they would be in a classroom of children with less severe disorders than they had but not regular ed kids.

Annie seemed to be thriving in this environment. She was picking up words and responding to language. Ruth was distant and seemed to be completely unaffected by anything in the environment. She had no interest in the other children, their activities, toys, or engagement in "circle time."

In all environments, Annie was outgoing and learning quickly to play with peers, communicate, and socialize with children and adults. She was using words to make requests—if not in full sentences than with eye contact, and her intentions were clear. Ruth was very withdrawn. She seemed to be correctly diagnosed with PDD/NOS. "PDD/NOS" back in the day of the DSM-IV meant "pervasive developmental disorder/not otherwise specified." Meaning, it is not mental retardation, it is not a genetic disorder, it's not brain injury, but it's got to be called something! Today in the DSM-V, she would have been labeled ASD—Autism Spectrum Disorder.

Ruth had no words, no eye contact, did not seem to understand language, and had no social contact with peers or adults. It appeared that she would be content to sit in a corner all day at school or just wander from spot to spot outside of school.

Their mother was outside the classroom every day looking through the two-way mirror on the door. She would be there the entire two-and-a-half hours without moving an inch. Mom spoke Spanish as a first language, English and Hebrew as second and third. She was a convert to Judaism from Morocco who had married an Israeli man, and they were trying to make a living in New York. Dad worked in construction, and Mom stayed at home with the girls. They had been married many years and were never able to have children until finally, after years of trying, they had these two precious little girls.

Mom would not accept, at first, that either of them had any problems, but when they did not talk by age two, she reluctantly agreed to enroll them in a program for early intervention at a different Center than ours. Before too long, she found reasons to take them out. One reason was that the girls were getting sick a lot, and Mom was convinced it was because of an environment with so many other children in it. Another was that she claimed she saw nits in their hair, and they had to have gotten them at school. So, just as quickly as she'd enrolled them, she yanked them out. Mom was convinced, luckily, by a service coordinator to have the children come to our Center and to continue with an ABA program in the home.

I was recommended to Mom because it was obvious that Ruth was going to be difficult to work with, as she did not like the highly structured environment. She would need an experienced therapist. A speech therapist was assigned as well as an occupational therapist. Mom had met me a few times at the Center, and we talked about her girls in both English and Hebrew. She was thrilled when she was told that I would be able to work with Ruth. I was also happy to have a crack at trying to get to this distant child.

They lived in a nice, second floor apartment. The main door opened to a little hall with the girl's bedroom on the right. Past the door was the living room. The living room was festive, as it had a fish tank, musical instruments, and Moroccan decorations all around. A feeling of joy was felt there. Beyond the living room was a small, attached dining room with windows overlooking the streets below. There was a bathroom off the living room and a kitchen with swinging, twin doors. The trouble with the living room, as in most houses, was that all their toys, their videos, anything they loved to play with, was in that room. It would be hard to hold Ruth's attention there. Not to mention the phone that seemed to be forever ringing, and Annie forever running in and out of the room wildly swinging those double doors. All this pulled Ruth's attention away from me.

I told Mom that in the beginning at least, we must work in isolation, as I needed to establish a rapport with her, and she had to feel that I was fun to be with, or I'd never get her attention and/or teach her anything. I could not compete with all the distractions.

There was an opening in the wall between their bedroom and the living room that Mom could look through whenever she wanted and as often as she wanted. I began to work with her in the girl's bedroom. It was small and cramped, but Ruth adjusted. She did better than I thought she might because she began to repeat words, actions, and respond to her name with eye contact on the very first session. She sat well for the whole hour. She did not want to stop and cried when I packed to go. She was given twenty hours a week of ABA, of which I was doing ten and writing the programs.

It was going well. She could sit readily for the hour, and I began writing simple programs, which were learned quickly. She did not like doing "discrete trials," and I adapted my teaching for her. Mom would often look through the window to see how it was going. She said that she heard a lot of laughing. Good!

After three weeks, we all felt that things were going well. One day, as I was doing the paperwork in the living room, I broke out a balloon for her and she said, "balloon" and "blow." Mom was thrilled. I hadn't taught her this, so it was obvious there was more to her than her evaluations suggested. The fact that she did not like discrete trial teaching was a good sign.

Then, it all changed. Dad, whom I'd never met, came home one day, walked into the bedroom where we were working, shook my hand, and thanked me for the work and progress. We spoke in Hebrew. The next week began the ten-day break for Passover. I was both surprised and relieved at how well Ruth was doing.

During the Passover break, I came home one day to find a message on my phone.

"My rabbi doesn't like it that you are working alone in a room with Ruth."

I called Mom, and she told me that she didn't care where we worked, but her rabbi didn't like it. I explained to her again how important it was to work in isolation for a while until we'd established enough of a rapport and consistency in our work.

She said, "My rabbi doesn't like it." I had a wild feeling that it wasn't her rabbi but her husband who didn't like it.

Judaism has a rule called, "yichud." It means, "oneness" or "being as one." It is forbidden for a Jewish man to be alone with a Jewish woman (or female child) in secluded environments if they are not man and wife. But, in this case, there was no problem with yichud because Mom was in the house and able to come in or peek in at any time. This is not considered a violation of yichud. I assumed that yichud was the problem with her rabbi. So, I went and got a bunch of responses from different rabbis and brought them over to their house to show them that what we were doing in the house was okay according to most of the people who judge these sorts of things.

They were not home. I had these responses in a plastic bag, and I slipped them under the door. I sincerely thought that this would clear up the problem, and we could continue. That night I had another, very angry message on my phone.

"My rabbi knows all this! This isn't a game!! We don't need those papers you threw under our door."

I was flabbergasted. I called her. She picked up the phone, and she was livid. She literally screamed into the phone, "My rabbi told me one thing, and my husband's rabbi told us something else, and anyway, I don't want you working with her in the bedroom anymore." Seems it was her all along. Again, I began to tell her about isolated environments, but she stopped me and said, "The other therapists work in the living room on the couch. Why can't you?"

Yes, why not indeed? The other therapists, speech, and OT came a few times a week for a half hour. What do OTs do with children on the spectrum under three years of age? Play pattycake. There is absolutely no research to verify that anything an OT does with pre-school children on the spectrum is credible. Yet, everybody includes them and pays them well for their "services." Great racket. Speech therapists might be helpful with young children on the spectrum but usually are not. I was always greatly relieved when I found speech therapists who knew about autism and how to work not on speech but on communication. In any case, neither of them had programs individualized for her or took data. Taking data is important because it suggests when to update a program of skills or how to work toward short-term goals and long-term objectives. What did they write in their quarterly progress reports? "Child is responding better." Evidently, that was good enough for the City. So, Mom was correct. The other therapists simply did not need to be in a therapeutic environment because they were just playing pattycake.

I told Mom that the other therapies were not as intensive as ABA and did not require work in isolation. (What I really wanted to tell her was, "Good thing you're not paying for the services. Let the City of New York pay for pattycake.)

She said, "Well, I don't care. You either work with her in the living room or not at all."

I suggested that she find another therapist. She said, "Fine!" then slammed down the phone.

I was glad to hear about six months later that even though Mom had stopped all ABA therapy, Ruth was doing much better.

Kim and Kenny

I must make an admission. It was over ten years ago that I worked with these guys. My notes from then are confusing. There was a huge mix-up about which therapists were assigned to which child. Kim and Kenny were quite different, but in the beginning, it was not so easy to tell them apart. I began working with one of the boys and as will be seen, I received a panicked call from the service coordinator that I was working with the wrong kid. As I write this now I don't remember which boy I started with, making this a confusing chapter to write. Such a thing would not happen today because all session notes are done electronically and recorded immediately. But in those days, everything was on paper and handed in once a month. I am going to try and rely on my notes that I wrote back then!

Kim and Kenny were not identical but similar in appearance. They were Black, from well-to-do parents who both worked full time. I worked with them at the paternal grandparents' house. Preemies born at seven and a half months, they were both considered lucky to have survived. These were the parents' first children.

I was asked to work with Kim. Kim was "higher functioning," as they say, than Kenny. They had been getting therapy for a few months already when I came on the team. I was not keen to take this case because the twins stayed, by day, with their grandparents who lived way over in East New York, which is right next to Queens. It would take at least forty-five minutes to get there and forty-five to get back. That's an hour and a half out of my daily work schedule, on good traffic days.

His teacher was a rookie, first year, and with minimal previous experience. She would be writing the programs as team leader. Once again, Ayelet, the service coordinator, was successful in getting me to go against my better judgement and accept the case.

Grandma's house was beautiful—very stylish, with expensive furniture and curtains. There were floor plants everywhere, which is not good around twin two-year-old boys!

I explained the program to Grandma. I could tell from her expression that she was not thrilled with this whole "therapy business." She did not like all of the different therapists tracking in and out of her immaculate house every day. She confined herself to the kitchen when we were there, which was just a short distance from the living room where we worked. The therapy up until now hadn't shown any progress to convince her that all this trouble was worth anything. Besides, "Ain't nothing wrong with them boys!"

As instructed, I began working with Kim, who was far more advanced than Kenny. I thought it odd because I was usually assigned the lower functioning children, as I was more experienced. We began in May. Kim was doing fairly well. He attended, learned quickly, and was readily amused. He was fascinated by my drawing a circle with a crayon! Connie, a therapist who was working also with both boys, suggested that I work with Kenny, as he was far more in need of an experienced therapist. But Kenny already had his two hours filled: one with Connie and one with somebody else. Five days after Kim and I began to work together, I received an urgent call from the service coordinator. "Hey! You are supposed to be working with Kenny, not Kim!" What? How could such a mistake be made?

I switched to working with Kenny. Kenny was a world away from Kim. So, the set up now was that Kenny had two experienced therapists for his two hours a day of in-home therapy, and Kim had Connie and Alex. Alex was a Russian with no background in autism or ABA.

After three months, Connie suggested that Alex be dropped, as he was not qualified to work with such children. Alex would sit and "work" with his iPad for the entire hour. It was very entertaining and kept Kim quiet but did nothing for him. Alex did not follow the programs or take data. So, he was taken off the team, and I took over an hour with Kim. Unfortunately, my first day back to work with Kim, Alex was also there for the session. I called the supervisor, and she told me that, as of this day, Alex was off the case, and I was to take over. Evidently, nobody told Alex! It was not my place, but I had to tell him, on the spot, that I was taking over.

It was going great with Kim, as he learned quickly and soon began to sing and interact. His rookie teacher was writing programs for him that were far too easy. Easy programs means a very bored child. Breaking the rules, I stopped doing the programs and let them rely on data from Connie while I probed for higher level skills.

Kenny was going nowhere. His programs were not well written and not at all appropriate. In fact, the typical discrete trial teaching was not appropriate, so I decided to use natural environment training which meant working out of the therapy chair. He much preferred this, but there was one big problem. Grandma did not like it. She would come storming into the living room telling him to sit down. I told her that I did not want him to sit down, but to act natural and we'd replace screaming and tantruming and running around with appropriate behavior and communication eventually. I tried to explain that each child must learn in a way that he enjoys and Kenny did not enjoy sitting in a chair for two hours a day.

Grandma would have none of it. He was "messing" with her plants, tugging at the curtains, jumping on the furniture, "destroying her home." She was right about the plants and the curtains. I tried to keep him away from them, but could not keep him from the plants as they were all over the house.

He was not jumping on the furniture—he liked to sit on the couch, but Grandma did not want him on the couch. She continued to come storming into the living room and scream at him, "Sit down, boy" (meaning, at the therapy table), while giving me the evil eye. What could I do? I had to continue working with him in the chair trying my best to keep him entertained, and hopefully, learn something. Grandpa was a sweet old man who just laughed.

At the team meeting with Mom, I asked if we could do something about her mother-in-law interfering. Mom smiled and said, "No."

I worked with both boys steadily from September of 2011 to August of 2012. By the end of March, Kenny hadn't moved an inch. There was no response, no eye contact, nothing to suggest that he had the slightest idea what we were both doing there together day after day. He hand flapped wildly and made funny vocal noises when he did like something. I found at times the only thing that I could do was hold him in my lap to prevent him from "destroying" Grandma's house and to keep his attention. Often when I did this, Grandma would storm in and tell me, "Don't hold him! He's a big boy and gets babied too much!" Meanwhile, his mother was asking via the communication book why no one was writing about his progress. Sigh, what could we write? There simply wasn't any.

And so it went until the end of August. My frustration with trying to help Kenny was intense. He was a beautiful little boy with a contagious laugh and bewitching smile. But there was nothing there. I tried both the teacher's discrete trial teaching, natural environment training, and sign language, but nothing helped. Would a different approach have worked? Verbal Behavior? Floortime? Pivotal Response Training? Dolphins? Diet change? I have no doubt that advocates of each particular method would assure everyone that their method would have worked. Maybe. I doubt it.

By November, his brother Kim seemed capable of imitating oral motor movements and repeating words. Kim seemed so smart and capable and I just could not accept that Kenny was not capable of these things. Therefore, I continued to push Kenny, but it soon became obvious that I was pushing too much. Once I started working on oral imitation, his behavior decreased rapidly. I had to back off, at least until the December break.

When we started up again in January, I tried again. The team wanted to try sign language with Kim, but Mom opposed this idea. I suggested a communication board, but this idea was also rejected. He had begun, since returning from the break, to repeat some sounds—Sss, Mmm, Pppp—though he didn't like it much. Mom was with us one day after the break, and I asked her to join us. She watched as Kim verbally imitated a few sounds, played the harmonica, and operated various toys.

By the end of January, Kim was saying choo-choo, go, wind it up (with help), juice, and trying very hard to repeat other sounds/words. He could say the alphabet. He was starting to understand that words caused events. I concentrated our work on verbal imitation and verbal requesting. On February 29, we had a staff meeting with Mom present. She reported that she was very pleased with Kim's progress. Then, in the first week of March, Kim began to use words! It was very exciting to see this little boy go from "non-verbal" to verbal. By mid-March, he was answering "wh" questions. That put him in a whole new category. He understood that words make things happen, and due to his intelligence, he would get frustrated when he didn't know the words. He would suddenly scream or throw things due to this frustration, as we hadn't taught him the critical skill called, "Help me," yet.

When he did this, Grandma would come flying into the room and scold him with an evil eye on me. I asked her how would she feel if she suddenly found herself in Japan? I'm not sure she got the analogy, but she left us after that. Thankfully, Grandma was now a bit more enthusiastic about therapy, as she saw real results with Kim. The bad side of that, of course, was seeing how little Kenny was advancing. Not at all actually. How do you balance the joy for one against the heartbreak of the other?

Kim's aunt took him to church every Sunday, and one particular Sunday, toward the end of June, he burst into song. We had a few weeks remaining, and Kim and I just sang a lot from that point on. He loved music, and so that's what I used to get him to communicate. He had to request songs, make eye contact, and answer questions to get his plastic microphone, which he loved to hold as he sang. He had to verbally request the microphone.

It was so gratifying to see such growth in a child. I thought that someone could use the twins as a case study to show that some kids will improve, and some won't. It could be the method that makes the difference, or it could be the skill level of the therapist, or it could simply be that the child was not capable of making much progress. Kim did great. Kenny made no progress at all.

Hugo and Ruth

The family was from "the Islands." Haiti, to be exact. The father was a certified preacher, and Mom was stay-at-home with the twins. I know it's not supposed to be this way, but truth is, you just really like some kids more than others. Hugo was so cute, I really enjoyed just being able to be with him. His sister was as well. The two of them together were a riot. They were all over the place but so incredibly happy and fun. I soon came to be calling him, Hugobi Doobi.

His sister was, supposedly, fine except for continual toe walking. I had my doubts about her not being on the spectrum, but Mom insisted that she was fine. She wasn't. Ruth was not brought in for evaluation, though she went along with Hugo for his, and I don't know how they missed it!

This story is one that had a happy ending after a long, long trial of not going well at all. Dad was a short, fiery little man, profoundly serious, and I think, somewhat taken aback to have an Orthodox Jew as a therapist. Fortunately, he never brought up the subject of religion. Mom was a nice lady but overwhelmed by having twins and one so obviously disabled. Grandpa also lived with them in their upper story apartment in a middle-income part of Brooklyn. Mom's sister visited often, and they sat just off the kitchen at a table in a little room between the kitchen and the living room. The apartment was small, but they seemed content.

Hugo had a habit of hanging on door handles—one in particular in the kitchen that opened to a closet. His father did not like this at all, and it seemed to be his main complaint that Hugo engaged in this behavior. Dad did not seem to be concerned that Hugo did not talk, or his wild "stimming" with his hands. He just wanted me to get him to stop hanging on the door handle.

I tried to explain that this behavior was, like hand flapping, a self-stimulatory behavior, and it really wasn't worth all the effort it would take to work solely on that. He'd stop eventually. But no. This bothered Dad a great deal, and we had to work on his stopping it. And so, we did, but I did not interrupt my programs for it. On breaks I would just make sure playing with me was more fun than hanging on a door handle. Simple as that, the behavior stopped. Now we could concentrate on more important goals: object ID, picture ID, imitation, following one step instructions, and joint attention.

He did not go to the Center, taking all of his therapy at home. I wrote the programs. He had a new therapist that worked with him for two hours at night, after my two hours in the afternoon. For some reason, Mom did not want a Center-based program. Although we did a four-hour-a-day home program, I tried to convince her that it was always better to be Center-based, with a few hours of home therapy. Eventually, she agreed because for over four hours a day, plus speech and OT, his sister had to be "out of the way," and in this small apartment, there was no "out of the way." Because we could only work in the living room, the TV had to be off, and this was a big problem for Ruth and for Mom, who used the TV as a babysitter.

His night therapist was a rookie and not well trained. I insisted that she follow the programs, but she seldom did. I was getting no feedback on what she was doing with him, as she also did not write in the communication book. When I asked her why she did not write in the book, she told me simply that she didn't have time. She was there for two hours with a low functioning child! How could she not find time? When I complained to our supervisor that the ABA therapist was not doing the programs and not taking any kind of data, the supervisor informed me that there was nothing she could do, as they found this therapist working at another agency and our supervisor could do nothing. The only other option was to fire her, but then finding a replacement for her would be difficult, and the Center would be "out of compliance" for not servicing Hugo with his allotted hours in the meantime.

Eventually, Mom gave in and sent him to the program. I was no longer team leader, as the classroom teacher took over that role. I was relieved, as now she could worry about missing hours and therapists who don't take data or use the communication book. It also meant that we would both see him for just one hour a day. Further, we'd all have to change our times working with him after he got home from the Center.

The change of schedule brought a new problem, however. The schedule changes interfered with the OT's schedule. Either an ABA therapist had to give up time for OT, or they would have to find an OT who could work at a different time. I let the service coordinators figure it out.

Mom went to the Center with him every day. In the building where the Center was, they also did evaluations. I convinced her to have her daughter evaluated, "as long as she's there anyway." Mom was reluctant mainly because she did not want to hear that both of her kids had autism. After my continual nagging, she had her evaluated. Now, she was sending two kids to the Center and getting home services for both.

Ruth was "higher functioning" and immediately learned well and began to converse, follow instructions, and master programs. She was obviously, to me at least, on the spectrum, but it was evident mostly in social/communication skills. Cognitively, she learned fast. I began to work with both children for an hour, and another therapist worked with them both for an hour every day.

Time went on, and Hugo's father continued to be thoroughly unimpressed. I couldn't blame him, for there really was not a lot of progress for Hugo. Fortunately, after six months in the program, Hugo started to respond. He had begun to make full eye contact, learned the names of things, began to imitate verbally, and was more social. I'm not sure what made the difference, but at this point he was clearly on a much higher level. He could answer one-word questions and name colors, shapes, and letters. One thing that really helped was a toy bus that had the alphabet in buttons around it. He loved to push the buttons of the letters and repeat the names. I found this with many of the children that I worked with. People familiar with autism know the importance of the ABCs. Unfortunately, many special education therapists, speech therapists, and others simply do not know anything about autism. They have their master's degree in special education or speech, and that is sufficient to be hired to work with such children. It's not. There are many characteristics that you find in autism that you may or may not find in other children.

The importance of using the alphabet is vital to know when working with children on the spectrum. What attracts children on the spectrum to the alphabet? I'm not sure, but my guess is it's regularity (it doesn't change), it's cadence (singing the song), it's predictability, and a love for naming things and putting things in order, over and over again. While many professionals will insist on beginning with "manding," which is fancy jargon for "requesting," I have always found that "tacting," or naming objects and pictures, has "higher reinforcement value" than manding. If you think about it, it makes sense. If you don't communicate or understand language, why would you think to ask others for things? But, if naming pictures or objects is a passion, the child is far more likely to do as such. In any case, knowing something about the characteristics of a particular disorder is vitally important in directing people on how to help others.

Hugo had another common problem found in autism, which was food selectivity. Ruth would eat anything you put in front of her. Hugo was more typical in that he only ate a few things. Mom ground his food into a mush, as so many mothers do. Supposedly, the speech therapist was working on this, but like most speech therapists I've ever worked with, she had no idea how to help with this. As always, the OT said it was a "sensory issue."

The first thing that must be determined with food selectivity is whether there is a physical reason that the child will not chew or swallow or bring anything to his mouth. If it is physical, the doctor will address that. If it's physical, and an ABA therapist tries a behavioral intervention in order to "increase eating behavior," it simply won't succeed and will cause the child more suffering. If it is not physical (which it usually isn't), then you can try different methods to get the child to try new textures, tastes, and consistencies.

Fear of unknown things is called Xenophobia. While today it's used primarily to mean fear of foreigners, it actually means fear of anything unfamiliar. What might cause this fear of eating with pre-school children?

Here is an example familiar to all of us: When you go to the doctor, he'll ask you to open your mouth and say, "Ah." Suddenly, he's thrusting a stick into your mouth and pressing down on your tongue! What in the world? How far is he going to stick that thing? How long is he going to keep it there? What if I throw up? What might be the basis of your fear? In my opinion, it is your lack of control, lack of predictability, pain, and not understanding why the person is sticking this thing down your throat! Now, add to that an inability to communicate and having no theory of mind (knowing the intents/thoughts of others), and the problem is much worse. So, how can someone try to spoon-feed such a child? One other problem is that to the child, "eating" means McDonald's pancakes or chicken nuggets. Due to "rigidity of routine," such a child will not tolerate anything else.

I had one technique that often worked, and I tried it with Hugo. We knew Hugo had no physical issues. So instead of trying to "reinforce eating behavior," I simply told Mom to keep him hungry until I got there. Then, as we worked, she would bring out foods that he would never touch, such as pretzels, nachos, and crackers. I just carried on working with him, and I ate as we worked, all the while saying, "MMMmmmm, this is good, yum." I would "accidently" drop a few on the table.

I tried it first in December. Nothing. He would not go near them. Then, on February 17, as Mom and Dad were home watching the session (a rare event!), for the first time, he picked up and ate chips, pretzels, and crackers (which became his favorite), and we were all absolutely stunned. Mom shrieked, and Dad's eyes grew wide. I had to pretend it was no big deal, or Hugo might be put off by my reaction. There was, of course, no "sensory issue." It was simply a phobia of unfamiliar things. From that point on, he began to eat all kinds of different foods and textures, though he would still refuse certain textures that he didn't like.

In the end, after they "aged out," Ruth had made a lot of progress, and Hugo had made some. I was sorry to leave them. His parents were sad to see me go, too. Things had changed for the better in that house. I often drove by their house and really wanted to visit, but it is never a good idea. Parents have to move on to new therapists, new programs, and a new team. Hopefully, better than the one we had been on.

CHAPTER SIX

More Twins

Yeshiah and Nessie

I'm not sure how to write this next case. It is an extraordinary case that will live in my memory forever. The children involved are eleven years old now, and I'd give anything to know how they're doing. But I can't because of "confidentiality." I left them at age three, as always, and have had no contact since.

This case is an incredibly sad success story. It is the kind of "case study" you read about in college in "social worker 101" classes but are sure you will never see in real life. The children's names fit the story beautifully, as Yeshiah in Hebrew is pronounced "Yeshia," which means, "God helps me," and Nessie's ("my miracle" in Hebrew) recovery really was a miracle.

They lived in Bushwick—a section of Brooklyn on "the other side of the tracks." The inhabitants there were mostly Black, from the Islands, or Puerto Rican. In this case, the female caretaker, Ana, was Puerto Rican, and the male, Reg, was also Puerto Rican but grew up in Arizona where he met his wife, Ana. These caretakers were not the parents of the twins. Their biological mother was a young lady who had also been raised by Ana. The mother, whose picture was on the wall over the cribs of the twins, was dying in a hospice somewhere in New York. There was never any mention of the father.

For many months, I did not ask who the picture was hanging there, nor had any questions about parents. Such information would make no difference in my work with them, but it did account for one thing. I never got a feeling that Reg was very much interested in the children. They told me that Ana had a lot of "health issues," which I interpreted to mean that she had some serious illness, possibly life threatening, and spent a lot of time by doctors in hospitals. She often visited the mother of the twins and was told that she probably wouldn't be around much.

There was another boarder—a young Black man, about eighteen years old, who was a quadriplegic. Apparently, it was cerebral palsy from birth. He could not move a muscle nor talk. Reg and Ana were his caretakers. There was also an eighteen-year-old girl, Ana's daughter. I was never sure where she slept, as there were only three bedrooms. Another daughter was married and lived upstairs from them, but she was often in the house as a babysitter. Maybe she slept up there. There was also a seven-year-old sister of the twins there. She had been labelled, PDD. She followed me around and continually kept repeating questions. I did not see her at home much, however, as she was usually in school when I was there.

Ana indeed was hardly ever home, leaving the children in the care of Reg. This was highly unfortunate because Reg's idea of babysitting was putting each twin in a crib and putting straps over the top so they could not get out. There were no toys. They would be left like that only to be taken out to eat and change their diapers. (Remember those infamous experiments where they did that with orphan children to see its effects? Most of the children died!)

We began the first week of October. Reg showed me around the apartment before we began formal sessions. The children were in a back bedroom where the windows were covered, and the room was absolutely packed with big boxes. It was like a cave. Reg showed me teeth marks in the railings on the cribs. The varnish was almost completely stripped on the upper handrails where they bit into them. He told me, "They have pica." Pica is the continual eating of non-edible things. Paint chips, for instance, come to mind. Older buildings were painted with lead-based paint, and many children got lead poisoning from eating the paint chips.

As I walked through the apartment, I saw paint chips hanging everywhere. The floors were full of all kinds of dirt and plastics from containers. I thought it very strange that children with pica should be in an environment full of tempting things like these for them to eat. Their evaluations did indeed say that they had pica. I asked Reg how often the children were in the cribs. He told me all morning and parts of the afternoon. I asked why.

He said, "Well, it's hard to watch them." Reg did not work and sat in front of the TV all day. He smoked. A stuffed ashtray and cans of Coke adorned his TV chair and table. He showed me that Nessie's crib had been bolted to the floor. He explained that she often violently rocked the crib, and they had to bolt it down. As we entered the room, the children were crying and standing as well as they could in order to be lifted out of their cages. We walked out of the room and back into the living room, which was incredibly cluttered with knick-knacks, a four-foot-high statue of Don Quixote, and hanging ornaments.

There was clutter everywhere, but I did not see any toys. There were dirty, empty baby bottles on the coffee table. The conditions were deplorable. The twins had dirty hair and clothes, and their nails needed cutting. Their noses ran continually. There was a constant stream of moisture from one of Yeshiah's eyes.

What should I do, report this? Obviously, social services were involved and made periodic visits! Could it be that social services approved of the living conditions? Evidently, because here they were. The children struck me as mentally retarded, as I did not see any symptoms of autism. I was to spend one hour a day with each child. They also had speech therapy and OT. Yeshiah attended the Center as well. At least the services would get them out of their cribs, so I reluctantly took the job but told the service coordinator, "Look for a replacement." I really wanted no part of this job.

I was to begin four days later on a Monday. Monday, I arrived with a small table and chairs, but no one answered the door. I heard nothing inside the house. I called. There was no answer. I left the table and chairs in the upstairs hall leading to the sister's apartment and wondered what was up. The next day when I arrived, Reg let me in after I'd waited outside in freezing weather for about ten minutes. He gave no explanation for the delay. He just let me in and went back to his TV chair and cigarettes. The eighteen-year-old boy with quadriplegia also sat in front of the TV. Did he understand what he was seeing? Did he understand anything? It was sad.

I set up the little table by squeezing it in between the two cribs. I removed the straps from Yeshiah's crib and lifted him out. His sister went nuts when I took him out of his crib and did not take her out of hers. I took her out, brought her to Reg, and told him that I couldn't work with her screaming in the room. He'd have to watch her in the living room. He put her on the couch and returned to his big armchair directly in front of the TV. I knew this wouldn't last. Sure enough, within minutes he brought her back because, he explained, "She won't stay on the sofa, and I can't run after her all the time."

Really? He'd put her on the sofa with no toys, no food, no drink, and told her to "Sit down!" Surprise, she did not "listen" to him. She did not like being separated from her brother. I took her back and played with her a bit while her brother engaged with the toys at the table, and then I put her back in the crib but without the straps. I worked with Yeshiah right next to the crib and occasionally handed her toys to keep her occupied. This strategy worked.

I was able to do the basic programs with him, and he mastered them almost immediately. His eye contact was good, he looked at me, and he repeated words. There was a continual running of fluid from his right eye. His nails still needed cutting.

I also began that week working with Nessie, but she did not attend the Center. It was hard, as one child had to be in the crib while the other worked with me at the table. And the one in the crib, I had to keep occupied, or he or she would scream. Both of them enjoyed being at the table and playing with my toys. They loved the attention. They both did well. I really didn't see any autism. The thought of "neglect" entered my mind.

Yeshiah and I had started working together on October 11. By November 11, I had written in my private notes that he definitely was not on the autism spectrum—probably not very delayed at all, though he did not speak other than to repeat words. I had to continually request that his teacher update his programs, as they were too easy for him. I had also sternly reminded Reg that their nails must be cut! Reg did not respond. On November 11, I finally met Ana for the first time.

Ana was present for the session. She watched for about twenty minutes and was impressed with how well Yeshiah did and how happy he was to be at the table with me. She wanted to talk. We went into her and Reg's bedroom. Reg was not invited for the conversation. She wanted to talk about the children's head banging. I was surprised, as I had never seen it.

I told her as much and further suggested to Ana that neither child had pica. She was surprised, as it had been written in the evaluations that they did! She asked me if they didn't have pica, what about the wood on the cribs being stripped due to their biting? I asked if she had ever seen them eat things off the floor when not in the crib.

"Well, no."

I suggested that if they were biting the cribs (didn't want to say it, like caged animals trying to get out), it wasn't because of pica. They just wanted out of the cribs! It would also account for the continual crying and head banging (if, in fact, there was any) and violent rocking of Nessie's crib. She said that she would talk to Reg about keeping them out of the crib. I knew where that was going to go.

Often the speech teacher would work with one child, while I worked with the other. One day, she told me told me a secret that she was not allowed to tell. She lowered her voice and whispered, "The children were born HIV positive." Their biological mother was dying of AIDS. For some strange reason, at least in New York, no one is allowed to tell the therapists that the children are HIV positive! Confidentiality, supposedly. This worried me because when I work with children, there is a lot of touching, nose wiping, the occasional vomit, and diaper leaks. When I called the supervisor, quite angry about this, I was told, "They were tested again at six months and were negative." Two more tests, every six months, and each time they came back, the test was negative. Thank God.

I thought that it was important for Nessie to also go to the Center. It wasn't clear to me why she wasn't going. She certainly needed it. I got the service coordinator to submit a request for Center-based service. She was accepted right away but was not put into the same classroom at the Center with Yeshiah. That meant I had to deal with two different teachers. Her teacher was experienced, and I knew she would write good programs.

Nessie worked readily and happily with me from the beginning. But if she did not get something she wanted, immediately she would throw back her head against the chair or rock violently and/or hit me. I knew that I would have to adjust my style with her. She appeared to be higher functioning than her brother, but she was not good with the programs and did not like doing them (actually, this is a good sign!). She would imitate verbally and physically when not in session, but never in session.

She excelled with the speech teacher. She would still run away from the table with me if she did not get what she wanted. In order to get her to stop that, whenever she ran away from the table, I would put my head down, hands over my eyes, and ignore her. She did not like that and soon she would come back. If I continued to ignore her, she would push my head up. I had to make the work more fun.

By mid-November, they were both moving well. Their progress was good, but their living conditions remained a disaster. Their nails still needed cutting, and they could have used more baths, but what could I do? One day, in late November, I went into the kitchen, away from Reg and the TV, to do the paperwork. The kitchen was right next to the living room where Reg sat, as always, watching TV, cigarette smoke wafting ominously into the air. I stood over the stove when suddenly, it seemed like something moved quickly at my feet. I looked down and saw nothing. A few seconds later, the same strange feeling. This time I looked down and saw mice scurrying under the bottom of the oven.

I called out to Reg, "You know you got mice in here?"

He said, "Yeah, well, we got most of them."

I was not astonished by the presence of cockroaches in people's apartments, as they were prevalent in New York, but mice running freely in the kitchen? This was too much. As a "mandated reporter," I was legally obligated to report such things to social services. But social services were already "on the job." I just shook my head. What could I do? It made me sick to think that mice were infesting the kitchen, yet, if I "reported" it, I would lose the children, as the parents would certainly fire me.

This is a systemic problem in the industry. Imagine what a parent would think if they were "reported" to authorities about mice or bugs. Would the parent say, "Gee, thanks?" I doubt it. They would be angry and immediately fire the therapist. Yet, this is the procedure that is mandated by the State of New York. I once wrote a professor who lectures on this topic about this question, and she told me that, yes, indeed, I am to report it, and I could lose my license if I failed to do so. She told me that the parents are not "in trouble," they need assistance.

I suggested that "reporting them to an agency" was not a helpful way of finding assistance. Maybe we could give the parents a phone number and have them call for assistance? No. I did not "report" them.

At the end of November, Nessie's IFSP (individualized family support plan) was due, so I had to stop working with her until they made decisions about how to continue. Continue in the Center? At home? More hours? Less hours? Continue OT and speech? The last week of November was tumultuous in any case, as the entire family had to leave the house! They had been approved for a new, wheelchair accessible bathroom and shower, which meant completely tearing down the old bathroom, knocking out walls, and installing a new floor, handrails, and hoses. This way, the young man in the wheelchair could wheel right into the shower without being lifted. This was going to take a few weeks.

The family was informed that they had to vacate, as work would begin within a week! Ana was in a panic. Fortunately, I knew just who to call in Manhattan, and he arranged for them all to stay in a few rooms at a local hotel for the duration paid for by The City. Thank God, one less crisis. It wasn't my job to help with this, but it seemed that no one else knew what to do about it.

I began to work with them in the hotel. It was very cramped, and there was no room for a table. I thought I would use this time just to work on verbal communication skills and social skills and not do the table work. To them, it was just play: balloons, bubbles, bouncing on the beds, but this was actually very influential in strengthening our relationships.

Things changed when we went back to their apartment. Both of them had made big gains in skills across programs. Verbal skills were increasing, but spontaneous speech was still lagging, as they would still point rather than verbally request something.

Our relationship was now very good. I called Nessie, "Mishmish" (Hebrew for "apricot"), and she began to call me the same. Yeshiah, I called JoJo. I was getting very attached to them, which is, supposedly, unprofessional.

Nessie's IFSP was finished, and it was determined that she would continue her present schedule. Unfortunately, I had taken on another child and could no longer work with her as of December. They brought in another therapist, and to my horror, it was George. George was in his late thirties, highly inexperienced with autistic children, and had a bad habit of simply not showing up for work. No calls, no excuses, he just did not show up!

I called the service coordinator to ask why she'd sent him and not someone more experienced and dependable. I got the usual answer: "There is no one else." That could mean one of two things. Amongst the thousands of therapists in NYC, this late in the year, all the therapists were indeed booked. Or, it could mean, "No one is going into that neighborhood!"

George was Black, from the Islands, and had no difficulty with Bushwick. There were two major incidents in the neighborhood during my time there that would have given anyone pause about Bushwick. One was that my car was hit by a UPS truck while parked outside. Neighbors saw it but did not take down the license or number of the truck. When I called UPS to complain, they told me that without a number, since they have thousands of trucks out, they would not be able to verify the incident. Yeah, sure.

The other incident was far more serious. A teenaged boy was shot to death, on the sidewalk, by the side of their house. When I came to work the next day, there were TV cameras all over the place, and they interviewed the daughter who lived upstairs. Ana set up a display there and a donation pot for the family. This was not my first time that someone had been shot at a worksite in Brooklyn.

Our work together was going very well now. The children were not locked up all the time, and they were increasingly running about the house. The eighteen-year-old sister would watch them, as she'd just finished high school. She tried to enlist in the Navy, but she said, "They didn't take me because I'm too fat!" She wasn't, so I don't know what was up with that other than I was glad she was home to watch the kids. (They say standards for entry into the military change in peace time. When I went in the Navy during Vietnam, they were happy to take anybody.)

When George came on the scene, the plan was that I would work one hour with JoJo, and he would work in another room with Nessie. Nessie did not like this arrangement at all and began to tantrum as soon as she was alone with George. This went on for days, and George did not know what to do. I suggested that both he and I work in one room until she got used to him. That is what we did, and that worked great. Eventually, George was able to work with either she or JoJo separately.

While things were going well at home, the twins were not doing well at the Center. They were crying, throwing tantrums, and hitting. When they did work, their scores were exceptionally low. I went to the Center to see what was going on. I entered the classroom to see JoJo working with someone who was in the wrong business. The poor kid was crying very hard. I told the teacher, Ora, "This kid should not be crying. And why the low scores?"

She told me that she had no assistants. She was a new teacher. The supervisor and this new teacher did not get along, so the supervisor would not help her, and she had no time to write new programs. I went in to talk to the supervisor. She told me that they needed to hire more assistants, and she would check on the children's progress.

At home, they were doing great while in session. The problems were what happened when they were not in session. Evidently, according to Ana, both JoJo and Nessie's head banging and tantruming had increased. I was surprised to hear this. I had noticed bite marks on Nessie's wrist and fingers. I called an emergency meeting with the OT, speech therapist, George, the service coordinator, and both parents. The service coordinator asked the other therapists if they had ever seen this behavior. Negative.

Reg's solution was to fit the kids for helmets and chest restraints. Typical—blame the victim! Ana did not want this. I was completely opposed to this idea, and we began to discuss what exactly "head banging" is and what it indicates. In my opinion, they were not head-bangers, even if they did hit themselves occasionally. Head-bangers continually hit themselves for no apparent reason. JoJo and Mishmish hit themselves when they were angry. Reg was unmoved by my explanation and insisted on helmets and restraints. The next day, a man showed up to measure them for size. He said to me that they didn't appear to need it.

Fortunately, while the City was happy to pay for the fitting and the manufacture of these very expensive pieces of equipment, they were never used. Over time, I brought their head banging "under control" in my sessions simply by reacting to the behavior by dropping my head and closing my eyes. They both hated when I did that. Once they stopped the tantruming, we would work on replacing the tantrum with pointing to what they wanted. Nessie would stop her screaming, come over and try to get me to pay attention to her. It was very cute. As for JoJo, all I had to say to him was, "Ok, go away."

He'd say, "No!"

I would respond, "Go away, you're not my friend." Then, I would give him a hug and say something like, "Okay, you're my friend. Let's try it again," and all would be fine.

If I ignored Nessie too long, she would stop the aggressive behavior and would simply go into the corner and pout. I loved these kids! They were so cute and funny and obviously dying for attention, yet they had no way to communicate that except for crying. We could change that!

The OT told me that she used time-out when they "don't behave." Reg, of course, only knew time-out. Many times, when I came to work, one or both were in their cribs crying, and when I asked Reg why they were in their cribs, he told me that that were in time-out. Obviously, this was not a prescribed use of "time-out." Rather, it was that no one else was home, and he couldn't be bothered with them.

I was angry. I let him know that he could not keep them in the crib. They needed stimulation out of the cribs, and this would have to change. Ana, at this time, was flying up and back between

Arizona and Puerto Rico due to some family emergencies. When she got back, I let her know that keeping the kids in the cribs leads to head banging, tantrums, self-injury, and they would not learn to communicate locked in a cage. The language I used was strong. The message was understood.

On December 28, I stopped working with Nessie, as her hours were cut due to good progress. She continued with George. I saw her every day and often included her with me and Yeshiah as she would not be separate from him for too long. I didn't mind. I used her to work on verbal skills with him. Yeshiah's progress was remarkable. He was using words to communicate; his programs became far too easy for him, and he laughed a lot. His eye was no longer leaking.

One day in March Mom told me that the following day, JoJo would be reevaluated because the agency said that he had been misdiagnosed and was functioning normally. Uh, okay. The evaluators, who had tested him originally, were incredibly surprised by his progress. He lost his diagnosis of autism but was still able to continue services because his cognitive and speech were far below age level.

By the end of May, both children were using longer sentences, answering yes/no questions appropriately, and were just fun to be with. They were learning, they were speaking, and we laughed a lot. It was amazing to see how protective Nessie was of her brother. If I had a toy that he wanted and would not give it to him for some reason, usually because I wanted him to use words, Nessie would snatch it from me and give it to him. If I took something away from him, Nessie would grab it and give it back to him. However, if she wanted something and he also wanted it, she often would not share. It was only if I did not let him have it that she would step in and get it for him.

As their hours had been reduced, George worked for the next few months alone with Nessie. She was, by far, further along developmentally. I worked alone with JoJo. Still, every day I had to play with her, or she would get angry. In the middle of August, for some reason, George quit. So, while she was officially not getting services until George was replaced, I brought her in to work with JoJo and me. I could not charge for the hours. I didn't care about that. Their sessions were scheduled to end August 31, in any case. I was glad it was almost over because they had done so well and really didn't need this anymore. As far as their home life, there was nothing I could do.

On August 31, my last day, Ana told me that the children's services had been extended until December 31. I told her that I was not sure if I could do the hours, as September brings in a new batch of children. The service coordinator told me to stay until December. That was a problem because come January 1, I would have a two-hour hole in my schedule. But she said that she had nobody else. What could I do? I didn't want to go back because they did not need me any longer, and seeing how they lived—mice and cockroaches and floors needing vacuuming—really bothered me. Too bad for me. I had to go back until a replacement could be found, and so I worked with both of them for another month until they found someone to replace me.

The twins were now using full sentences, understood everything, their SIBS (self-injurious behavior) had stopped, and they went into the advanced classroom at the Center. The things they needed most, I could not help them with. I knew Reg would go right back to "putting them in time-out" in the cribs, ignoring them when out, and failing to understand how important stimulation and human interactions were. He would not apply the techniques I had taught everyone for communication and replacing SIBS with an appropriate behavior. It broke my heart.

On October 11, both Ana and Reg were home. I told them that someone named Dan would be taking over for me for the last two months. Reg, said, "Okay." He could care less. Ana looked shocked but said nothing. I gave the kids a hug and walked out of the house. No one said, "Goodbye" or "Thank you."

I had to go to the Center a month later on some business and went upstairs to the classrooms. I had forgotten they were up there or I would not have gone. Too late! As I turned around in the hall to leave, they saw me. They broke ranks with their class who were moving to the playroom and came running to me. Nessie was saying, "Mishmish!" I picked them both up and hugged them. I did not want to let go…. (Tears flow as I write this eleven years later.)

Yair and Yossi

I am not sure whether to include this case under "Different Kinds of Mothers," or "Twins," but since Yair was a twin, it will go here. His twin's name, I forget. I never worked with the twin, as he was a TD (typically developing) child. They were clearly fraternal twins. Yair was diagnosed PDD/NOS, in other words, on the autism spectrum. There was no doubt.

This case is only noteworthy for two reasons: His mother was antagonistic from day one, and it eventually led to my leaving. The other was that all food had to be ground into a liquid and he took it from a bottle. Despite having a "feeding specialist" who was supposedly a specialist in food selectivity/refusal, they had made no progress in the six months they had tried to overcome this problem.

As I have stated elsewhere, in my many years of working with children who would not eat or would eat only a few things, it has invariably been the case that the reasons for the selectivity were behavioral and responded well to a behavioral approach. The story with Yair is the perfect example.

There was a team meeting before I began to work with Yair in the second week of June. It was very unusual to start working with a child in June toward the end of the school year.

I had to squeeze Yair into my already packed schedule. The team leader who wrote the programs for him was a very experienced woman named Lacy. She and I had a particularly good working relationship and had worked with many children together. I did not know the eating specialist. The subject this night was his "regression" and eating problems. I learned that there had been other therapists, and they "had to leave the team." I would find out why shortly.

The parents were Israeli, Orthodox Jews. They lived in a part of Brooklyn called Boro Park, which is a small section started in 1948 by survivors of the Holocaust. The predominant language is Yiddish. One reason I took this case was because it was close to my apartment as I also lived in Boro Park. The other reason is that the Center wanted someone who spoke Hebrew as the mother's English was not that good. I was sure that this case would go well.

I was to work with him three hours a week—one hour a day on Tuesdays and two hours on Thursdays. This was very unusual for me, and very unusual for a child to get services like this. The usual is five days a week, one to two hours at home and going to the Center for a few hours as well.

Boro Park is hot in the summer. As I mostly worked in "the projects" with poor people of color, I had gotten into the habit of removing my shirt and "tzitzits" and working in my t-shirt alone. No one ever complained. I could tell that the mother did not like this and I suggested that she turn on the air conditioner, as it was a sauna in their apartment. She refused. I soon got a call from the director of the Center who told me to put my shirt on. I told him that it was ninety degrees in that apartment and I couldn't work under such conditions. Certainly not for a two-hour session. He suggested that I "try it." I didn't.

Another problem was that every day, without exception when I rang the doorbell, I had to wait outside for anywhere from five to fifteen minutes. Upon entering, without fail, Yair would be fast asleep. I had to wait while she woke him, changed him, fed him a bottle of milk and then we began our sessions. On a day when I saw him for two hours, okay, maybe this was not so terrible but on Tuesdays, a one-hour day, it wasted half our session. As he had been getting services for a long time, he had a lot of programs and there was no way to do them in a half hour. When I suggested this to Mom, she became angry. I was beginning to get a hint as to why the other therapists "had to leave" the team. Already on my second session I had written in my private notes, "Mom does not strike me as the appreciative type."

We had to begin our sessions in a peculiar way. Yair lay on the couch with his blanket and bottle, and my job was to get him to finish the bottle! Naturally, this was not in his best interest. I wanted him to eat normally and sit down to do his work. But Mom insisted on this and then we could go to our worktable.

Yair was easy to work with. He did most of his programs easily, tried to repeat words, and though he seemed socially aloof, he responded well to me. However, he completely ignored his twin brother. I tried to include him in the sessions, but the TD twin would dominate the activities and my attention such that I had to stop.

By the end of June, Yair was making good progress for his cognitive level. That is to say, he did all of his programs and his behavior was good. He was still quite aloof. I did not feel like we had a real rapport at all. He loved my toys and the activities but I didn't feel that he had any connection to me.

On the twenty-ninth of June, his mother told me that he attends much better in the bedroom and I should work with him in there. I doubted this though sometimes it is indeed the case that in a more isolated place with fewer distractions a child will respond better. I did not get that sense with Yair, but Mom insisted. I had a feeling that she just wanted to be in the living room where we worked and she did not want to get involved with the sessions (no parent training in this family).

I tried it in the bedroom. Sure enough, his responding did not change. Mom asked me on the way out how he did. I told her that he seemed distant today. She said, in a very accusatory tone, "I wonder why that is?" Mom did not like me—at all—in English or Hebrew. This went for another two weeks. In the meantime, we had another team meeting. Upon every suggestion I made, Mom was quick to say, "No, I don't agree." On everything. The feeding specialist had little to say, as she had made no advancements in the case. Just some dribble about mixed textures, and "bolus" problems in swallowing. All medical reasons for his not eating had been ruled out. I suggested that the problem was behavioral, i.e., he was used to eating that way. He liked lying down on his blanket and being fed his bottle. Simple. Naturally, the feeding expert did not agree, and the suggestion made Mom angry.

On July first, everything changed. His mother was not home. Yair would not take his bottle from his father. We began our work as usual at the table and then, about twenty minutes into the session, Dad came in with a plate of food—shredded cabbage, two pea pods, three baby carrots, pieces of cold chicken, French fries, garlic bread, and water. I looked at Dad like he was nuts.

"What am I supposed to do with this?"

He said, "See if he'll eat anything."

Eat anything? This kid had never eaten real food in his life. But okay, Mom wasn't home to intervene and throw him on the couch with blanky and bottle, so, I decided to see what happened.

I put the plate on our worktable. He immediately grabbed the purple cabbage and started chewing! What's this? He grabbed some more. *Oh, so you like cabbage, aye?* I thought. Good, we'd use that for a "reinforcer." The first trick was that whenever he grabbed cabbage, I would turn on the music. Then, after he swallowed, I would turn it off. The next trick was to offer him something else, put it in his hand, and prompt him by the elbow to move it toward his mouth. If he took it in his mouth, I would turn on the music and give him a bite of cabbage. This simple "stimulus transfer" trick worked. Yair ate the entire plate of food, except for the carrots and drank from a full glass of water from a cup! The child was hungry!

He had been taught to eat like a baby, so he ate like one. Not today. Today he ate age appropriately. His father came back in the room later and was astonished. Shortly thereafter, Mom came home and the feeding specialist was with her. I showed them the empty plate and told them what had been on it. Fortunately, Dad was home to verify this or neither one of them would have believed it.

The full impact of this hit Mom like the proverbial ton of bricks. She had taught him how to eat like a baby. The "feeding specialist" was embarrassed. She suggested that it was "too overwhelming" for the child to eat like this. I gritted my teeth and did not respond.

I continued to work with him for another two weeks and his scores were much higher than the other therapists. I had begun using a "delayed prompt" with him, which means instead of just giving a command and immediately prompting him to do the action, I would give the command and then wait three to five seconds before prompting. Yair was "prompt dependent," just like in his eating habits, and this delay was enough time for him to think about the task, understand the request, and figure out how to do it. I was thrilled. He was doing great.

On July 15, five weeks after we'd started, I got another phone call from the director of the Center. "Mom says you must keep your shirt on." I was furious. I called Lacy and said that I was sorry, but I quit.

"This kid really doesn't need an experienced therapist anymore; he's making rapid progress. He is eating now; he's beginning to use words. I think a less experienced therapist can work with him now."

She did not want me to quit. It would be hard to find another therapist this late in the year, and he was doing well. Her thought was, *If it ain't broke, don't fix it.* I told her that Mom had complained again about my shirt. She did not call the director to say, "I'm so thrilled with Yair's progress. I'm so grateful that he's eating normally now. Thank you so much." No, she'd called to complain about my wearing a t-shirt in a ninety-degree room and she wouldn't turn on the A/C. I was done.

They found a replacement for me—Pat, a nice Black lady with a lot of experience. Shortly after this I ran into Lacy at the Center, and she told me that Mom was not happy that I'd quit. At this bit of news, it was my turn to be amazed.

CHAPTER SEVEN

Savants

Years ago, they called them, "idiot savants." Today, there are two separate categories for savants: "savant syndrome" and "autistic savant." The standard definitions of both are as follows:

Savant Syndrome. "A rare condition in which someone with significant mental disabilities demonstrates certain abilities far in excess of average. The skills that savants excel at are generally related to memory. This may include rapid calculation artistic ability, map making or musical ability."[18]

Probably the most famous savant was Kim Peek, who was the model for the character in the movie, *The Rain Man*. Kim was not autistic. He had serious brain abnormalities making daily living and social interaction almost impossible for him.

Autistic Savant. "Someone with autism who also has a single extraordinary area of knowledge or ability."[19]

I am not sure why they say, "single." Autistic savants can be extraordinary in more than one area of knowledge or ability. Maybe they mean, "at least" one area.

Savants skills usually manifest as a child gets older. When younger, such as age three to ten, there are other names used to classify them. These include hyperlexic, gifted, miracle children, and little Einstein. As they age and the specific skills are exhibited, it becomes increasingly common to label them as autistic savants. There are many books about savants who are artists, calendar counters, sculptors, musicians, mathematicians, and people with remarkable memory skills. Even twenty years ago, I had never seen a book about a young autistic savant, except for Nadia Chomyn.[20]

In all my years of working with children on the spectrum, I had met many children who were above average in cognitive or verbal skills but no one to whom I would apply the label "savant" except for two children. Oddly enough, they were both Asian. One I included in the chapter on "Different Kinds of Fathers." I included it there because now, years later, I'm still enraged that his father fired me from that very unique case. That section is called, "Allan's Father," and you can read his story there. The other child was Filipino, and his name is Lonnie.

Lonnie

Lonnie and his family—Mom, Dad, and Lola (his grandmother)—lived in Brownsville, a borough of Brooklyn primarily made up of Blacks and Latinos. They lived in a NYCHA building. It was very unusual to find a Filipino family in the hood.

Mom was a nurse, and I am not sure what Dad did, but it had something to do with trade, and he often flew to Abu Dhabi. Lola was the mother's mother, and she was usually the one I was home with. She spoke very little English. Though I spent two years in the Philippines in the Navy, I did not remember much of the language except for "uh-oh," which means "yes" and "n'ndai" which means, "no." But Lola and I became very good friends and managed to understand each other despite the language barrier. Mom spoke very good English and Dad's was not bad. Lonnie was spoken to only in English—except for Lola.

We were together only ten months. In the beginning, he used to pop words out spontaneously. That is, not in response to questions such as, "What is it?" I would take out a toy, and he would name it, or I'd turn something off, and he'd say, "Off." Numbers and letters, he said often but again, without any prompting or requesting from me. He was not communicating anything to me. He was just labeling aloud to himself. If I asked him, "What is this?" he would just look away or stare back blankly.

On our second two-hour session, it was obvious that he could follow one step instructions, match pictures in a field of three, and be prompted to say, "Go" when I spun a top. He would make eye contact if you asked him to look at you; otherwise, he did not like making eye contact or being directed where to look. Asking a child to look and attend to something, "joint attention," is a very important skill for learning and usually children on the spectrum simply don't do it. Lonnie would, but he didn't like to.

There was one big problem with this case that I had no control over. I knew it would affect his future progress. At the Center, he had a rookie teacher who would be in charge of his programs. That, in itself, was not so bad as there were other teachers around to help her and a supervisor present, but I did not like this teacher. I had seen her in training and was thoroughly unimpressed. She was getting her master's while in training, and there was talk of hiring her as a classroom teacher once she completed her master's and training at the Center.

I strongly advised both the supervisor and the director not to hire her. Working with autistic children takes far more than a master's degree in special education or training in the discrete trial method they used at the Center. I did not see that this woman had it in her for this kind of work. She was moody, did not take any constructive criticism and when someone suggested anything, she felt personally offended. Worse, I did not see her ability to relate to children or form rapports with them. She was easily flustered when a child did not respond or "exhibited escape behavior." She did not know what to do in such cases. I was taken aback when they indeed hired her as a teacher and for the first time in my career, I wrote a letter of protest to the supervisor and the director. I would not want any of my kids working with her.

Another problem—other than her lack of experience—was that she was trained to work with children one way: the typical ABA method of discrete trial teaching. It is intensive, in isolation, and if one did not know how to work with children, any kind of children, they were going to be faced with tantrums, SIBs (self-injurious behavior), self-stimulatory behavior, and there certainly was not going to be any progress. In her defense, I would only say that she never had any training in other models of therapy, like most in the field today. While they do teach things like "working through" a problem (terrible method), errorless learning, increasing reinforcement schedules, decreasing task difficulty, task analysis, and other techniques, one had to know when and how to practice these things. She didn't. While she could easily write programs for children with no skills, simple beginner programs, she would not know what to do with a child such as Lonnie, who was clearly on a higher level.

We began working the day before his second birthday, October 1. It was clear from the start that this boy was not going to be like other two-year-old children with that heavy "autism" diagnosis. After two days, it was obvious to me that he was cognitively fine. He would do things that most children his age did, but reluctantly. He would make eye contact if I pushed him. He had joint attention if he was interested in something you were doing. He knew language, as words popped out often, and it was obvious that he knew the names of things. He could follow instructions.

What made him "autistic?" Lonnie was in his own world. He had "hard signs," such as no interest in others, including parents, lack of communication skills, and limited interest in activities—very limited. He also had many "soft signs," such as stereotypical behavior (lining things up), "edging" (looking at objects on a table from the table's edge), no response to name, and toe walking—although there was no self-stimulatory behavior such as hand flapping or verbal stims. No, as smart as he appeared, it was obvious that they had gotten the diagnosis right.

As always, when I started with a new child, I spent a lot of time finding out what he liked to do, what amused him, what he did not like to do, what attracted his attention, and also "pairing myself with reinforcement" (fancy ABA term for, "making him like me"). By the end of October, I knew that this boy would not like discrete trial teaching. Higher cognitive level children seldom do. To someone like Lonnie such programs were boring and meaningless.

His teacher had started him with standard beginner programs that were not "functional." Touch your nose, stand up, clap your hands, all rewarded with a toy or a resounding "good job!" The "reinforcement" (reward) for following such instruction had nothing to do with the behavior. A "functional program" would be something like asking a child to "push the button" and music comes on. The pushing causes something pleasant to happen. It has a purpose, a "function." But what function is there in "touch your nose?"

"Touch your nose" and then getting a cookie is fine for lower-level children in the beginning. After some time, when you have "established contingency" (do A get B) then you can drop the non-functional. But with kids like Lonnie, you don't have to establish contingency. A rookie teacher would not know the difference. His didn't.

I was supposed to follow the teacher's protocol, take data on the progress, and compare it to the data taken at the Center. When scoring reached between eighty to one hundred, the teacher would either add a new program or update the difficulty in the present task. Such is standard ABA procedure. The data should do the talking. If a child masters a program, and it is not updated, he will soon become bored. Boredom without the ability to communicate means tantrums.

Within that first month, he tantrumed a lot. As soon as I asked him to do a step he began screaming, crying, and running away. I had to work with him in an unorthodox way in order to implement the teacher's boring programs. Once we'd established a rapport, and he trusted me that all our time would not be an endless bore, he did the programs as written if I did them quickly and made it fun. I hated making him do them as he quickly mastered these beginner programs and his teacher was not updating. As she refused to write in the communication book, I had to call her and ask why she wasn't updating. She told me that he only tantrums at the Center. "I can't update if he won't do the programs!" It never occurred to her to change the programs or the method of presenting them.

We had a sheet of scores from the Center, and I noticed how he was scoring 0 for program A and 0 for program B, etc. At home, he was scoring hundreds and completing all of the programs in minutes. I told the teacher that I was going to probe more advanced skills for him to work on.

Silly me, I thought his classroom teacher might be interested in the skills I was probing. He was using words, imitating orally and physically, increasing eye contact, and more importantly, laughing, enjoying our long two-hour sessions. Yet, he remained aloof, as he often just ignored me and engaged in his favorite activities. He loved to take the wooden letters from my alphabet puzzle and line them up on the floor. I did an experiment with this. While he wasn't looking, I'd remove one letter and put the two next to it closer together so you couldn't see that I'd removed one. When he finished, he would look over his alphabet and knew immediately that one was missing. "R…R," he'd repeat, without looking at me. He did not know how to ask me for it. No communication skills, no theory of mind (understanding that I could help him), but he knew it was missing and was frustrated about what to do about it. I taught him to say, "Where is the R? Help me."

His other favorite activity was making little balls of Play-Doh, lining them up and saying, to no one, "Mercury, Venus, Earth, Mars," until he'd named them all. He made Jupiter very big and Pluto very small. He put a ring around Venus. He had just turned two years old! No one taught him this. He saw it on TV. Soon he was writing letters! He could read simple words.

I put those words together on paper and he could read the sentences. Yet, his teacher wanted him to "touch your nose!" I couldn't stand it. I called the supervisor and railed that I couldn't take this. "I told you guys that this teacher is incompetent and look at what she's doing!"

The supervisor told me that she'd "look in" on her. But nothing changed. I made a video of him doing much more complicated things and took it to the Center. I showed it to the supervisor and the teacher. They responded, "Well, at the Center, all he does is cry."

I asked Mom if that were true. She said, "Yes, pretty much."

I told the Center to get another teacher. More importantly, I told Mom, "Tell them you want another teacher." (It is out of bounds for a home therapist to tell a parent such a thing!) If all this wasn't bad enough, his in-home speech teacher also had problems with him. She thought that if she was very strict, he would listen. Sure.

I watched her work with him twice and couldn't watch anymore. She'd say things like, "Listen, Lonnie, you are going to sit for five minutes and do X." After thirty seconds, he'd be screaming. She would say, "Look, when I say five minutes, I mean five minutes!" Which meant, of course, that he'd scream for the next four and a half minutes.

By the end of November, they'd switched him to the other classroom teacher. This meant that I had to switch my hours with him in the morning to five to seven p.m. Usually, I would never work that late, but for Lonnie, I made an exception. Doing so just meant I'd get to the gym an hour later.

His new teacher was far more experienced, and I was relieved when she took over. He only stayed with her a month, until the end of December, and then they finally figured out that discrete trial teaching aggravates him. They put him into the "mixed" class, which is for children with all kinds of different diagnoses, but these were children who could follow a story, do crafts, sing along, sit in circle time, and work together. No more highly structured teaching in isolation. I would continue the intensive one-on-one teaching at home, which was good because he did need it for specific skill acquisition. It also meant that I would now be writing all of his programs. No more, "touch your nose, clap your hands."

In January, he made rapid progress. He was repeating words when I asked him to. He never liked that, but he did it. He was starting to ask verbally for things. If I handed him a jar he couldn't open, he would say, "O-o." Speaking, getting the words out, was hard for him, but getting easier. I wrote higher level programs for him and he learned them all quickly. In the meantime, he was naming letters, numbers, shapes, and colors and understanding categories like furniture, clothes, animals, and food. He was able to learn concepts, such as, "same" and "different" and spatial relations—under, over, behind, next to. In short, he was showing that not only was he learning things appropriate for his age level, but he was also learning things beyond his age level. He also learned one other thing, and this was causing problems.

He was a first-born son. Incredibly cute and good natured but, like all two-year-old children, when he didn't get what he wanted, tantrums were not far off. His mother always gave in, and the few times that she wouldn't, he would hit her. This did not disturb her, but I saw that he understood that aggression works to get you things. I had to do parent training with her and Grandma to let them know that Lonnie cannot hit. That when he hits, he does not get what he wants, rather, he learns that hitting leads to being ignored, so not a good strategy for him to use.

But he couldn't talk! What should he do? He had to learn two things: one was a "replacement behavior" for requesting. Getting things by appropriate communication. He could point and use his limited speech. The other thing he had to learn was going to be hard to teach. He had to learn that sometimes in this cold, cruel world, the answer is that dreaded word, "No."

"No." So much debate about the use of that word. Heated debate. According to some, if you use the word, you are a sadist, "not sensitive," unprofessional, incompetent. "You **never** say no to a child!" I was told this by the director of a developmental Center in Pennsylvania upon making a visit. The program there was very impressive. I was surprised by that actually. After the tour, the director and I went for a short schmooze. It went really well, until the end when she told me, in deep seriousness, "We never say 'no' here." I responded, "Oh really? That's interesting." I was not about to ruin a good visit by debating this heated topic.

The supervisor at the Center I worked with in New York also had a meeting one day to tell the staff that henceforth, we would not use "no" or any other negative instruction. Instead of saying, "Don't run," we would say, "Please walk." Instead of saying, "Stop," we would say, "Let's try X, or Y." Nice. Politically correct and "sensitive." But, to me, a big mistake. Hearing "no" is part of life.

I'm not sure when the word "no" became evil. My parents and teachers told me, "No," many times growing up. I can't think of anyone I know who was not used to hearing the word in their upbringing. None of them became serial killers. It's a powerful tool to have in your toolbox. When a child is doing something dangerous and it needs to stop immediately, you say "No." Then you explain. When a child is engaged in SIBS (self-injurious behavior) or aggressive behavior towards others, and it needs to stop now, you say, "No." Then you work on a less aversive alternative.

In the beginning days of ABA, there were videos of children making a wrong decision during a task, and the therapist would bang on the table and shout, "No!" There are old "Lovaas" tapes you can find that show this.[21] This "technique" scared the children to death! They had some kind of weird theory about "implanting an aversive" to the wrong response. Today, you watch such tapes and are shocked and amazed that they ever did such things. The stigma for ABA stuck and punishment became known as part of the method. They haven't used this "method" for over twenty years now, but the stigma remains. Hence, the over-correction of the use of the word, "No." In therapy, I seldom use the word simply because I have little use for it. But when it comes to hitting Mommy, or banging oneself in the head, the word is necessary in my opinion, to let the child know that doing such will not be tolerated. He doesn't like that? Sorry, that's life.

In any case, it soon became unnecessary for Lonnie to hit or tantrum because his language skills were advancing, and he could speak to get what he wanted. He even began to enjoy working with his speech teacher who was working on two and three-word requests: "Give me water," "The top is blue," and many other such sentences.

By February, he was really moving. He tried very hard to vocalize when he couldn't. I wondered if he didn't have apraxia, but I would have to let the speech teacher worry about that. He "stimmed" on the alphabet. That means he would line up letters and say them—over and over again—for hours, if you allowed him to.

As previously noted, "limited interest" is one of the hard signs for autism. A typically developing child might engage in a favored activity but eventually, he'll become bored. Not so for kids on the spectrum. What is the difference? DIF: duration, intensity, and frequency are signs that normal behaviors become self-stimulatory behaviors and are no longer in the realm of "normal." The good thing was that you could get him to stop that and focus on something else with just about anything except, you guessed it, the iPad. Try to take that away and you'll need shoulder pads and a helmet for yourself! I found this often with children on all levels of the spectrum—typically developing children as well. My humble advice for children with communication problems: never let them use an iPad. Never.

Lonnie was sick a lot. He would often have a very runny nose, cough, and it would last for up to two weeks. It turned out that he had allergies that often blossomed into colds. However, in March, his lips were swollen and his tongue seemed discolored, so Mom took him to the doctor. He was diagnosed with "hand, foot, and mouth disease." I'd never heard of it. Hoof and mouth disease, yes, but that was for cows. What could this be? I Googled it. Sure enough, it is a real diagnosis and a real malady. It was serious but would pass.

He just kept getting better and better which made it hard for me keep him engaged for two hours, as he just didn't need such intensive therapy anymore. He was bored. I had to introduce something new and fun. Luckily, I found just the thing: The Play-Doh Factory [22].

He was fascinated by all the things he could do with this toy. Hours went by like seconds as he learned to make all kinds of things. I told his parents not to let him have it except when I was there or I'd lose my edge. What remained, autism wise, was his absolute aloofness. He didn't seem to care if I, or anyone else existed. How much of that is "autism" and how much is "personality" is debatable. His communication skills were still far below age level.

By the end of April, I did not want to continue to work for two hours with him. He just didn't need it. I asked the Center to find someone else to do one hour. In any case, he needed to be able to generalize his skills across people, not just me. The parents were not happy about this. I would have suggested cutting his services to one hour, but it was late in the year, that takes tons of paperwork, and then the approval process. Not to mention that his parents would not have agreed. Better just to find someone else to do the other hour until we finished at the end of August.

His speech teacher showed me that he could label activities with two words: boy running, dog barking. I probed to see if he could do it when not looking at cards. It's an important point and often overlooked by therapists who use a lot of two-dimensional tasks—that is, using pictures to teach things. She had taught him to look at a picture and tell her what it was. Show a picture of a child clapping their hands and teach him to say, "clapping hands," and the therapist will think that now he's got it! Good. Unfortunately, it's not good. His response is only a step in the process. Now you have to be able to do it in three dimensions. You model clapping hands and ask him, "What am I doing?" Or ask someone else in the room to clap. Or ask him to clap then ask, "What are you doing?" Simply showing a picture and expecting a response that you taught him is the same as getting a pigeon to tap the red button to get a crumb. Show the bird the word, "red," and then she'll tap that red button. You can see this in early films by B.F. Skinner where they show a pigeon the words "turn around," and he turns around! Show him the words, "peck blue," and he'll peck a blue button. Amazing.

Clever Hans, a horse, could do math supposedly. It was nothing more than stimulus-response training and had nothing to do with comprehension. Actually, I was also making this mistake with his "reading" program. Sure, he could actually read words put into a sentence, but he could not tell you what he'd read. For instance, if he read a sentence such as, "The black bear sat under a red roof," and then I asked him, "Where did the bear sit?" he would just stare blankly back at me. Or "Who sat under a red roof?" There'd be no response. But he was only two years old. The fact that he could identify single words was already amazing.

In late May, Lonnie had to take a whole new set of psychological exams for placement in his next school in September. The psychiatrist said he scored "pretty low" on the battery of tests. I thought, *Yes, well, so did Thomas Edison.* But it was good that he'd scored low because otherwise, he would not have qualified for services. Despite the fact that he was a genius, he still had serious communication and socialization problems. Even though he was naming the planets and lining them up in the correct order and could label the names of different dinosaurs, these were just "splinter skills." These kinds of skills would not help him navigate the world. He still couldn't tell someone that his diaper was wet or that he couldn't find something.

One time I pretended to eat Play-Doh, and he cried and ran away. I had to teach him how to tell me, "No, don't eat Play-Doh." We also worked on telling others, "Stop it." If he asked me to make the letter K with Play-Doh, or write it, and I purposefully wrote another letter, he would tantrum. I had to teach him to tell me,

"Stop it." But he overgeneralized that. If he bumped into his mother by accident, instead of saying, "Excuse me," he would say "Stop it."

We worked on requesting, "I want K," instead of tantruming. He would have to learn how to generalize these skills to other things. It would take time and practice. But that was better than tantruming. His most amazing achievement was that he could write letters and read words that I would write! He could spell things like dog, sun, go, and up. Self-taught!

By mid-August we had two weeks left together. In ten months, he had gone from a non-verbal, aloof, iPad-addicted child to a child who could write, read, interact, exhibit extraordinary skills beyond his age and make progress with socialization. Rare child indeed. It is now many years later, and I wonder how he's doing.

Chapter Eight

Different Kinds of Mothers

There is often an underlying tension between therapists and the mothers of children with special needs. There is not much trust. A therapist has to earn that trust. Mom knows her kid. Therapists know theory and method, often assuming that whatever they know is just what this kid needs. Mothers are only interested in one thing: Is this so-called professional going to hurt my kid?

Now that we've established the above, I will state most emphatically that I've encountered some really strange mothers. It's unavoidable. You can't work with over a thousand kids and not run into some strange people—in any profession. It would be tough for me to decide which was the strangest. I'll list a few and you can vote on it.

Cindy's Mother

I only worked with Cindy for three months from late September to December. She was a cute, chubby, little blond thing—like an over-inflated Shirley Temple. The parents were White people living in a small house in an Italian neighborhood. Cindy was definitely from planet autism, as she was completely aloof. She did not respond to much of anything—not toys, videos, books, objects, or picture cards. She never made eye contact in response to a name or speech. In short, she was not going to be easy.

We were doing a complete home program, meaning that she did not attend the Center. I was to lead the home team, taking over for the previous leader, who Mom had fired. The speech therapist would follow her own protocols, and so would the OT and PT. A young lady, Queenie, had just gotten her degree and had been working with her for three months doing ABA. I would sit with Cindy for two hours, five days a week. Queenie would work for an hour, and the other therapist, Ralph, would work for an hour. Speech, OT, and PT were a half an hour, a few times a week.

I was not expecting much from Cindy, as she was so distant. To my great surprise, however, she did comparatively well. She would sit in the chair at the table I brought for her. We took a lot of breaks, but she sat far longer than I thought she would. In the course of our work, she began to respond, make eye contact, point to desired objects, and occasionally repeat a word. She began to respond to affection. Although she seemed very distant, after a few weeks, she would crawl into my lap as she liked physical affection. Perfect, right?

Cindy was not a problem. Mom was. Mom had the living room roped off so that Cindy was in a continually safe environment yet could not leave the confines of that room. The main reason she did this was that Mom smoked outside, in the winter cold, on the porch, and would leave Cindy alone while watching her with a camera on her phone. I thought, *Okay, a little strange but no big deal.*

There was a program book already in place that I had not seen yet left by the last team leader. Mom told me that the last team leader had been fired because Cindy cried for two hours when she attempted to work with her. This Mom made me nervous, as she was high strung, monitored all sessions with a camera, and complained about the other therapists, which indicated to me that she readily finds fault.

The reason she smoked outside was because Mom was clinically OCD. The house was immaculate—every chair in place, no shoes allowed in the house. Lysol was the predominant odor in the house. Once her father came to visit, and they had a big fight because he did not want to take off his shoes before entering the living room. Against her vehement protests, he entered the living room wearing shoes. She went berserk. To avoid contamination, all things had to be in an order that only someone with severe OCD could recognize.

She scrutinized every item anyone brought into the house. How did this affect me and the others? I always came with two bags and a cushion to sit on the floor. One bag was full of toys and other materials. The other, her program and communication books. Mom did not allow me to bring my bags into her little sanctuary where we worked, that is, the living room floor. My bags had to be left on the other side of the barricade, at the front door. I had to take out all my stuff and bring in each little toy, each little puzzle, and lay them out in a designated area. Soon, even this precaution was not enough. Soon, I could no longer bring my bags into the house at all because, she explained with great exasperation, "I saw little flakes coming off of them." Okay. This was a pain but for the sake of the little girl, I complied with Mom's wild imagination.

I brought a table and chair for Cindy to do table work for some programs because Mom's table came up to Cindy's chin. Mom did not like "foreign" objects in her house. I told Mom that no one can work with a table at their chin. She said, "The other therapists use it!" The other therapists were a young lady fresh out of training and an older guy, Ralph, supposedly trained in ABA, who had no idea what doing a program meant. He had no use for a table, as he did not follow the programs.

Previously I had asked Ralph about his experience. He told me that he had many years working with such children. He explained that he did "holistic stuff." I reminded him that he was part of an ABA team and was supposed to be working specifically on the goals as laid out in the program book. To this he responded that he worked with "the whole child." So, I asked him if the rest of the therapists, myself included, were only working with "part of the child." He went into a verbal jungle, and I just walked away.

When I suggested to both the supervisor and the service coordinator that this man was not qualified to work with such children, they all gave me the standard reply: "There isn't anybody else." That was true. I told Mom that I was sorry, but Cindy could not work with a table at her chin. "I am going to use mine." Mom angrily left the house for a smoke.

There were cameras all over the house, and Mom watched us on her phone outside as she smoked. I didn't mind the cameras. Actually, I always wished that all sessions, with all children, were filmed for two reasons: One is that I could then be sure that the parents, at least, saw how the therapy worked and second, if there were any wild accusations, such as I had with another child, all would be on film.

In any case, such was our beginning. The first thing I would do every day was check the communication book. There were no entries. When I checked the data sheets, there was no data. I had shown Mom the program book—how it worked, how we kept data in order to decide when to move on in a program, and how all the ABA therapists would follow the program book and keep data. Evidently, no one had ever explained this to her. I also explained how to use the communication book so that all therapists and the mother would know exactly what each other was doing.

I asked Mom what the other therapists were doing if not the programs, not taking data, and not communicating. She said that she didn't know and didn't care because "Cindy likes them." I told her that there is a protocol to ABA therapy, and if the data is going to be accurate, we need to stick to the method. Mom said that the others don't need the program or the communication book. I saw that I had to be more forceful and tell her that I was the leader now, and it would go according to the protocol or I wouldn't be able to work with this team.

At the first team meeting, I brought up the programs and communication issues to the team. "How can we accomplish goals if everybody is doing their own thing? How can we incorporate and reinforce each other's goals if there's no communication?" Silence. Mom blurted out that she didn't care, as long as we were "helping" Cindy. Whatever I said, Mom contradicted. Any suggestion, any idea, Mom disagreed.

I told the other therapists that they either do the programs and take data, or I'd request a replacement for them or I would leave the team and they could all do as they wished. Also, at the meeting we all agreed, except Mom, that Cindy would benefit from being in the Center with other children in circle time, eating together and working on peer relationships and social skills. Mom said, "No way, she's not toilet trained." I told her that none of the kids at the Center were toilet trained. She responded as if I were nuts: "No one else is changing my kid!" So much for getting her into the Center program.

I didn't really get what her objection was to Cindy's being changed by people at the Center. They were paid to change all the kids. She told me that there were perverts out there who would abuse her. I assured her that all of the women at the Center have had background checks, have been working there for years, and the door to the changing room was always open with plenty of people around. But no, according to Mom the risk was too great.

One day, I listened in as Mom changed her in a bedroom right off the living room. "Cindy! Stop it! Lie still. STOP!! STOP!!" Cindy was screaming. Later that day, as we worked, Cindy sat forward in her chair, as she was interested and engaging wonderfully with me. Mom entered the room and screamed, "Cindy! Sit back." Then, when Cindy "didn't listen," Mom came over and pushed her back in the chair.

I asked Mom, "Do you think she understands you?"

Mom replied, "Oh yes. She understands every word I say to her."

Really? A non-verbal, low cognitive, very delayed child understood every word?

I pushed back. "She does? So why do you suppose she doesn't listen to you?"

"She's stubborn."

Sure, stubborn. Blaming the victim.

A month passed and Cindy made small but steady progress. She was able to sit for longer periods, do simple imitation, and follow simple one step instructions: stand up, sit down, clap hands, tap table. I was pleased with her progress. Mom asked if I could cut back to one hour.

"Why?" I asked, incredulous.

"It's too much for her," Mom replied.

"But she's doing fine," I insisted.

"I don't care, and I want you to come at a different hour."

I explained that changing schedules meant I would also have to change my other children's schedules, and all those therapists would also have to change theirs. It would be impossible.

"Okay, then come at this time, for one hour and that's it," she said with finality.

Mom's OCD was creating more problems as well. I was using the table that I'd bought for Cindy and put Mom's in the kitchen in a corner, out of the way. She told me one day that she could not store the old table in the kitchen corner because "there's no room." I asked her where I should put it. Again, she said, "Use it." And again, I said, "Sorry, it's not good for her height. Mom went wild, but I did not budge. She would have loved to fire me on the spot, but there would be no replacement. She was stuck with me.

One strange day, she sat down next to me as I worked with Cindy and broke out a bottle of Lysol. Every time I used a toy with Cindy and then put it down, Mom would spray it and wipe like mad. Next toy, more Lysol. She did this one day and never did it again. Why did she do it one day and never again? When I asked her what was up with this, she said that I had a cold and was infecting her.

Another month went by, and now Mom was never in the room with us. She sat out in the winter weather, on the porch, watching on her phone and smoking. Progress was good but painfully slow. Again, the therapists were not doing the programs and not taking data. I wrote in the communication book, but no one read it or responded. I wanted to quit the team, but the service coordinator begged me to hang in there.

"Please?? There is no one else!"

I bit my lip and continued on the team. There was no teamwork, no communication between therapists, no data being taken, and no supervisor—hopeless situation.

Cindy, like so many others with autism, was a big toe walker. At the next team meeting the PT suggested that Cindy toe walks because of "sensory issues." For the first time ever, an OT disagreed. OTs are famous for saying everything is a "sensory issue." Not this time. She tore the guy's head off. I suggested that everyone go home that night and look up "autism and toe walking." It was not discussed again. I brought up the program and communication book again. There were no responses.

Occasionally, Dad would be home with Mom. It was astounding to me how this man survived. Everything he said, she attacked. Everything he attempted to do, she criticized non-stop. He just kept his mouth shut. Hero or dishrag? Once when he was there and Mom was out, I told the father that I found it very difficult to work with his wife, as she was contrary, critical, and unreasonable. Dad nodded his head but did not respond. During team meetings, he never said a word.

Things were going better by the middle of November. I'm not sure what happened, but Mom was suddenly very agreeable. There were smiles, no arguments, no complaints. I wondered what was up. In the meantime, Cindy began to crawl into my lap. This amazed mom. I wasn't. She was a little girl starving for affection, which apparently, she didn't get.

The other therapists continued to ignore the communication book, and Ralph was not doing programs at all. I didn't know what he was doing. Queenie did the programs and was in constant communication with me. Cindy was showing some temper now and then, but that was nothing unusual for a non-verbal child. What recourse did she have? I did not know what the speech therapist was working on for communication.

Then, suddenly, in mid-December, a miracle happened. Somehow, Mom was convinced to send Cindy to the Center. That meant that I would no longer be team leader, as the teacher would take over writing programs, checking data, and being responsible for the performance of the other therapists, including me. But now that she was going into the program, her home therapy hours were cut. Either me or Ralph had to quit the team on January 1. So, of course, Mom decided that they did not need me anymore, and I was fired. I was absolutely thrilled!

During the last week, I decided to watch Ralph, the man who worked with the "whole child" and used a "holistic" approach, to see exactly what he did with her. He sat on the floor, not facing Cindy, and read a book "to" her. It wasn't "to" her because she sat near him, completely unaware that he was even in the room. Occasionally, he'd say, "Oh look, Cindy, see the horse?" and, of course, not understanding language and unable to follow a story in a book, she just stared off into the distance, happy that this guy wasn't bothering her. Ralph obviously had no idea what joint attention was. Nor that Cindy had very little receptive language such that she could not identify a horse in an illustrated book and was completely unaware of his presence. But she didn't cry, and Mom was satisfied with that.

December 31 was to be my last day. I came on December 30, and only Dad was home. He told me to come again tomorrow. Later that day, Mom called and said not to. That was it for my little blond-haired, blue-eyed sweet girl. I felt bad leaving her but was simply overjoyed that I did not have to go back into that house.

A few months down the road, I found out from Queenie that Mom was upset because she "had gotten rid of Ben." I asked her why. It was obvious that we did not like each other. At all. She told me that Mom said, "All Ralph does is sit on the floor and read a book to her. She doesn't pay any attention, and Ralph just sits there reading away while Cindy ignores him the entire time."

Jimmy's Mother

My fingers start to tremble as I write about this case. I almost lost my entire career because of this mother. Nine years later, as I recall what happened, it scares me and angers me—but mostly it upsets me because this difficult child, that no one else had any success with, was doing so well, and I had to leave him.

The Center called me at the end of June to see if I could take another case, "Just until September." This was odd. It's always a bad sign when you get a call in the summer for a child who is aging out soon. If this kid needed a therapist in June, that meant his previous therapists had quit or were fired.

He did not live too far from my house, so I agreed to add him to my packed schedule. I was told that there had been others there before me, and that Mom had fired them. Word was that he was extremely difficult to work with. Okay, I'd heard that before.

They were a fairly well-to-do Black family and the second generation from "the Islands." Mom obviously took great pride in her Black heritage, as there were portraits of famous Black people on the walls—Martin Luther King Jr, Malcolm X, Harriet Tubman, and Nelson Mandela. She also had African statues, paintings, weavings, and knick-knacks everywhere. She told me that she was very active in the local Black community. Her mother was often in the house with us. She was interested in her grandson and wanted to help. Grandma's Jamaican accent was thick.

At this first meeting, I asked her to show me the program book that they had been using until now. She looked at me quizzically. "Program book? What's that?" I was dumbfounded. "You mean he hasn't been following a program all this time? What have the therapists been doing with him?" I thought, *Nine months with no programs?* Where was the supervision? What was going on here?" I had heard that some previous therapists had quit. Mom told me that she'd fired the OT, a White woman. In this case, color made a difference, as we will see.

When I came on the scene, a Black woman named Connie, an ABA therapist, had been working with him for quite a while. I knew her. She was good. Mom explained that mostly they just played, as Jimmy would not sit at a table or in a chair. She explained that the therapists just kind of followed him around and tried to interact with him.

There had been no speech teacher assigned. That was odd for a non-verbal child on the spectrum. The OT had been fired. I asked Mom why, and she told me, "Well, I found her being too rough and abusive with him." I highly doubted that, as OTs are usually doing fun things that don't help much but don't hurt either. Mom explained that she'd confronted the OT about it, and the OT supposedly said, "With some kids, you just gotta treat them rough."

I stored that information in the back of my mind, as I didn't believe any professional would ever say such a thing to a parent, even if they believed it, which I doubted. Later on, those very words would come back to save me.

For sure, he did not like to sit—not for a second. He could not talk, so he was used to running and grabbing whatever he wanted instead of asking for help. He seemed to understand language, but he was unresponsive to commands, instructions, or reciprocal interactions.

I saw that I had to try and get him to sit at a table; otherwise, he was just all over the place. He would sit whenever I broke out a toy that interested him and stay in the chair until bored with the toy. Then, suddenly, he would whoosh up and out and into another room. When Grandma was with us, and he would run into another room, she would run after him, grab him, and physically drag him back to the table. I explained to her that I could also drag him back, but I'd prefer that he come back because he wanted to. I needed to be more interesting than whatever was, "over there."

She backed off. I introduced a table and chair in the living room, which is usually a disaster, but I didn't want to isolate our work area until I had established a rapport with him. I would just try to find out what he liked to play with (a "reinforcer assessment," in fancy ABA terminology). He really seemed to be just super-hyper, running from room to room, jumping on the furniture, up the few steps between the kitchen and living room, down again, up again, endlessly.

The first week, either Mom or Grandma was home watching the sessions, as we all sat in the living room. He did surprisingly well. The beginner programs I wrote for him, he learned quickly. He could sit and attend and follow instructions. He was also toilet trained, which is rare, and made good eye contact with me. In one of these early sessions, he continually held a metro-card, which he fixated on. Mom snatched it away from him, and he began to wail.

I explained to her that whenever you find things that children like, metro-cards or whatever, don't take them away, use them to get his attention. I showed her how to use it.

"What do you want? Oh, a metro-card? Good. Can you point to it? Good job, here it is." But, instead of seeing the potential for using a highly desired object to elicit communication, she considered this "giving in" to the child and spoiling him. She explained that she was a strict disciplinarian.

Within weeks, he began to respond well, and I was writing harder programs for him. He was doing great with object ID, picture ID, following one step instructions, and imitation came easy. He enjoyed the sessions. Mom asked me if I could take over for the other ABA therapist as well. I didn't have the time, or I would have been tempted. He was doing great, and I wasn't sure how he'd gotten such a bad reputation. Still, he did have this urge to run and no way to ask for a break. One time when he ran away, Mom suddenly appeared with a long wooden spoon. It was about a yard long, with a ten-inch bowl. She held it in front of him and shouted, "SIT DOWN!" He didn't. He ran away with her in hot pursuit. I didn't know what to make of this, and she brought him back, showed me the spoon, and said, "This is what I use to get him to listen." I probably should have reported it, but, hey, it's her kid.

They didn't expect me on July 5, and Dad was home. He seemed like a nice, quiet guy. Jimmy did fine that day, as Dad watched. The next day, however, was a disaster. He had been running a lot more than usual. After the session, he began to cry, and for this, Mom gave him a few smacks with the spoon and made him stay in bed. He howled.

This was a first child for this young mother. She came across as arrogant and trying to impress others with superior knowledge. I did not much care for her personality, but I was hoping to convince her that hitting a child and placing him in Time-Out is never a good plan for a non-verbal child on the spectrum, although I knew that she would not accept these ideas. She was pretty convinced that such ideas were "giving in" and "spoiling." I thought it was time to try and work in isolation. We went to his bedroom, which was not very visible from the living room, as it was up a few steps and in the back of the apartment. I was hoping that with fewer distractions, he wouldn't be tempted to run so much. We began the first week of July. It was harder for him to jump and run there, so he produced a new trick to "escape" his work. He would begin to giggle and fold himself up and fall into my lap. I would just continue with the programs, and he usually came back to work with no problem.

At this point, I was told that he was doing far better with Connie, the other ABA therapist, as well. Me, Mom, and Grandma were all very happy with the change in Jimmy, and the two women and I had a great rapport. We would laugh and joke after the sessions as I did my paperwork.

I was thrilled because just a few short months ago, this boy would not sit in a chair, did not respond to anything, and was seemingly unable or unwilling to follow instructions. Now, he was doing great. The other therapists had programs to follow, and we were all happy about his progress. He would start in a new school program in September, and it now appeared that he would be able to sit with other children, attend to instruction, and hopefully, start to use verbal communication. He still had his moments when he wanted to bolt, but we could usually work past them.

Then came the fateful day of August 12, six weeks after we'd started. Everything exploded. On this day, he was in a particularly bad mood. We worked for about a half hour with no problem, and then he started crying, pushing the table, throwing objects, trying to get away, and I let him up. After the break, he came back to work, but again, he began to fidget.

I said to him, "C'mon, Jimmy, you know we have to do some work." I could usually persuade him to do some more. This time, he did something that I'd never seen before. He started to wildly blow his nose all over himself and me, then he started hitting himself on the head. I was afraid that he'd really hurt himself. I gave him a tap on the shoulder and said, "Stop it!" I wanted him to know that he could not hurt himself.

I wiped us both off and gave him a hug. He continued to cry, but soon, he calmed down and went on to continue to work well until the end of the session. When Mom heard that the session was over, she came roaring into the room and exclaimed, "Today is your last day. You hit my child!"

Then, she ran out of the house, called her mother and an uncle, who both came flying over to confront me. I was sitting on the sofa in the living room filling out paperwork while Grandma continued to berate me. "You don't hit a child!"

Then Mom said something extraordinary.

"If it was me [meaning, "because I'm Black"], and I hit a Jewish child, I'd already be in jail!"

I told her, "Let's not bring race into this, okay?"

She said, "I ain't signing no papers, so no point in you filling 'em out." Then she put Jimmy into his highchair, in front of the TV, and he sat happily watching TV and eating his lunch. All was well, as far as he was concerned. I left while she got on the phone to the Center.

A few minutes after I left, my phone rang. It was the director of the Center. "You'd better come right down here." When I got there, I was facing the director and the ABA supervisor. They told me that Mom had said that I was too rough with him, and when she asked me why, I had supposedly told her, "Sometimes you have to be rough with children."

These were the exact same words she had said to me about why she'd fired the OT. I told them that she had said the same thing about the OT, and that I had not said such a thing, nor could I imagine any professional working with such vulnerable children saying such a thing, even if they believed it.

They also told me that the City had already called and they put me on suspension pending an investigation. Mom had called Quality Assurance, the Special Education Office, the Board of Education, and later, the police. The investigation took six weeks. Six weeks where I was not allowed to be near children. Six weeks where I had to cancel my other children including a new little Spanish girl no one else had had any success with. She had to sit in her mother's lap with other therapists, but with me, she sat at the table and played with my toys. Mom was amazed. Mom started crying when I told her that I had to quit. She begged me to stay. That really hurt.

For the next six weeks, I was petrified that I'd have to give up my career, lose my license and my professional insurance, and would need to find a lawyer to handle my case.

The director of the Center showed the various offices who investigated me that I had over ten thousand hours of excellent work and no complaints. Not one. The Office of Quality Assurance called other mothers I was working with or with whom I had worked. They gave rave reviews.

After all of the different offices finished investigating and taking my statement and reviewing the facts, all was dismissed. The verdict came down: "Unsubstantiated allegations." Mom was livid. She told the director of the Center that it was her goal to make sure that I never worked with another child again. Then she called the police. The police called the director, and he informed them that all had been dismissed and that the allegations were false. End of story.

I worked for many years after she tried to make sure I never worked again, and in all those years, I helped many children—many of them needing someone with a lot of experience to progress. I cringe to think of how many I may not have been able to help because of this mother.

Yonkie's Mother

Yonkie is a "Sephardi" Jewish name. He was a sweet little Orthodox Jewish boy who learned quickly—very quickly. It was such a pleasure to work with him. He was very short, like both his parents and looked like a little wind-up doll. He was very good natured, easily entertained, and sociable. He wasn't talking, and I guess that's why he had been diagnosed with autism. I wasn't so sure that diagnosis was correct. Unfortunately, I did not work with him very long.

His father was an extremely sweet man, but his mother was a very unhappy young lady. This was their first child, and they also had a newborn daughter. They lived in a nice house next door to her parent's house. It was obvious that she had been a "privileged" child growing up and was very attached to her parents. I had met her mother a few times and she also seemed like a nice enough lady. She was very interested in her grandson's progress and involved in decisions.

Yonkie was fun to work with. He attended well and laughed a lot. He had one problem though that drove his parents crazy. The second his father or mother entered a room that he was in, he started crying—especially the kitchen. In their presence, he cried a lot. Very strange. Mom was very frustrated and irritated by this. He did not act this way with me or any other therapists. Just his parents. Mom seemed quite distressed that he acted so normal with others. He was improving across skills and with communication. He behaved beautifully and laughed a lot.

I got the feeling that Mom resented that with his own mother/father he acted so unhappy and was always crying, but with these strangers, he seemed so normal! I never found out what she was thinking as I was not there long enough to figure it out. She never watched a session and never had any questions for me. What she did have was a lot of complaints.

She would complain to me about all kinds of things. For instance, he liked to stand on the windowsill, looking into the backyard while I held him, and we would point out trees, flowers, birds, and clouds. He repeated the words. I was thrilled. In order to do this activity, I had to roll up the venetian blinds. They just cleared his head as he stood in the window. Mom came in one day and said, "Don't roll the blinds so high."

"Uh, why not?" I asked.

"Because my mother said that they are not made to go so high."

I told her that she was mistaken, that they are indeed made to go all the way to the top and that Yonkie loved to look out the window. She stormed out of the room. The next day, I rolled them up again, and she was wild. She ran next door to her mother's house and called her husband.

Another time I wanted to work with him in different rooms as he did not need to just sit at a table. We could walk around the house and identify objects, learning the names of different rooms and furniture. She did not like this. I was instructed to stay in the back bedroom.

One day, as we were in the kitchen, just out of the bedroom, Mom walked in. Immediately, upon her entrance, he started whining and crying. This was perfect for an experiment. I had her take Yonkie out of the kitchen, and I sat at the kitchen table alone. Then I brought Yonkie back into the kitchen and we played there at the table while she stood outside of the kitchen. Next, I asked Mom to come into the room. As soon as he saw her, he started to cry. I just watched. She took him over to the cupboard and gave him a cookie. He stopped crying.

One didn't need a degree in psychology or behavior analysis to see what was going on here! It was pretty clear! I told her that because he couldn't talk, he had learned an alternative way to communicate in order to get what he wanted. This was his system. I explained, "He cries, you take him right to the cabinet and give him a cookie."

She did not believe me. On the spot, I taught him how to sign for "Give me cookie." I had her review this procedure with him, and henceforth, to give him a cookie only when he signed and was not crying. It worked for her, but she seemed stunned and not happy—because it worked!

It wasn't long after the team started working with him that he was making great progress across skills. He was beginning to use words to communicate. His IQ jumped. He seemed pretty much like a normal kid. Yet, Mom continued to complain. She would say that I tickled him "too much," or I picked him up too much, or she had some other complaint, and this complaining was on a daily basis. One day, I just lost it.

"Is that all you do is complain?" I asked her.

Her eyes grew wide. She jumped out of her chair and ran to her mother next door, who came over to confront me. I told Grandma, "Get another therapist."

The next day I was at the Center, and there was an announcement on the speakers. "Ben, please pick up line three." That was strange, as no one ever called me at Center. I didn't work there. It was Yonkie's father. Evidently he had called the service coordinator to "straighten out the problem" and they passed the call on to me. He asked me to please continue working with Yonkie. I told him that I had no patience for people who did not appreciate when others helped them. Then I asked him if he had seen any difference in his son from the day we'd started until today. He said that of course he had, but when I'm in the house, I should respect his wife's wishes. He brought up the example of not raising the blinds too high. I told him that his wife finds nothing but things to complain about and that I could not work in such an environment.

A week later, I got a letter from him. In it, he apologized for his wife's behavior and thanked me for all I'd done for Yonkie. He asked if I could finish out the year. I called him and said, "Thank you for your letter. No, sorry."

Yonkie continued at the Center and went on the following year into a regular education classroom.

Tommy's Mother

This was a sad tale and a strange tale. Tommy, Mom, and his eight-year-old sister lived in a packed, one-bedroom apartment deep in East New York (ENY). ENY is a high crime (violent crimes) area where your average therapist will not go. It wasn't always that way. In any case, I was asked to go there because, being one of the few male therapists, I never had any problems in any area I had worked in New York.

We began our work in May of 2013. Tommy was one year and ten months old. I don't know if there was a father anywhere on the scene. No man was ever mentioned, and there were no pictures on the walls except for one of Mom's sister standing on the tarmac near a private jet with Barak and Michelle Obama.

Tommy started in May, as he had just been diagnosed after his evaluation. The plan was to do a home program until September, and then he would go to the Center for both Center-based and continued home therapy. My colleague, Lacy, wrote programs for him, but when I came on the team, she left the team to me. On the team was a man named George. He was about thirty years old, Black, and I'd worked with him before, unfortunately. He was not meant for this kind of work and knew nothing about ABA. He was not "child friendly." He also had a continual habit of simply not showing up—not for sessions, not for team meetings. No calls, no messages. He just did not show up!

Tommy's speech teacher, Yaffa, surprisingly, was an Orthodox Jewish woman who was also willing to go into the "bad" neighborhoods. She was a rare, good speech teacher who incorporated ABA procedures into her work.

The family was another "from the Islands." Mom was a tall, very tough lady who seldom smiled. She never laughed. She was just a very serious lady. She did not like her son's diagnosis and did not agree with it. According to her, he was simply a late talker. His evaluations by the staff indicated all the typical kinds of things usually found with a "PDD/NOS." He was, no question.

In retrospect, I can say that I did not handle Tommy's program very well, and it blew up. Tommy was "low functioning." He had very little patience. He might sit for one minute and then run away to the pantry with a window that looked out into the alley, the next. That was one of his favorite spots. Because the apartment was so small, it was not easy to get to him if he ran to there. It meant moving past Mom at a small table, going through a very narrow kitchen, not much bigger than a closet, and coming into the tiny pantry. He would stand there and stare out of the window for hours.

Every time this happened, Mom had to get up so that I could run after Tommy and bring him back to the table. I should have immediately given up the table and worked with him "out of chair." If he liked the pantry so much, I should have tried to engage him there. Big mistake on my part!

His other favorite spot was on his mother's lap. Once there, he would not leave, and she would not force him to leave. Another thing that greatly bothered me was that the little girl was sent to the only small bedroom for the entire time any therapist was there. One hour for me, one for George, and a half hour for the speech and OT therapists. She was allowed out only for bathroom breaks.

In those days, it was considered essential to get "stimulus control" in a "highly structured environment." What that meant in plain English was this: get the kid to sit down and do his work! Like most in ABA at the time, I bought into this belief. And so, that is what I tried to do. Unfortunately, Tommy was not much interested in sitting at a table nor in the vast majority of things I offered to hold his interest. Your average professional would blame the victim and evaluate him as, "unable to maintain focus" or "inability to attend." I did, too.

I managed to find things that Tommy liked, and for the first few months, he sat well and was learning. He sang songs with me, laughed hysterically at some of my toys, made eye contact, and occasionally repeated words. On a good day, he was great and fun to work with. On a bad day, he'd be out of the chair continually and either at the back window or in Mom's lap. George was up to his old tricks of simply not showing up. Mom did not seem to care about that.

We had started working together in May, and he picked up some basic skills by the end of June. After we had moved on to higher level skills, I decided to review previously learned skills. He had forgotten them! Programs he had mastered were completely gone! This was probably due to another mistake I made. The fancy ABA term is "temporal generalization." It simply means remembering what you learned. With children on the spectrum, it was important to do "maintenance" of skills—that is, occasionally, along with the new skills you are teaching, go over the skills previously learned, or they may disappear. I had not written maintenance programs.

Throughout July, George simply had not been coming. A day here, a day there, but he was supposed to see Tommy one hour a day, five days a week. Tommy was losing a lot of therapy time, and it was hard for me to determine whether his lack of progress was due to this or simply his inability to learn. The method we were utilizing, called discrete trial teaching, required, according to research, a minimum of twenty hours a week to make progress. Tommy was getting ten in a good month.

In late July, we had a team meeting with me and Mom and the speech teacher. The speech teacher wanted to try sign language with him, even though he hadn't done well with imitation skills. Mom claimed he understood everything, and he was just bored and ignoring us. She did not want to try sign language. I asked if she wanted George replaced, and she said, "No."

During the meeting, Mom was quiet, as Yaffa and I went through his progress (or lack thereof). Throughout, Mom grunted disagreement and displeasure at what she was hearing.

I asked Yaffa after the meeting how she got along with the mother. She told me that Mom rarely said anything, and she was obviously not happy about what we were doing. Yaffa only saw him for a half hour, so she was able to, "get in and get out," and have little interaction with Mom.

Tommy was supposed to start at the Center on September 1, so I figured that his hours would be cut to five at home, and I would no longer be team leader and responsible for his programs. Maybe someone else would have better luck. At that point, if it happened, I could be replaced. I was hoping it would go that way, but then I got a message that he needed an EpiPen and as a result, he could not attend the Center.

He was getting increasingly impatient at the table. There was little progress. Mom was very unhappy about this. She asked me what was going on. I explained that there was no consistency in his therapy, as the other therapist never showed up and did not follow the programs. I asked her again if she wanted George replaced. She said, "No."

Instead of discussing what options we had to improve conditions, she took two buses to talk with the director at the Center to complain about the service and the program. For sure, I could not deny that it was not going well. Mom started to cancel sessions fairly regularly, and when I did come, she was not at all welcoming.

She did not look at me or speak to me unless it was to complain. Tommy would get out of the chair and run into her lap, where she would hold him as they watched a small TV together. She would give him a cookie. I told her that if she kept letting him jump in her lap and eat cookies, he would never come back to work with me. She did not respond to me; she just held him there and ignored me.

In September, his health appeared to be deteriorating. He was often sick, and when Mom took him to the doctor, he was given the diagnosis that so many young children with autism are given—ear infection. I had so many children given that diagnosis so many times that I came to believe it was the thing doctors told mothers when they really did not know why the child was sick.

It was getting nearly impossible at this point to do anything with Tommy. I tried working out of chair with him, but he would run to Mom the first time I tried to get any kind of response from him—into her lap and a cookie. Not being able to attend the Center meant that he would spend another year with me. My heart sunk at the news.

Mom requested that we all take a break until September 9. When I came back, George had been taken off the case. I was now supposed to do two hours a day with Tommy. I found that one day, Tommy would do well. The next, there was no response at all. I was able to change my afternoon hours to morning hours now that George was gone. Tommy seemed to work better in the morning.

The speech teacher again requested using sign language. I incorporated it into our sessions. Mom was to do it as well. She was not to give him anything unless he signed for it after she modeled how. But no, she wouldn't do it. She knew what he wanted and just gave it to him. I was happy about one thing. His sister was in school from nine to eleven, so she was not locked up in the bedroom while I was there.

After the break, his mother wanted us to spend about twenty minutes first thing at the computer singing along to sites of children's songs. Okay, so we sang, and I tried to get verbal imitation.

Aside from this activity, he was very cranky and didn't want to do anything but hang on to Mom.

One day, I put him on the countertop in the kitchen and turned on the water. He loved this and learned quickly to "turn it on/off." Then I put a cup in and prompted the sign/word "cup." He said it once and eventually let me prompt the sign. This was good. Maybe our "breakthrough." We did this for two days in a row, and I was hopeful after these two days.

For the next few weeks, things went well enough, but there was no real progress. At least he was out of the chair and not running to her as often. It went like this until mid-September, when the Jewish Holidays began—Rosh Hashanah, Yom Kippur, and Succos—so there were a lot of breaks.

In late October, I was out sick for a week, and Mom had cancelled a few times. He missed two weeks straight. When I returned, Mom said that he had tubes put in his ears, and that's why he never spoke. Supposedly because he couldn't hear. I had a lot of children over the years who had tubes put in, but it didn't affect hearing, it was simply to drain excess fluid and hopefully, stop all of the "ear infections." It seemed to me that Tommy had no problem hearing.

The next problem was that Mom complained that the speech teacher was locking him in the highchair to work with him. I asked her if she'd told Yaffa not to do that. "No." I called Yaffa, and she said that it was impossible now to work with him at all, as he ran away all the time. I asked her if she'd spoken to Mom about this, but she told me what I already knew: this Mom was not one to sit and discuss things with.

November came, and things were looking up. He was beginning to repeat words and occasionally make requests verbally without a prompt. He loved the sunglasses that I brought him. He wanted to wear them all the time, so I used them to get him to request with words. Mom did not like this because, "It'll hurt his eyes."

On December 10, everything changed. He had throat surgery. He came home from the hospital tired and very clingy to Mom. It became impossible after the surgery to continue as all he wanted to do was sit in Mom's lap. As soon as I walked in the door, he ran to her lap, she held him, and that was that. I suggested that if he were happy in her lap, maybe she and I could work with him in her lap? I got him to work on a puzzle that he liked, but as soon as I introduced something he didn't like, he would turn into his mother and bury his head in her chest. This wasn't going to work.

We went back to the table, but he would not sit for a second. As soon as I introduced anything that he did not want to do, out of his chair and into Mom's lap. I asked Mom what she thought I should do. Maybe she could make a suggestion on how we should proceed. She said that she'd ask her doctor.

Her report to me from the doctor was that he was healing, and "it'll take time." She told me further that I was to stop trying "to force him" to sit at a table, as the doctor said that you can't force a child. I asked her, "So how do you suggest we proceed?" She gave no response. What I did daily from that point on was to take out toys and play at the table. If he wanted to join, he could but rarely did. I had two-hour sessions daily with a child who would not leave his mother's lap, was recovering from surgery, and there was nothing I could do.

I called the service coordinator and suggested that she ask Mom if she wanted me replaced. She told me that Mom doesn't like what I'm doing with him and it "should be fun."

Well, she was right about that. It should be fun. But all Tommy wanted to do was stare out the pantry window or sit in her lap in front of the TV. I could not compete with those things. He was difficult enough to work with before his surgery. Now, it was impossible.

I asked Mom soon after this call what she thought I should do. She went into a tirade about how I am not nice to her, and not friendly or respectful toward her, and that I am boring her son. I asked if she would like to have me replaced. Her eyes grew wide, and she said, "What? Why?"

I was stunned. Wasn't it obvious? "Well, if you are not satisfied with the service, maybe another therapist would do better with him. I really don't think I can help him." She angrily responded, "Ok!" I gathered my things and walked out the door.

I was in my car across the street from her house doing some paperwork, and my phone rang. It was the director of the Center telling me to apologize to Mom. Further, to not drop the case. I told him that I can apologize if that'll help anything, but I could not see continuing to work with him. Not for his sake, not for mine. I hung up and immediately called Mom. I told her that I was sorry that it was not working out. Her response was a very cold, "Ok."

I continued, "But in the best interest of Tommy, I really don't think I can continue with him." She readily agreed. I was relieved, she was relieved, and the director was not happy!

I walked back to the apartment to retrieve the program book. She met me at the door, looked away from my face, and held out the book. I took it and turned to leave.

Looking back, I see that I made a lot of mistakes. The first one is that I should have abandoned working at the table immediately upon indication that the child did not like the structure. The second was that there was no rapport between me and Mom. She did not feel confident in me nor that I was one to confide in. Was it just me? I don't think so, but having a good working rapport with a mother is vital. She's part of the team. However, in this case, I tried my best to get along with her, but it just never happened. If it had only been that way with me, then I could say that it was all my fault, but the fact that the other therapists felt the same indicated that maybe the entire fault wasn't mine.

Israel's Mother

There's an area in Brooklyn that is well known amongst the Jewish population. The area is where the Jews from Syria live. It is a very wealthy community. I had never been there before and only heard rumors. Good things mostly—wealth, strong community, philanthropists, kept the customs of Orthodox Jewry from Syria, spoke Arabic, Hebrew, and English. I was told that they were "tribal," meaning they stick to their own, marry their own. Autism doesn't care where you're from, and neither did I. But I was kind of curious to see what it would be like in one of their majestic homes.

Unfortunately, I didn't get into the big fancy home. I was to see Israel at a cousin's house in a less wealthy part of the neighborhood. The babysitter spoke Arabic. She led me from the living room door immediately to the basement where we were to work, amongst tons of clutter, in a small area hemmed in by an old couch. She brought him down to me as I set up a makeshift table.

He was young, only seventeen months old. I was left alone with him for our first session. He was able to imitate, which I did not expect. His eye contact was good. Good, as in normal. He responded to his name and would look where I asked him to. He struck me as pretty normal, though he had some "secondary signs" such as toe walking, self-stimulatory behavior, and being non-verbal. In any case, I expected that he would be one of those kids who, after a few months of stimulation, would probably get reassessed and have his diagnosis changed. This was not the kind of child I preferred to work with. He was perfect for a rookie therapist.

I was not sure how a child so young, and so attentive, had even received a diagnosis of PDD/NOS. But then, that label could include a cat.

Mom worked, but she was able to join us for our second session. His sister also joined us. She was about five years old. The sister appeared to me to be gifted. She was very smart, very quick. I presented shapes to Israel, and he was able to match them immediately. I presented five nesting cups, and he figured out how to stack them inside and build a tower, also upon one showing. Obviously, his performance skills were excellent—above age level. This, at least, was typical: high scoring on performance scale and low scoring on verbal scale. But then, a lot of different kinds of disorders fit that description.

It was not easy cramming into that spot in the basement, but we managed. Israel was a very happy little boy and was easily and readily engaged. I was not sure what to do with him because the beginning programs were too easy for him, yet the advanced programs, he was not ready for. I told Mom when she first joined us and participated for a while that I was not sure why he'd gotten the diagnosis he did and that I was not sure what I could do for him, as he didn't seem to need much. I suspect that Mom was simply worried because he hadn't said any words yet. But then, he was only fifteen months old, and that's concerning but not terribly out of the realm of "normal."

A few times I did get to work in the parent's home. It was in the wealthy area, and the house was huge, furnished with expensive Arabian furniture and servants. After a few weeks, Israel was simply having a good time while I tried to figure out what exactly to do with him. He simply did not need much. But before I could figure it out, it all ended.

One day, I came to the house and Israel had a terrible cold. Really bad. There was no way to work with him, as he was miserable and could not breathe. I spent the entire session wiping his nose, his face, and trying to comfort him. I told the babysitter that I could not believe they had not cancelled the session! She asked me why would they do that? I gave her two reasons: One, he is not capable of working in this condition. It was torture for him. The other was that I did not want to catch his cold. I didn't bother explaining to her that if I caught such a cold, that would affect my ability to work with other children. I assumed she didn't care about my problems, so I didn't mention it.

After about forty minutes of my wiping his nose and his continual crying, Mom came home. She sat on the floor beside us, and I asked her why she hadn't cancelled this session. Her eyes grew wide.

"Why would I do that?" she asked, astonished.

I said, "Look at him! He's sick and probably contagious."

Her reaction was outrage!

"What? He's not that sick! You never wanted to work with him anyway. Just get out."

That really bothered me. I reminded her that I had told her that he probably didn't need much because he's on such a high level, not that I didn't want to work with him! This deliberate twisting of words really angered me. I wanted to just pack up and leave, but I had spent over an hour with him and was not going to give up two hours' worth of wages.

I told her again that, thank God, he did not need much, as he was doing so well and that I was not leaving until she signed both sets of session notes so I wouldn't lose the money. Surprisingly, she waited for me to finish the paperwork, and then she signed it. I suggested that she get another therapist. That was one suggestion that I didn't have to make. I was glad it was over.

Sally's Mother

While visiting the Center one day in early August, I saw a little girl whom I did not know. Her name was Sally, and I inquired about her. They told me that she was very difficult to work with and did not respond well—mostly cries and/or tantrums. The teacher told me that they couldn't find a home therapist for her because of where she lived, which was in the west thirties blocks of Coney Island. That was NYCHA housing and notorious for drugs, violence, theft, and truancy.

Though only a five-minute drive from the famous Coney Island Boardwalk, with all its amusements and tourists from around the world, going to the hood there was like entering another world.

The teacher told me that the Center was desperate to find a home therapist, and could I take her? My schedule was pretty packed, but I said that I could squeeze her in on Tuesdays, Thursdays, and Sundays from five to seven p.m. I did not like working past six o'clock, but I felt a real sympathy toward the girl. She was always dressed in pretty clothes and braided hair yet seemed so utterly helpless and hopeless.

My first attempt at a home session, I caught Mom on the sidewalk. She told me that Sally had a fever and had to go to the emergency room. She couldn't call me, she said, because she did not have my cell phone number. I doubted that, but okay. First time and all.

At my next attempt, there was no answer at the door. A little boy said through a window that the mother had gone to a store, but her daughter, meaning Sally, was home! Home alone with a little boy? I was hoping that he was wrong. I went back at five-thirty. No answer. An old lady next door poked her head out of her window and said, "She was home a half hour ago." Then she asked if I was the therapist. I told her that I was. So much for confidentiality!

Hmm, ok, twice I was there, and twice I couldn't see her. These kinds of things happen when you begin a new case, so I didn't think anything of it. I was just anxious to start working with her, although I did call the Center and told them that I was not driving way out to West Coney Island again until I heard from the mother that she'd be there. They informed me at this time that the mother was unpredictable. It seems she was in a program for addicts and was not the most dependable of people. I didn't care about that. None of my business, but if I was going to go out of my way and work late, I at least wanted to be able to see the little girl.

A week later, I hadn't received a call—not from Mom and not from the Center. I pretty much wrote this case off.

The second week in August, a service coordinator called and said that Mom called, wanted services, and would be home. She also had a new phone number, claiming that her old one was broken, and that's why she'd never called me. I decided to give it one more try. Evidently, there had been some mix-up in the phone numbers and who knows what. But, if Mom called, that told me that she was serious. Maybe now we could get started in earnest.

The service coordinator also explained to me that her little sister, Brenda, was about eighteen months old and had just been diagnosed with "failure to thrive." She asked if I could work with her as well. I did not have time to add to my schedule, and I had never worked with such a diagnosis before. It sounded like they needed an eating specialist or a living coach. What would a behavior analyst or special education teacher be able to do for a little girl who wasn't "thriving?"

I called Mom after this. No answer. I called Mom's sister because I had been told by the service coordinator that Sally's aunt was more dependable. The aunt was married, both she and her husband worked, and they had a fourteen-year-old daughter. They lived in one of the NYCHA buildings a block away. They often contacted the aunt instead of the mother when they needed to communicate something and suggested that I do the same.

I tried again at the home. I got there at a quarter to four. I banged loudly. No answer. I waited a few minutes and banged again, louder. This time, a child banged on the window next to the door in response. I waited another few minutes and banged again. This time, it hurt my hand to bang so hard. Again, some child banged on the window. I called Mom's new cell phone and heard, "No incoming calls." I called her sister and got her machine, and I left a message.

I banged again. No answer at all this time. While driving home, my cell rang, and a lady asked if I had called this number. I said that I had and that I was looking for Mrs. X. The lady said that I had the wrong number. It wasn't. By eight p.m. that evening, no one from the family had called to ask if I had been there or not that day. It had now been three weeks of playing hide and seek.

Sally was getting to school every day, but I just could not seem to get her at home. At school, they told me she continued to tantrum and threw up fairly often. They assumed, as good behaviorists would, that the throwing up was a "behavioral response." I never was able to get ahold of Mom. She never called me, and neither did her sister. I never saw her. Sally turned three and aged out of the program.

A very interesting postscript to this case:

Her caseworker told me that she'd suggested to Mom to have Sally assessed for reflux. Sure enough, it was very bad, and she began taking medication for it. Now, she said, Sally was a calm girl. There was no more screaming, biting people, and vomiting. Amazing. This was, for me, a very important lesson. Behaviorists always assume that any "behavior," such as vomiting, is "learned behavior"—that is, purposefully done for a "function," or reason. One of the myriad problems with behaviorism! If something like vomiting is present, the first assumption should be that there is a physical cause. A doctor should examine the child before attempting any kind of behavioral intervention. While it is true that such is explained in behavioral classes, there is so much emphasis on behavioral explanations for everything that it is often forgotten. Golden rule is that before working with a child, check to see if he/she has had a hearing test, a visual test, an allergy battery, and whether there are any eating/digesting problems.

Chapter Nine

Different Kinds of Fathers

I did not have much interaction with fathers in my nineteen years in Brooklyn. There are only a few who come to mind, and this because they were so crazy. Were there good fathers, too? Of course. Some of them were the sweetest, caring, most involved people in the world who would sacrifice anything for their children, with autism and without. Some were Black. Some were White. Some were Chinese. Some were Japanese. Some were Jewish. Some were Christian. Some were Muslim. Get the picture? I had kids from everywhere on the planet, and being a good or a bad father had nothing to do with race or religion.

There is a big myth out there in Autismland that the divorce rate is considerably higher in families with children on the spectrum. Don't you believe it. There are studies that show a slightly higher incidence, and there are studies that show that there is no difference at all! In cases where there is divorce, there is no reason to assume that having an autistic child was the cause. There is stress to be sure. Sometimes there are shattered dreams. However, of these divorces, you must consider the age of the parents, their financial situation, their commitment, and the amount of support available to them. There are a lot of reasons that people get divorced. Could having such a child be one of them? Maybe. But why assume that's the reason?

The main reason that I saw few fathers was simply that most of them worked during the hours that I spent with the children. I would usually see them at team meetings, which were always held in the evenings. I know what you're thinking: "You worked in the 'projects,' the 'hood.' There's no fathers there." I do not recall in all my years that there was a higher incidence of no fathers in the hood vs. not in the hood. I would have to go through all my notes to compare, and, truth is, the subject just does not interest me enough to do that. I simply want to recall the few fathers who were so bizarre that it affected the outcomes for their children.

Beverly's Father

Beverly was a sweet little Italian two-year-old. She presented with pretty much "classic Kanner syndrome" autism—no eye contact, toe walking, non-verbal, tantrumed quickly, no receptive language, limited interests, mostly TV (kids shows and videos). She had a five-year-old sister with the same diagnosis, but the sister was "high functioning" and went into regular education by kindergarten. ABA services greatly improved the sister's abilities.

They had a small house crammed in between apartment houses. The living room was small and crowded, with an oversized couch and chair. Worse, they had three dogs—two small ones and a German Shepherd. They had to be removed when I came, and that took time. Dad was not thrilled with this. He was the second husband of the mother and appeared to be about ten years older than her. Mom worked, and Dad was usually home. We began in the beginning of May.

When I started there, Mom made sure to be home to see what I was going to do and how we would get along. Both parents sat in for the entire session. Beverly had a reputation for being difficult to work with. Other therapists had come and gone because of an inability to control her tantrums. She might be perfectly fine one second and screaming and kicking the next. Her tantrums lasted a long time. Thankfully, our first session went very well, and Mom enjoyed it. Beverly was fascinated by my toys and engaged with me at our little table.

Already during our first session, I got her to make eye contact, point to what she wanted, and she laughed a lot at my windup toys, electric tops, and magnets. She was echolalic and also did verbal and physical imitation—all signs of a child who should do well. The parents warned me that she could stop and tantrum in a heartbeat, and once she started it was very difficult to stop. Evidently, that's why other therapists quit.

I was to see her an hour a day, and another therapist, an hour up to fifteen hours a week. They could not find another therapist, so I saw her six days a week for an hour.

Mom was also home with us on the second day, and Beverly gave me a taste of what her famous tantrums were like. Beverly really liked the toys that I brought. So much so that she began to tantrum the second I took them off the table in order to clean up. This would happen every day. Whenever I wanted to take off a toy that she liked from the table, immediately her head went back, a loud wail would begin, and then a flaring tantrum. The "function" of the behavior was obvious: lack of ability to request something. I was hoping that I could replace the tantrum with some kind of communication skill. I could see that this would have to be done in very small steps and would take a lot of time.

By the end of the second week, she would smile when I walked in and was able to begin formal programs. She was able to ask for a toy bus with a prompt. She repeated many of the letters in the alphabet as we did the puzzle. She made eye contact more often. In our two weeks, there was only one short tantrum burst at clean up, but it quickly extinguished. Mom was thrilled with this progress. Dad never said anything.

By the third week in May, she was making some consistent progress. Tantrums were still always just around the corner, but there seemed to be fewer and they were easier to control. She was doing imitation with objects very well but not imitation without objects. This was very typical, as imitation with objects are "functional" programs (bells ring or lights come on) and those without objects were "non-functional" (do this and get a cookie). She would absolutely not do imitation without objects. This was fairly common with children.

It seemed that when she did tantrum at the table, I was able to stop it by ignoring her. That is, I would turn my head away from her, with my hands down, and just wait it out. My guess was that she tantrumed to get attention as well as to request, so "extinction" or purposeful ignoring should work.

On one day in early June, when both parents were present, Dad intervened when she tantrumed. He said, "She does that when she doesn't get what she wants." I was glad that they were aware of that. I was hoping I could convince them not to give in but to help her learn to request.

By the end of June, they had found another therapist for her. His name was Ion, and I did not know him. Mom told me that he was using an iPad to work with her. I called him and told him to please stop using an iPad and to work on the programs. As I've said previously, therapists don't "use iPads" to "work" with children. They use iPads to babysit for them. Give any child in the world an iPad, and you can just sit back and watch them play with it. Sure, they'll learn that if you push this icon, you'll get Mickey Mouse, and so it looks like they "really know how to use it." But they don't. It's the same as a pigeon picking a red circle to get food. The bird learns nothing about "redness" or "circles."

Beverly was doing programs, identifying objects and pictures, repeating words, and our sessions were going well. I encouraged Ion to concentrate on those things. Tantrums were still with us, however. In June, I started to just say, "Uh-oh," and pull away from her whenever a tantrum began. Oddly enough, this worked!

By the middle of July, I thought all of our tantrum problems were over. Things were good. She was learning, controlling the tantrums when I said, "Uh-oh," and the only thing that was a real problem for us was that Dad, whenever he heard her cry, would come flying into the room, pick her up, give her juice, and/or turn on the TV. I told him that he should not do that, as she's learning to control herself when she doesn't get what she wants, but Dad was not one for taking instruction.

Then, her father started cancelling sessions. Often. My biggest fear was that due to these long breaks, we would have to rebuild a rapport and start all over with the skills she was acquiring. After one of these long breaks, and we began again, she was fine for a few minutes while Dad sat two feet away. I told him that he must let me work with her on tantrums. On that day, there were four tantrums. Each was short in duration. I would ask her to do something like match cards, and she would tantrum. When it happened, I removed the chair, gently put her down on the mat, and let her scream. Dad wanted to intervene, but I wouldn't let him. She lay on the floor and tried to kick the table. I moved it. She tried to bang her head. I did not let her. When I began to spin musical tops on the table, she stopped the crying, came back, and sat down. I told her, "Good. Sitting nice? Good."

Three more times it happened, and three more times, I ignored her and introduced a new toy. She came back, and I reinforced good sitting. She looked at me to see if I was watching as she tantrumed. The fact that she watched me as she tantrumed suggested that she was fully aware of what she was doing, which was, using a tantrum to get what she wanted, as opposed to just losing it and screaming for no reason. This was learned, that is, reinforced behavior. Her parents had reinforced her using tantrums to get what she wanted by giving in to her. My technique was to ignore her (though keeping her safe as she kicked and banged her head) and introducing something else to get her attention.

The last week of July, I was informed that Ion had quit. Something about a dispute over the parents taking a vacation and his losing money. I hadn't heard anything about his quitting. Being team leader, I should have been informed immediately. Now, we needed to find another therapist to fill his hours. This would not be easy to find in July. No one had an opening in their summer schedules!

July 28 was the second time I went to work with her to find that nobody was home. Again, I was not informed that they would not be home. It's not the end of the world, but if I know a child is not going to be home, I can do makeup hours with another child, or at least, save myself the time it takes to drive to their house. Maybe I could even afford the luxury of squeezing in a nap! It was always a little irritating when I arrived to find no one home at any child's house.

Dad also increased his habit of cancelling sessions. On August third and fourth, he cancelled sessions. On the fifth and sixth, I was on vacation. On the tenth, he cancelled again. They found another therapist, Olga, and I did not know her or which agency she came from or anything about her experience. She did not offer any information.

Shortly after we had finally found this new therapist, and Beverly's schedule was set, Dad decided that he wanted to change the session times. What? Everything was settled! There was no way that I or anybody else could change now because it would affect our working hours with our other children. This guy was driving us all nuts. The Center did not want to lose the case, and fortunately, Olga and I were able to rearrange our hours again because most of our cases would end soon on August 31, as many children would age out.

Olga would see her from ten to eleven, and I would see her from eleven to one. Three straight hours of therapy for a two-year-old girl. I was not thrilled with the idea of spending two hours with her, as her progress was not so good lately, and her tantrums were still not under control. I simply did not have enough programs for her to fill two straight hours. But ok, she was approved for fifteen hours a week starting in September. There were plenty of other things that I could work on other than programs.

When I got there for our first two-hour session in September, no one was home! No one called. I waited ten minutes, and they pulled up. Because Mom was with him, I let it slide.

I had just learned this thing called "texting." I was almost sorry I had, as Dad sent me my first text: "We may not be home." They weren't. The next day, another text: "We won't be home." I called Helga, the service coordinator, and told her that this may be over soon.

The next day, "We have appointments. See you tomorrow."

I did not see her again until September 11. Mom was home, and Beverly would not sit for anything. She began to tantrum. Mom immediately gave her the iPad, and she began to calm down and "use it." As long as Mom was home, I went against my principle never to use an iPad. I used it this time because it was one of those rare days when Mom was home. She did not want to see a tantrum. I did not want to go through with Mom why she should not use things like iPads with kids. I had explained all this to Dad and wrote about it in the communication book for Mom, who read it religiously every day.

The middle of September arrived and brought in the High Holy Days on the Jewish calendar. I took off for Rosh Hashanah and Yom Kippur. The next day, when I should have returned, Dad cancelled. When I finally returned, it seemed to me that Beverly was getting worse. Her tantruming increased, and her working well like she used to was not nearly as consistent. It was like we were completely starting over from scratch. She would not work, whined a lot, and tantrumed every day. Her tantrums were bringing Dad into the room, where he would turn on the TV, give her a bottle, and walk out.

When I came back and found this, I decided I'd have to start over, and this time use the iPad, then slowly wean her off of it. Her tantrums were too serious, not to mention dangerous. Since nothing else would work now, we could start over by using the iPad as a reinforcer. She had to do her work to get access.

On September 21, Dad came into the room, saw it, and grabbed it out of her hands. He carried her to the TV and turned it on. TV is, of course, even worse than the iPad, but I was not going to argue with Dad anymore. I tried to discuss with him other possible strategies that we could try but silently had doubts that anything would change. She cried, he put on the TV.

I called the service coordinator, Helga, and told her that this father was making it impossible for me to work and that all his cancellations were wreaking havoc on her learning consistency. Evidently, Helga was also having a lot of problems with the family, before I got there and after. She told me that hopefully, Beverly would be leaving in January. "Hang in there a few more months."

Mom wanted to enroll her in the school with her elder sister in January, even though she was too young to attend there. The school knew her and were sure that Beverly would make as great a progress as her sister did. Okay. Maybe she would. I hoped so anyway. My only hope was that I could hold on until the end of December, as Dad was increasingly hostile. He kept interrupting the sessions when Beverly cried by turning on the TV and giving her a blanket and juice. This was getting impossible.

One day, shortly after I returned from the September break, I pulled up and Dad was outside, smoking a cigarette. Dad told me that I wasn't supposed to come today.

He said, "It's a holiday, and I've got appointments."

I told him that today was not a holiday. He insisted that it was, and he would call the Center to verify this. I told him that there was a holiday calendar in Beverly's book, and he could check there. I also told him that his continual canceling could not continue, and it led to a vicious argument.

Here is how the argument went down: When I pulled up in front of the house, I saw Dad outside smoking. I approached with my bags and gear, and he said, "What are you doing here?"

I said, "What? What do you mean?"

He said, "I cancelled today."

I was in shock. "No one told me that."

Then I asked him why he'd cancelled if obviously he was home and she was home. "What's the problem?"

He said what he always said when he cancelled. "I have an appointment today."

This was about it for me. I told him, "Look, I do this for a living! I'm not making any money here."

He said, "I don't give a [fill in that word] about your money."

I told him, "Well, I do. How about Beverly? Do you care that she's missing so much therapy?"

He became quite angry at this suggestion. He told me to get the [different word, same intent] out of here. He took threatening steps toward me. I did not back off. I sincerely thought it was going to come to blows. When he saw that I was ready to fight if he attacked (I studied martial arts for years, by the way), he turned, ran into the house, and slammed the door.

I went up to the door and knocked. He shouted at me from the inside to get the [same word as last time] out of here. I knocked again because I had all my materials in the house, her program book, and some rather expensive toys in there. Finally, after about fifteen minutes of knocking (I wasn't going anywhere) and calling on the phone, he came to the door and asked what the [Oh, there's that word again!] I wanted. I told him that I need all my stuff. By this time, the dogs were back in the living room, barking like mad. If he opened the door, the German Shepherd would surely bolt.

He gathered my stuff, opened the door just enough to slide stuff out, and held back the dogs. Then the door slammed with a loud thud. I drove a block away, then called Helga and told her what happened. Helga had worked there almost twenty years as a service coordinator and had never heard such a thing. Bottom line, I wasn't about to go back. She said she'd look for yet another replacement for Beverly for the last few months. I drove off, and about ten minutes later, my phone rang. It was the father. In a jovial voice, he said, "So, you coming tomorrow?"

I immediately knew what had happened. He, or Helga, had called his wife. Mom went ballistic when she heard that I was not returning and laid into her husband. So far, I'd had the most success with Beverly even though it was nothing to brag about. I told him that I quit, and good luck, pal. He tried to console me. "Oh look, it's no big deal. Heh heh. I was just joking. Will you come back tomorrow?"

I told him that I was far too angry right now to make any kind of decision. I called Helga again and told her that there was no hope.

"I know this guy is going to be cancelling all the time as soon as this blows over. My work with her is going nowhere, and the guy is nuts. I mean, it very nearly came to blows!"

I never went back. I never heard another word about her. Though I was relieved, I really felt like I'd let this difficult little girl down.

Allan's Father

This was another heartbreaker; however, it was also maddening. I was with a child who was a pure genius! An extremely rare child. One in a million! I had had very bright children before but never on the level of Allan—and never such incredible results in so short a period. I was not there long, as Dad fired me, rather abruptly. Our sessions began in the winter. Right after the New Year. Here is the story…

Upon entering the house, everyone took their snow-covered boots off in the hall downstairs where an old Chinese lady lived. In this part of town, almost everyone was Chinese. Then, up the stairs and through the door. Immediately to the left was the living room, kitchen off to one side, and a bedroom just beyond it. Grandma slept in the bedroom. She was a tall, elegant Chinese lady who spoke no English. None. They say that her husband lived there as well, but I never saw him.

Grandma was not very keen on the whole idea of this therapy business. As far as she was concerned, there was nothing wrong with Allan. But, as she was the one who was mostly home with him, she went with the program. What that program would be, I was not sure at this point.

His mother was a very tall Chinese lady. She was highly intelligent and had a high-tech job in Manhattan. She spoke English like an American, so I assumed she grew up here. The father was from Argentina. His English was also perfect, so maybe he also grew up in the U.S. I wasn't around long enough to find out. I was warned by the service coordinator that Allan was "very autistic." As we say in Yiddish, "Nu?" What'd you expect? She told me that Grandma did not accept the diagnosis, and this caused some tension in the home. His evaluations indeed suggested that he was pretty bad, as he'd scored zero across skills.

Upon entering the home for the first time, everyone was home. I walked through the door from downstairs and saw Allan playing with alphabet blocks on a big rug on the hardwood floor in the living room. The second I walked in, a look of sheer panic came to his eyes. He was scared out of his wits! He sat there petrified, eyes filling with tears. Mom came to him, lifted him to his feet, and he ran deep into the hallway just past the main door I had come through.

This was strange. In all my years in the field, I had never seen a reaction like this. Most children on their first day usually completely ignore me. To your typical child with autism, I was just another object in the room. Allan responded in a way that left me baffled. Had he never seen another human being? From whence this panic? This was not the usual stranger anxiety kind of thing. It was way beyond that. So, I talked to Mom. She told me that he wasn't used to strangers. She also told me that he names letters, numbers, colors, and objects. He liked to tear paper to as small a size as he could, and he liked to lines things up. He grunted instead of using language.

I stayed in the living room while everyone tried to coax him into coming near me. He would not budge. Not on day one, not on day two, not on day three. I was stumped. What could I do with a kid who kept twenty feet away from me? They all tried to take his hand and lead him to the living room. He was not having it.

On the third day, I decided to try something that often worked with children with Down syndrome. I just sat on the floor and played with my toys: spinning musical tops, turning on a cassette player, stretching Slinkys, and dropping balls down a ramp. Allan would watch from the hall with interest but not come near.

Then, for some reason, I got a wild idea. I showed him rubber letters that go into a frame, and then I threw them at him! He found this absolutely hysterical. I threw another one. He burst out laughing. The next step was to throw them at him, but only about halfway between him and me. He had to get the letter and throw it back. That was the plan. This was very tedious, as I slowly closed the distance between us. After a few days, he was within a few feet of me but would not hand me the letter.

My next step was to throw it and then pretend that I had lost interest. I would throw a letter at him and then turn away. Now he had to get my attention to continue this great game. It finally happened: he handed me a letter. Rather than making a big deal of it, I pretended like it was just the natural thing to do, and we put them in the frame together. He would answer when I asked him, "What letter is this?" So ended our first week.

He kept a distance and cried when I walked in the following Monday, but I used a ball and the alphabet and was able to get closer. Then I brought out the magnetic toys. He loved them, and by the end of that session, I was able to get him to take them from my hand. He laughed a lot that day.

Mom was not home much. Dad wasn't either. When Dad was home, I found him to be very odd. There was no eye contact, no small talk, hardly any talk, actually. I could not engage him in conversation. He was often on the phone in Spanish and English making business calls while sitting on the living room sofa. He might watch a session and never say a word, never ask a question, never try to join our activities. He was like a plant. Was Dad on the spectrum?

I thought it odd that he did not speak to his mother-in-law either but wrote it off to her not speaking Spanish and his not speaking Chinese. Grandma, however, who was opposed to the whole idea of therapy, turned completely around. She saw Allan's engagement with me and was thrilled. She became my biggest fan—big smiles, offering me food all the time, sitting and laughing through the sessions.

I suggested to Mom that Allan needs two hours a day, at least. She agreed, and we submitted the paperwork. Allan, by this time, while able to be in the same room with me, was still sitting on the floor. I wanted him to sit at the table where I could do programs with him, take data, and refer to the program book. He would not sit down. So, I tried the same technique that had brought him into the room. I would sit facing the table and ignore him when he wouldn't come to the table. The old trick worked again. He came, sat down, and we began to work in earnest. The first day of February was also our first two-hour session.

After only two weeks together, he was learning incredibly fast. Two hours was perfect. I loved working with him, and he loved the activities. He cried every time I left. At night, after work, I would search for ideas on the internet and in books on what to do with him next. Allan was going to take a lot of imagination and thinking beyond a typical two-year-old child. He could already use flash cards, name the letters, and say the name of an object. It still amazed me that he would not verbalize at all to communicate. But okay, he had a speech teacher, so hopefully, she'd come up with something.

Working with such a child was a rare break for me. Two hours went quickly, and he could easily continue beyond two hours. So, I was shocked when Helga, the service coordinator, called me at home that evening to say that Mom wanted to go back to one hour because it "messes up his schedule." I should start tomorrow!

Schedule? What schedule? He was home alone all day, every day. I didn't know at the time, but what really happened was Dad did not like me being around for two hours every day. It messed up *his* schedule, not Allan's. I told Mom the next day that it would be therapeutically a mistake to lessen his hours. And it would also be a strategic mistake because the City would never give her those hours again.

None of the arguments convinced her. Her mother and hubby were pressuring her. Grandma thought it was too much for him, and Dad just didn't want me in the house for two hours. Because Grandma sat in on most of our sessions and was seeing progress, I was sure that she'd come around, but Dad was unapproachable. So, I said to her, "How about ninety minutes a day?" She agreed to this. I got them all to agree to ninety minutes, but there was no such thing as a ninety-minute session. In New York, all ABA sessions are one hour. If you work two hours with a child, you bill for two, one-hour sessions. There was no ninety-minute billing option.

What I had to do was legal but technically, not so legal. I had to bill for two full hours. It was legal because you can bill for a full hour even if you only work a few minutes with a child. Why? Because kids fall asleep in session, mothers have appointments to get to, and we have to stop early—the ever-present things happen. I did not want Allan to lose a half hour a day due to billing problems. Nowadays, all billing is done on cell phones, and a therapist cannot manipulate the time. If he tries to bill for a full hour after only a half hour, it will not accept the billing. That's good and bad. Good, because there's a lot of therapists who try to cheat by doing forty minutes and then leaving, and bad because what if a child does fall asleep in session? You have to sit and wait for the clock in order to bill. It is very awkward in many homes to do that.

I had not yet written formal programs for him. After two weeks, I was still not quite sure where to start with him. Do I follow typical autism programs for beginners? He seemed too smart for that. They would probably bore him to death. Do I analyze him using this fancy new thing called "The VB MAPP"? VB, or "verbal behavior" was the hot new therapy on the market.

I bought the manual and the evaluations book and used that with him. They have a curriculum based on the evaluations. Unfortunately, this fancy new evaluation tool did not tell me anything I didn't already know, and their beginning program wasn't much better than the typical one I was using. But I had to do something, so I went with this VB program, as it seemed that in Autismland, this was the hot new thing that every competent therapist should know. As usual in Autismland, anything new brought vicious debates for and against. But the pro-VB people won, and now, you cannot get any kind of certification without taking tons of VB courses. There was no research then, but that did not seem to make much difference to the VB advocates.

The speech teacher had been having problems getting Allan to work with her. However, it seemed that now he was becoming more social and less afraid of people. Why was he afraid of people? Was it a deficit in "social skills," or was the speech teacher making a common mistake? The speech teacher told the mother previously that Allan "stimmed" on the alphabet, and Mom should keep letters away from him. "Stimming" means he has a fixed or "limited" interest in something. The common mistake therapists make is to try to "break" that stim and get him interested in other things. I always did just the opposite. This was the advice I had been given by Temple Grandin when I met her in Jerusalem. She told me, "Whatever the child likes, use that to keep his interest and expand on it." She told me this after I had remarked to her that I was surprised that she found the work in Israel with dolphins so interesting. I suggested to her that it was just another bogus "therapy." That's when she gave me the advice.

Allan loved the ABC puzzle, and I Centered much of what we did around that. I wrote up a program book for Allan, but he did not much like the programs, which were boring things such as imitation, matching pictures, and receptive object ID (where is the cup, spoon, duck). It was very hard to get him to attend to instruction. But he had to learn these things. My job was to make it fun.

One day in early February, Dad watched as I probed some new skills. I probed imitation, one step instructions, and verbal responding. He did well. Dad suddenly said, "Well, I guess he's come out of his shell." It was the first time Dad ever made a comment on progress! The next day Mom was home, and she watched how the programs worked and what we were doing. Her main interest was that Allan enjoy it.

Then, on February 19, something extraordinary happened. I had the letters laid out on the table. Suddenly, he said, "Ben, B-E-N." How did he know that? I never spelled out words for him. How could he possibly know that my name took the three letters, B, E, and N? I was astounded. I tried something. I spelled out CAT with the rubber letters, and he said, "Cat." I asked him how to write, "Sun," and he said, "S-U-N." What? How? Turns out that Allan could spell a lot of words, and if I would begin to spell them with the rubber letters, he knew the word before I got the last letter in place! Don't tell me it's *Sesame Street*! This kid could read and spell words and seemed to have learned it on his own at age two.

Two years earlier I had worked with another two-year-old named Lonnie, a Filipino boy, who also learned to read and write at age two. Finding kids like that is like playing in sand and finding gold. Now, there were two things I did not know about Allan: One, that he had this precocious skill, and the other, why in the world would he not repeat words verbally on a consistent, contingent (when I asked him to) basis? He could. He had imitation skills. He understood instructions, so what was holding this back? Why wouldn't he talk to me?

The next day, his father was home while we were going through the alphabet cards, and I was trying to get him to say them contingently. Allan was learning so many other things so quickly. Why not verbalizing? I thought it was time to press a bit, to try to get Allan to repeat one simple phoneme: M or R, a "labial," as they call them. Easy to make without moving your lips much or your tongue. Allan would not even try. By now, we had such a good rapport that I could hold him or tickle him, and he would do anything I asked. But not this.

As I tried again, his father suddenly lunged off the couch, sat down next to Allan, and demanded, "Say R! Say M." I wasn't sure what to do, as any good therapist wants parent interaction, but this seemed a bit much. Too pushy. Allan was not enjoying this, and the last thing I wanted was our trying to force him to talk. I backed off, let the father take over, and went to the bathroom. When I came back, Dad was still at it, and it was time for me to go. I left him on the floor with his father.

Later, on that fateful day, I got a call from the service coordinator. "Allan's parents do not want you to come anymore."

"What?!" I bellowed. "Why not?"

She said, "I don't know. Mom won't say, but you can't go back there."

I was flabbergasted and terribly upset because it had taken so long just to get Allan to come near me, build a beautiful rapport, and then discover his genius—and with a phone call, it's all over? I told the service coordinator angrily, "Okay, but you're not going to find another therapist that can work with him."

She said with a sigh, "I know."

I was not going to just walk away. I was not sure what to do. I even thought about reporting the parents for neglect, though I would never do that, and besides, they did not neglect him.

That night, my phone rang. It was Mom. She was calling, I had hoped, to say that it was all a mistake, and they would see me tomorrow. No, what she was calling about was, "Could you please return the family pictures you have been using with him?" One pic of her, one of Dad, and one of Grandma. I thought, *You're kidding me. That's all you are concerned about?* I told her that I was really upset about losing Allan and reminded her that he was an exceedingly difficult child to work with—not because he had autism or because he was not smart, the opposite. He was a genius, and your average therapist would have no idea what to do with him.

She said, "I know. I'm sorry, too." Then she asked me something that blew me away. She said, "I hope you don't get insulted, but, uh, do you wash your hands after you go to the bathroom?"

I was in shock. "What? Do I what?"

"Well, his dad says that you don't, and that's why Allan is sick all the time."

I told her that I do indeed wash my hands after the bathroom. (In fact, Orthodox Jews not only wash, but they also say a little prayer of thanks that all of their organs work. We've been doing this for over three thousand years.) Then I asked her, "How does your husband know that I don't wash my hands?" The bathroom was way down the hall. Not at all close to the living room where we worked.

She said, "I don't know."

Then I suggested, "You know what, let me continue with him, and I'll wash my hands in the kitchen sink so Dad can see that I do. You don't fire a competent therapist over something stupid like this, even if it were true."

She said, "I'm sorry."

I told her, "Look, I've got some good news and some bad news for you. The good news is that Allan is a genius and probably will be famous someday. He probably won't need therapy for long. The bad news is your husband is nuts and needs a lot of therapy." Yes, I really said that. Unprofessional? Probably.

The next day, I called the service coordinator just to see who they were considering to replace me. She did not have anyone yet, of course. Then I told her what the mother had said about the washing hands business. She told me, "I know. She told me, too." So, I asked her why the mother allowed this. She obviously knows it's crazy. She told me that Mom said that she knows that Dad is a little strange, and she's just tired of fighting with him. And Grandma was very upset that I had to leave.

Stopping my work with Allan was losing a good friend. Someone I had come, in such a short time, to love and appreciate. For years afterward, whenever I drove by their house, my heart skipped a few beats.

Marty's Father (and Mother)

Truth is, both parents were strange, but I had no problems with Mom. Dad was a really strange dude. He was American and did not work, as far as I knew. Mom did. He had a therapist come to the house a few times a week to work with him, as he had some "emotional" problems.

Mom was Russian and about ten years younger. It was her second marriage. Their son, Marty, was very autistic. He was completely aloof, non-verbal, a toe walker, and cognitively was about as low as they come. He was like a little floating angel—didn't laugh, didn't cry, and was interested in nothing. Just happy to float through the day.

He had a sister who was about ten years old. She was very bright and quite the talented artist. She also liked to make up and perform little plays for people. She was very lonely, however, as her father insisted that she be home schooled. Mom worked and would teach her when she got home. I asked Dad why she wasn't in school, and he told me, "I don't want them to be in control." What that meant was anybody's guess. The poor girl was really starved for attention. There was also a seventeen-year-old girl from Mom's first marriage, but she could not stand her stepfather and went to live with her grandmother.

I'm not sure what Mom did for a living. They had a nice enough apartment in a slightly more expensive part of Brooklyn. Unfortunately, Mom also had MS, which often left her very tired and weak. Dad claimed that she was just lazy whenever the laundry got behind, or shopping needed to be done. No mercy.

I began working with Marty two hours a day, as the father wanted a home program instead of a Center-based program so that he could "keep an eye on things." I began with the usual beginner sorts of programs, but Marty was completely unresponsive. I was dreading this because two hours a day with absolutely no response was going to make for a long day.

We worked in a bedroom with the door closed because his sister would be at my side every second I was in the apartment wanting to talk or play or show me her new artwork. His father would often barge in and say, "Well? Anything? Anything new? How's he doing?" Day after day, I had to tell him the same thing: "So far, he's not responding." Not to food, not to toys, not to tactile or physical play. He was a rag doll. The father could not accept this. His only son, a rag doll.

"Well, do something else! Try something else!"

I asked for suggestions. "What does Marty like to do most?"

The father stopped to think. "Uh. Do? Uh, well, nothing really."

As I said, the sister wanted to be in the room with us. It was entertaining for her. At first, I thought that I could use her to get Marty's attention, but he paid no attention to her either. She would, however, try to get mine and would continually interrupt, grab at me, and grab the toys. I told the father that she had to leave the room. The father had absolutely no control over her. He came in, told her to go out, and she simply ignored him.

"Suzy, you have to get out right now!"

Nothing, as if he were a wall poster. He would start to pace because he didn't know what to do, and I saw that I would have to do something or quit the case. This environment was impossible. I told her, "Suzy, you have two options: One is to walk out of this room like a lady with dignity, and the other is to be dragged out screaming. You choose how you want to leave the room."

Her father said, "Wow! You don't fool around."

Fortunately, Suzy stood up and walked out of the room. I told her that she could come in on breaks.

Back to work with Marty and back to no responding. Worse than this, when Mom was home, and Dad wasn't, she would sit in the room with us and tell me all her problems. She sat in a corner by the window looking down onto the street two floors below while Marty and I sat about six feet away on the floor. I paid no attention to her, but she continued talking. She said that she did not love her husband and she felt that God had sent me to her to take her away from him! The first time she said this, I was taken aback.

"What?"

She assured me that yes, God came to her in a dream and said that I was her real soulmate and that I was sent to take her away from her husband and marry her. She would go on and on about how Suzy loved me and how good I was with Marty, and it was so obvious why I was "sent" there.

I told her to talk to her rabbi. She told me that she had spoken to her rabbi before about leaving her husband, and he told her to stay and be patient.

I told her, "Next time, don't talk to the rabbi, talk to his wife!"

Fortunately for all of us, Mom was not home much.

Dad decided one day that he wanted more therapy for Marty. I told him he was pretty much at maximum level—full schedule of ABA, speech, PT, and OT—and I sincerely doubted he'd get any more services from the City. (Not that it would help anyway, unfortunately.) He started to whine like he always did when something did not go his way and then used his ever-present ace in the hole: "I have big friends! I have friends in the government, and I have friends in Hollywood." He told me that he wrote movie scripts. I sincerely doubted it. He called the service coordinator at the Center. "Sorry," she told him.

The service coordinator knew that Marty was getting the max that the City would pay for. I heard the conversation in the other room: "I have big friends in the government! I'll go to them if I have to." When it got to the point that the service coordinator could not listen to him anymore, she transferred him to the manager of Center, who told him politely that there was nothing he could do, that the City made those decisions, not the managers of Centers. The manager was introduced to the whining.

"But, but my child needs more." The manager excused himself and hung up. Dad called back. Same conversation. He called again, and again that same day. Finally, the manager told him that if he called again, he would bring charges for harassment. So, Dad came running in to me with the same story: "Marty needs more services. I have friends in politics, I have friends in Hollywood." I ignored him, and he left the room ranting. I would hear this "I have friends" argument many times in the future.

Suzy would poke her head in a few times every twenty minutes or so. "Can I come in now?" Usually the answer was, "No." However, on break, I would let her in. She would give me pictures that she had drawn of me, or me and Marty, or me and her. They were beyond her years and had a most unique style. She drew me inside of bubbles, as I often used bubbles with Marty. They were very imaginative pictures. I still have them somewhere. Some days, she would do a new dance or put on a play that she'd written. It was obvious that this girl was very talented and intelligent. It drove me nuts that she wasn't in school in a gifted program, making friends and having a normal life outside of this labyrinth apartment building. It was like a penitentiary. But, being there simply to service Marty, it was none of my business. I was not allowed to interfere, and that's that! But no, I could not ignore this. I confronted the father.

"Why isn't she in school?" I demanded to know.

He said, "I don't want them to control her."

"What do you mean, 'control her?'" I asked.

He fumbled to explain. "Filling her head with nonsense, brainwashing her."

I reminded him that she would be going to a well-established Jewish religious girls' school with a thousand other girls, and she needed peers and friends. He resisted. I told him that he was destroying her, and she needed to be in a normal environment for kids her age.

I asked what her mother thought. He told me that the mother agreed with me. I lost my temper and told him that he was nuts and killing his child. To my surprise, he relented, and by the next week, she was in school. Lucky I didn't lose my job! I was way out of bounds doing this, but I felt I had to take the risk.

The work with Marty was going absolutely nowhere. There was no imitation, physical or verbal. No language, receptive or any kind of communication skill. He couldn't do a picture/card exchange program for the speech teacher. Every single day it was the same—nothing. Yet, after the session, the father would excitedly approach me and ask, "Well? How's he doing? Is he improving? How's it going?" Dad didn't get it. Marty was not likely to show any improvement anytime soon.

The Center was pressuring me to take on new cases. There were children waiting for services, and either the mothers asked specifically for me, or they felt at the Center that they needed someone more experienced to work with these new cases. Or, as was often the case, they were in "the hood," and no one else would go there.

I made a deal that if they would find a replacement for me working with Marty, I'd take on two new, one hour, cases. I couldn't help him in any case. I tried everything. To my great surprise, they agreed.

I had started working with Marty in September. When I told the father that two days before Christmas would be my last day, he went crazy. He insisted that he didn't want or trust anybody else, and he began his whining. I told him that I was sorry, but I had to drop the case and besides, obviously, I wasn't helping much. Maybe somebody else would have better luck with him.

He told me that his wife had to work on my last day, and asked, could I also come on the following day? I told him no. I had plans to go see my mother in another state over the break. He grew upset and said, "Oh, c'mon, it's not fair. His mother needs to see how to work with him."

I told him that she'd seen it many times. The programs were all there for another therapist or for the parents to follow. I would videotape a session for her to use, and after New Year's, Marty would have a new teacher.

Dad would not hear it. "No! You've got to come. She's got to see you work with him again."

Again, I said, "I'm sorry, I can't come then. I am leaving the state that day."

Now he was frantic. "Oh no! This is terrible. You must come that day!"

His annoying whine began to increase in volume. I lost my temper and told him that he was really getting on my nerves, and he'd better knock it off." I stood up. He ran out of the room wailing, "I have friends…."

Franky's Father

I first went to Franky's house in mid-January 2009. It was in Brownsville, an area of Brooklyn that was pretty run down. January is late in the year to start working with a child, but evidently, he had not been identified until he was two, or maybe Mom had trouble getting the paperwork in. They had no car. I was to do two hours a day with him, and when he was approved to start in Center, we would reevaluate how much home therapy was needed.

Franky's father was quite normal—a nice, quiet man from Haiti. He was a big man. The proverbial gentle giant. I do not have a chapter that Franky would fit nicely into, so I am putting him in this chapter because his father, as will be seen, made a horrific mistake—a mistake that changed everybody's life forever.

Dad was often home, as he had just recently lost his job—or so he said. I did not see him much, however, because he slept a lot in the only bedroom they had in this sixth-floor apartment. As you walked in, the bathroom was in the hall, then the kitchen, then a small living room to the left, and the bedroom, off the kitchen to the right. Mom was usually home unless she found some work around the town. Ironing, folding towels in a factory, cleaning, whatever she could find. She was twenty years younger than him. This was her second marriage, and his as well. Mom told me that she had a teenage son in Haiti who was being raised by his grandmother.

She told me the most amazing story. It seems that kidnapping and holding children for ransom is a fairly common occurrence in Haiti. Her son had been kidnapped and locked in a basement. When Hurricane Hanna devastated Haiti in 2008, the house that the boy was locked up in simply blew away, and he was able to escape back to his grandmother.

They had two children together. Franky was two and diagnosed with autism. He had all the typical symptoms. His brother was a baby, always strapped into a stroller when I was there. Mom was usually busy sitting in the kitchen or on the computer looking for work. On days that she found work, I would get to the apartment to find Franky bouncing continually on the sofa while watching cartoons. His brother simply sat in the stroller.

If Dad was home, he was usually asleep in the bedroom. Sometimes, I had to ring the bell many times because he was fast asleep. He would put on the TV and leave the kids on their own. Dad also had another peculiar habit. He would take a bunch of incense sticks, about twenty, and put the stick ends into the electric outlet as a holder and light them. The house was always alive with the scent of whatever flavor he picked that day. I suggested to him that maybe putting the sticks in the electric outlet was not such a good idea. He told me that there's nothing to worry about because the electricity does not touch them, and they simply burn out before they get to the outlet. He did this in the bedroom and the living room whenever he was home. They had a fire alarm, but the batteries were dead. I kept meaning to bring them new ones, but I always forgot. Okay, it was his house!

I called Franky, Fabby. He was very cute, with the most beautiful smile I'd ever seen. We all saw that smile a lot, as he was happy child and enjoyed engaging with people. It soon became evident that he was also very smart. I was his full-time teacher, as he had not been approved for the Center yet, and I wrote the programs for him. I started with beginner programs, but he learned them almost instantly. Once he learned them, he did not forget them. I never had to do "maintenance" programs with him. Already by the third week, it was obvious that he was on a higher level than his evaluations indicated.

Could it be this simple? In less than a month, he was readily working at the table, enjoying the sessions, excited when I showed up. Even when Mom or Dad turned the TV off, he made no objection but came right to the table. This was very unusual. He made my job easy! He was beginning to repeat words as well as sing and say the ABCs.

There was one program that he did not like, however, and that was imitation. I would make an action—clap, for instance—and he was to imitate it. He didn't. He obviously could, but he did not like this. He would begin to cry every time I tried to get him to imitate any action. Actions like tapping the table, waving, clapping, and raising arms were all non-functional beginner programs. As I've explained elsewhere, these programs usually bore children on a higher cognitive level. So, it seemed here.

By the end of our first month together, I was very happy with his progress. He continued to work well through March and April. His paperwork still had not gone through so he could start school, and I was completely baffled by this. It usually takes a few weeks for approval. What was the holdup? Dad had no idea, and I needed to talk to Mom to see what the holdup was. When I finally talked to her, she also did not know. Usually, this kind of thing is none of my business. It's between the parents and the service coordinators. It was obvious to me that nothing was going to get done, so I called the service coordinator, who does not have to answer to me, I'm just a therapist. But she did. She told me that the paperwork had never been signed by the parents! What? The parents never turned in the paperwork?

Sure enough, it was all sitting on top of the fridge collecting dust. I could not believe it. There it was, right on top of the fridge. As I reached to get it down, I noticed that their fire alarm was pretty dirty. I asked them if it worked. They told me that it needed a new battery. I kept meaning to bring them one, as I had tons at home.

In any case, on April 20, I told Dad, "Tomorrow, I'm taking you and the paperwork to the Center, and you can sign it all right there and make sure it gets submitted to the City." He agreed.

The next day, off we went in my car for the half-hour trip to the other side of town. On the way, he told me that he'd lost his job because of a voodoo curse someone put on him back in Haiti. He was dead serious. He said that this person put on a curse that he should have bad luck and die! Silly me, I suggested that these things weren't real. He looked at me and let me know, most emphatically, that these things were very real! Uh, okay. He told me other things. His family, also in Brooklyn, did not like his wife. Not at all, evidently. They said she was lazy and stupid, and he should never have married such a young girl. I was locked in the car and had to listen to this.

His wife had told me a few times that she was not happy in her marriage as well. Therapists become like bartenders and barbers. Clients tell you far more than you would ever want to know.

Within a few weeks, Fabby was in school. They took over his programs, as is customary, and I would implement them at home. I also had to switch hours and could not see him for two hours every day, so they brought in someone else to work with him for an hour.

She was experienced, and I had worked with her before, so I wasn't worried. Besides, he was so smart!

They started writing the programs for him at the Center and found that they had to "dumb them down." It seems Fabby would not work well at the school. His new therapist at home reported, after she'd been there a few months, that all he did was scream for an hour! What was going on? She suggested that their turning off the TV when she walked in caused his screaming, but we had been working like this for months with no problems. Something was up.

I made a video of me and him working and showed it to them at the school. They told me that they were happy he was doing well at home, but at the Center, he would not cooperate. Okay, what could I do? At home he was doing great, and by June, he was talking. He simply started using words. His in-laws came to watch and were amazed at how well he was doing. Mom was not home, of course. They would not come if she was home. There was one time when they did come when she was home, and the ice in the room was visceral.

On another occasion, a social worker came for some reason, and she was also surprised at how well Fabby was doing. I could not take credit for his amazing recovery. Obviously, he was spontaneously recovering, and whatever had been holding him back simply was not any longer. He was fast approaching a normal kid, and I suggested that he be reevaluated.

June, July, and the beginning of August, he continued to make good progress. He was saying things like, "Where's the light? Oh! There it is." He had speech now, but his communication skills were still poor. That suggested that maybe it was autism, as he could speak, but it never occurred to him to do so. His other main problem was selective eating. It was getting late in the year to start working on that.

The school continued to report that there was no progress! I decided to go visit there while they worked with him. I saw him at school and listened to the frustration of various therapists exclaiming that Franky would not work at all for them. I made a suggestion of taking him out of the classroom and sticking with one therapist until he got used to her. I knew, however, that no teacher would ever allow one of her kids to be taken out of the classroom. They did it for speech and OT, why not ABA?

As I watched them try to work with him, I saw that he was just being stubborn. He could do this stuff easily, but he just didn't want to. I tried with him there and made a huge mistake. I reprimanded him and told him sternly, "Fabby, stop fooling around and do your work!" His teacher went wild and said, "We do not use language like that in my classroom."

I told her that at home, if I said this to him, he would do his work. It wasn't that he didn't understand, he simply did not want to do his work and had to know, like any kid, you have to do your work!

No, she was furious, and this was a big mistake on my part. I knew that the vast majority of the children you work with, you should not use reprimands or the hated word, "punishment." It really is bad policy most of the time. The child should enjoy what he does, and then you'll have no problems. But Fabby always worked for me, and he was doing nothing at school and nothing for the other therapist. I believed it was because he just didn't want to, and so I'd scolded him. Therapists, like all people, make mistakes. This was one of my biggest.

Fortunately, I learned from it. There may have been some truth to my theory, but then, scolding is still not a good idea. Looking over his history, he was used to me for a long time, and I was his first therapist. Really, his first friend. He was in that tiny apartment since birth with no other contacts or peers. I was fun. The Center was not fun. The other therapists were not fun. So, he just shut down.

His communication skills were still very poor even though he could speak. I did not have that much more time with Fabby, so I decided to back off on discrete trial teaching (the method they used at the Center) and use only natural environment training to develop language by engaging him in fun activities that he preferred. Of course, I was criticized for not being a "team player" because I did not follow the programs. The programs stunk. They couldn't "fire" me because I was an independent contractor, but they could remove me from the case. I knew his parents wouldn't allow that, so I was free to teach him in an effective way with no fear of "not following the programs."

In August, he wasn't going to school much. The situation at home was grim, and it looked like divorce was imminent. He was working well through August for me but not for the other home therapist. At school, they told me that he would not work with the speech therapist either. They tried using candy with him, sour sticks, and for this he was willing to do his work. So, for now, things seemed well. I brought him a twelve-piece puzzle, and he loved it. He wanted to do it over and over again. It became the focus of our verbal communication sessions, as he had to verbally ask for pieces and answer "wh" questions. Where is the piece? Where does this go? Which one do you want?

One day he could not wind up a toy and said, very clearly, "I can't do it!" while making full eye contact. Mom heard it and laughed. He would ask for the puzzle when I sat down with him. Mom told me that he asked her for it as well. He slipped on the floor one day and said, "The floor is slippery." At times, he spoke perfectly normal! This was great progress from a few months ago.

On we went through September and October. Something changed. Maybe it was the heat. His apartment was hot, and there was no A/C. He was obviously fed up with this therapy business and would simply refuse to work when he did not want to do something. Not only at school, but with me as well. Was he simply bored to death? Probably. He seemed to me now more like a normal two-year-old that simply did what he wanted and refused what he did not. Still, I was a little concerned because the behavior change was fairly radical. When there is a serious behavior change, the first thing to do is to rule out any physical cause. If you don't communicate well, you can't say things like, "My tummy hurts," or "My head hurts," or "This is boring." I asked Mom to take him to the doctor. She took him and the doctors were alarmed because he was not gaining weight. He ate only baby food. He refused to eat anything else, except candy.

Fabby was one for the books. He could talk though he didn't much. For another month he was on and off with his refusing, but by the middle of November, he was doing his work and back to his old mischievous self. His brother would no longer sit quietly in his stroller and wanted to join us. I had fun toys, and he could no longer tolerate being tied into a stroller while we had such fun right in front of him. His name was Sabastian, and he was almost as cute as Fabby. It was really a pleasure to go there every day and just play with these two guys. At school he began to participate well and was bumped up to the advanced class. No more programs! Now there was peer interaction, Circle Time, crafts, and schedules.

By the first of November, he was his old self again both at home and at school. I'm not sure why he went through those rough patches. Obviously, using a teaching method that he didn't like was one reason. They were monitoring his health, as Mom still continued to feed him only baby food. "That's all he'll eat," she said. Otherwise, the tension between the parents and the in-laws was getting worse. I was not sure what I could do about that. That was the social worker's department. The status quo now was that Fabby was working, expanding his language skills, growing more social, and I was thrilled.

On Tuesday, November 17, I was driving to his apartment for our session when the speech teacher called me.

"Don't bother going to Franky today. The police have the entire street cordoned off." Probably a fire. More likely, being Bed Sty, a shooting. I figured, I'll just tell the cops that I have to work with my little autistic boy, and they'll let me pass. I had to park on another block. As I walked toward the apartment, there were fire trucks all over and tons of cop cars.

I walked through the crowd and toward the main entrance of the building. I was stopped there by a policeman. He would not let me pass. As I turned away, he said, "By the way, which apartment is the child in?" he asked.

I said, "6D."

He told me, "Stay right here."

I was approached by a plain clothes detective. He asked if I was trying to get into 6D. I said, "Yes." He told me that the fire had been in 6D and wanted to know who lived there. I had to call the Center to get all the information on names and contact numbers, and then I gave them over to the detective. He got his information and started to turn away. I stopped him and asked what the story was. He told me that there had been a fire in 6D.

I asked, "Is everyone okay?"

He stated, matter-of-factly, "There were casualties."

I'll never forget the way he stated those words. I asked him who the casualties were.

He said, "A male and two children."

Dead from smoke inhalation. The mother was not home, as she had found work that day folding towels. They had no way to contact her, and she walked home from work that day happy to have made some money. They told her at the door, hours after the fire. The three were already in the morgue when she arrived home.

The next day, Mom called the Center and asked for me. I found her by her in-laws in a kitchen chair, screaming. I had taken a few of the ladies from work, who had worked with him, with me to go see her. One of the ladies spoke Creole. It was a scene I'll never forget. She was sitting alone at the kitchen table screaming, non-stop. Her in-laws sat in the adjoining room on a sofa and in fancy chairs. The father's mother sat on the floor in another room and said nothing. The people spoke mostly Creole and some English. All present in the room were from the father's side of the family. She had no one. A few social workers from the police department came and spoke to everyone but her. It seemed to me that her in-laws saw her as a nuisance. They did nothing to comfort her.

At the Center, we raised a few thousand dollars for her, but I would not give the envelope to the in-laws. I did not trust them. I later heard that the family wanted to use the money for headstones, and she wanted to use the money to find a new place to live, buy clothes, and a few household items, as she'd lost everything she owned in the fire. She called me and asked me what to do. I told her, "It's YOUR money. Do what you need." Then I told her, "These people are not your friends." She repeated it and later told them that she would use the money to start a new life.

The fire inspector gave me a call to ask a few questions.

"Did they have a fire alarm?"

"Yes, but it had no batteries in it." I felt guilty about that, as I always intended to bring some and kept forgetting. From then on, whenever I started with a new child in the hood, I checked the fire alarm first thing. Then he told me that the fire had started in the bedroom on the bed, and did I have any idea how it may have started? Did he smoke?

I wasn't sure if I should have told him but felt at the time like I probably should. "No, he did not smoke." I told him about Dad's bad habit of putting incense into the electric outlets, and he'd probably moved the bed too close to the incense and the sheets caught fire. "That would be my guess." The firemen were incredulous that he'd put incense into the electric outlets.

A few years later, as I was driving through Bed Sty to see another child, Mom saw my car and came running to say hello. She looked good. Happy. She had remarried and had a typically developing baby girl.

Chapter Ten

Grandmothers

There are usually two kinds of grandmothers in Autismland. At least, two kinds that I've had the pleasure to work with, or the great misfortune to be stuck with. There are those who are immensely helpful and hopeful. They cheer every little step of progress. They hang on every move, every instruction, and work with the therapist to incorporate everything the child has learned in therapy sessions to attempt to generalize these things into his daily life. If I teach a child to make eye contact before requesting something, Grandma will make sure that he does this for her as well.

Then there are the other grandmothers. The others are the ones who are often said to be "in denial." But it's closer to delusion than denial.

"Ain't nothin' wrong wit' dat boy! He just don't talk. His mother didn' talk neither 'til she was five!"

To these grandmothers, you, the therapists who have invaded her happy home, are the enemy. The pages and pages of evaluations done by the psychologists and speech therapists and physical therapists and special education teachers mean nothing to her. She won't read them. Of the rare few who do read the evals, they will deny every word in it. "What's this say that he can't do? He can do that! He can't talk? He talks to me! He understands every word I say to him! I've never seen him bang his head!"

In fairness, the grandchild is usually the first, and Grandma is sure that her son or daughter is just doing a bad job of raising the child. If the grandmother is paternal, the problem is compounded, as Grandma is convinced that her daughter-in-law simply doesn't know how to raise children. The worst-case scenario is if you should have to work in the grandmother's house, as Mom and Dad both work. Grandma doesn't want you in her house—not for two hours, not for one. And she doesn't want the speech therapist or the OT or the PT or the other ABA therapist in her house either. Well, I can't blame her for that. Who wants a continual, extensive invasion?

In the chapter on twins, I introduced you to one such grandmother. Kenny and Kim's grandmother definitely saw me and the others as the enemy. I will relate a few others like her.

Carrie's Grandmother

Carrie's story is a short and unhappy one, and I only include it because of the outrageous facts concerning the case. Carrie was, like most kids I began working with, around two years of age. He lived in a dilapidated building on a major street running north/south through Brooklyn. This building was even more dilapidated than your average Brooklyn building. It was literally falling down, as if its only support were the apartments of the building on either side of it holding it up like a wounded soldier in the Civil War. The stairwell up to the first floor had huge holes, gaps, and paint chips that hung like elephant's ears from graffiti-ridden, dirty walls. The apartment was cluttered and dingy. There was a continual flow of water in the kitchen sink, but the dishes were clean, and the kitchen was tidy.

Through the kitchen and into the living room facing the street below was an altogether different story. The entire living room smelled of urine. There was an old couch covered with sheets and urine stained in large areas, as if buckets had been set there to dry. The couch faced the forty-four-inch TV. On a shelf over the TV was a picture of a young Black man with a bandanna around his head who looked to be about twenty-two years old. I guessed it was the father.

We started working together on May 19, 2006. Mom was a young Black woman with another child, about six years old, who had autism. There was also a normal (typically developing) brother about four years of age. Off of the living room, there was one bedroom to the left of the TV and one to the right. The left was for Grandma, and the right was for the boys. I don't know where Mom slept.

Upon my first visit, I found Carrie sitting on the couch wildly rocking. His autistic brother was on the floor paying attention to nothing. The other boy sat indifferent on the couch watching television. Mom and Grandma joined us in the living room. The expression on Grandma's face told me that she was not going to be a team-player.

Carrie was diagnosed PDD/NOS. That was a "soft way" to say, "autism" back in the DSM-IV days.[23] It was very difficult to get his attention, to hold it, to interest him in anything besides the television, or to befriend him. His world was TV and rocking and any attempt at intrusion into this world was fiercely resisted. He wore diapers that were often wet upon my arrival.

I always found that it was best to work in a quiet, isolated part of a child's home—somewhere with no distractions. In Carrie's house, we had nowhere to work except the living room, and there, the TV was on continually. I could not compete with a TV. Another problem was that he would scream if Mom or Grandma were not in the room with us. Usually, it's a good thing to include a parent. But Grandma interfered in the course of instruction often. Another major problem was that I did not want to sit down anywhere in the living room, as it smelled like a urinal.

I was eventually able to convince Mom and/or Grandma that if we had to work in the living room, the TV had to be off. Grandma would have to keep the brothers occupied for the hour somehow, or it would be impossible to work.

Grandma was polite enough, but I definitely got the message. She was not at all thrilled with this "therapy." As the older brother had obviously gone through a lot of therapy with no recognizable improvement, one could easily sympathize with her skepticism. Eventually I was able to convince them to let us try working in the cramped boys' bedroom. I asked that no one come in.

I arrived to work with Carrie one day about a month after we had started. My phone rang as I was about to get out of the car. I noticed that it was the director from the Center calling. This was highly unusual, and I wondered what he might want. He was angry.

"Did you tell this boy's grandmother that she could not be in the house during therapy?"

I was shocked. "No. It's her house!"

I walked into the apartment, and Mom was also very angry. She wouldn't look at me, and she answered questions in one-word sentences. I asked her what was up. She told me that she didn't like the way I talked to her mother. As Mom had not been home when the supposed conversation took place, it was obvious that this is what she'd been told. I saw no future in this house. I asked her if maybe she'd prefer another therapist. She readily agreed, never once looking at me. I turned and left.

There were two remarkable things about this case that had nothing to do with autism. One was that Mom told me that they paid no rent. None. I asked how this was possible. She told me that the building had no owner, and everybody in it just "moved in." I suggested to her that if there's a building in New York City, someone owns it, and this couldn't last. Mom did not like to hear that. Not at all. Sure enough, one day after I was off the case, the City came to look, declared the premises uninhabitable, and everyone had to get out. I heard later that the family was living in a homeless shelter.

The other thing was that one day, I walked into the apartment, and for some reason, Carrie blurted out, "Daddy!" Mom stopped dead in her tracks and said, "Boy, dat ain't yo' daddy. Yo' daddy's daid." I was a bit taken aback by this comment. The other boys were in the room. I pointed to the picture of the young man on the shelf and asked, "Is that his father?" She said, "Ya." I asked a question that only an ignorant White rookie from outside of New York City, would ask. "What happened to him?"

Mom said, "He got shot." Then she quickly added, "He was just hanging out on the steps downstairs, and someone mistook him for someone else and shot him."

Over the course of the coming years, working in the hood, I would learn two things: When you see a picture of a young man on a wall, and he's not around, don't ask where he is. If you do, and if they tell you that he's dead, do not ask, "Oh really, what happened?" Unfortunately, I would forget this lesson in other houses. One other time when I was stupid enough to ask, I was told the same thing: "He was mistaken for a drug dealer."

An end note: They never found another therapist to go into that apartment. Carrie's services at home simply stopped. He continued in the program at the Center for a while, and occasionally, I'd be there and check in on him. He was not doing well. About a month after I left, I was at the Center, and they told me that Carrie was no longer in the program. Lost souls in the bowels of New York City.

Terrence's Grandma

Our team worked with Terrence in the grandmother's house. This was a nice house in a middle-income neighborhood. The neighborhood was mostly Black people, many from "the Islands." Grandma was in the Islands, so we never saw her. There was me, another ABA teacher, a speech teacher, and an OT. Terrence's mother and father also lived in the house, and Mom had a very successful, fully licensed educational day program for young children that was located in the basement.

Terrence was a very difficult child to work with. Nothing, and I tried everything, nothing would get his attention. He would sit passively the entire hour and just look off into space. Never at me, never once. Even when using "primary reinforcers" like candy, pretzels, anything, there was only a vacant stare into space. His teacher at the Center wrote basic programs for him, but neither I nor the other ABA therapist, a Black lady with experience, were successful in getting any response. The speech therapist quit the team, claiming her schedule had to change for some reason. The next speech therapist also was unable to elicit any response from Terrence.

We worked in the living room, and the door to Mom's school program downstairs was right off the living room. Terrence spent a lot of time simply trying to get to that door and go downstairs with Mom and all the children there. When led back to the table, he would either try to run back to the door or sit passively.

All his responses in his programs had to be prompted. After a while, as there was no progress, I tried an experiment with him at home. I tried using a TEACCH approach. That is, using visual cues, a visual schedule, and materials that he could find by using the cues. TEACCH gets children into a routine that they can follow without the pressure of eye contact or highly structured, functionless trials. This approach also did not work. He paid no attention to the cues and simply stared past me as I attempted to train him. It was very frustrating. We had monthly progress meetings, including the mother. We all tried to be positive, but there was an undercurrent of hopelessness with this case.

I knew building a rapport was not going to be easy with Terrence. My main goal was to try to get some sort of "connection" with him. I was never successful. That's how it went, week after week, month after month. Nothing. He might do an easy puzzle or sing a few words in a song, but mostly he sat, unresponsive. My magic toys that usually got children's rapt attention had no effect on him.

After five months of trying to get any kind of response, I felt defeated. Mom asked me how he was doing now. I had to tell her the truth. There was not even "a little progress." There was no progress. Mom told me that she was bothered by his continually lining things up. Evidently, she did not take the advice to do some research on what autism was all about.

The ABA supervisor at the Center suggested not sending him anymore and to do a complete home program. I don't know why, but I suspect they were pretty frustrated at the Center. When I discussed it with Mom, she was not sold on the idea because she thought that the school speech therapist was good, and her home therapist was not. Sure, the Center speech therapist always wrote glowing notes home. "He's doing great!" He wasn't. And he was sick. A lot!

It took a few months of paperwork, but he finally began a home program. I would be the team leader and write his programs. Sadly, I soon found that home or school program didn't make much difference. I was writing programs that require more attending and were functional (puzzles, turning cranks on a music box), but it didn't help much. He continued to be ill, and his new programs were too intense for him even though they shouldn't have been.

One day, I noticed his father was standing on the stairs in the hallway, just out of sight and watching us. He didn't say a word and went back upstairs.

I was pretty much at a loss. If I tried more advanced stuff, he would tantrum. If I stayed at the level we were, he'd make no progress. I decided to back off and decrease demands or trying to "prompt" him through skills and just try to get him to enjoy our activities and hopefully, make some kind of connection. For the last seven months, nothing had worked. This is where we were when Grandma came back from the Islands.

For seven months, Grandma had been no problem. The reason was simple: she was away. When she returned home, immediately the problems began. She made it clear to me that there was absolutely nothing wrong with her grandson. "So, he doesn't talk, so what? Neither did his mother at that age." His ability to follow simple requests also did not phase her. "He doesn't want to do it, that's all."

Grandma would sit in the kitchen, just beyond a wall from the living room. If Terrence made the smallest verbal sound, she'd come running in. "What happened? Why is he crying?" He wasn't crying, of course, but Grandma made every scene dramatic.

She complained continually to her daughter that all this was unnecessary, and she did not like the way that the therapists were "tearing her house apart." We all used a small table and chair on the living room floor, which was carpeted. Grandma said that we were destroying her furniture and ruining her carpet. Her sofa had a polished wooden decorative frame that ran along the bottom and up the sides. Someone had backed their chair against it and scratched it. It was probably me. In any case, Grandma went wild when she saw it. No one else in the world would have noticed it, but it became exhibit A of the destruction we were doing in her house.

The truth is, we were not helping Terrence. Not at all. Until Grandma came back, we kept plugging along happily, but once she came back and worked on her daughter to get rid of us, and to continually insist to her daughter that there was nothing wrong with the boy, it became tense in the house. Our last team meeting was one of accusations and hostility between therapists, Mom, and Grandma.

It became untenable to work any longer. Grandma was continually complaining and wanted us out of her house. Mom was upset because I was "so negative." Terrence hadn't moved an inch since we'd started, and she wanted to hear how wonderful he was doing, and how much progress he was making. I do not lie to parents. We had three months to go until he would turn three and move on to public school services. Yet, I knew I could not walk into the house if Grandma was going to be there. She told me straight: "There is nothing wrong with him, and someday I'm going to send you a letter to prove it." I told her that I hoped she was right.

At the end of that day, Mom requested that I not come anymore. I was replaced by Lacy, who I had worked with many times before. Lacy knew her profession well, and I figured that it would go better for Terrence. I hoped so because we had gotten nowhere all this time. It was a shame. Grandma won. She got rid of me, but the team remained on, with Lacy as the new team leader.

After a few months, I ran into Lacy and asked her how it was going. She gave me a look that said, "Oye!!" She told me that the old speech teacher had been replaced by someone with no experience with autism, and hence, knew a lot about speech delays but nothing about communication problems. The other ABA therapist, who had been there from the beginning, just attempted to do whatever was in the program book but had no ideas of her own, after all this time, on how to approach Terrence. It was a no-win cause, even with Lacy on the team.

I never heard another word about the case, and it hurt me that I'd failed so badly with him.

CHAPTER ELEVEN

Angels

Different ethnic groups all seem to have favorite names for their children. In the Spanish community in New York, Angel is pretty common. I had three children named Angel—all Spanish. So, I thought I would write about them for no other reason than that they all had the same name, the same diagnosis of autism, were the same age, and were all in the same socio/economic class. The only exception was Angel S. His mother was Anglo, and he was spoken to only in English. There was one other thing they had in common: all three of them did excellent.

Angel S

You would not know by looking at him that there was any Latino blood in him. He, like his mother, was very blond, blue-eyed, and had pale white skin. His father was Latin. He looked like a miniature Pillsbury Dough Boy. He was a very beautiful child, but he had some serious behavior problems that made working with him nerve wracking.

They lived in the top floor of a six-story Housing Authority building. The apartment was tiny—small living room connected to a small kitchen, down a short hall to the bathroom, and then a small bedroom. They were in it illegally. The apartment was assigned to someone else who took rent from them. It was none of my business. Mom was pursuing a degree in education, and Dad drove a truck for Snapple. Mom had a suspended license, so she was not supposed to drive. But she did. She had to.

During our first session, despite what his evals said about him, I found him to be high functioning but with no verbal skills. There was one thing his evals were accurate about, unfortunately. They wrote that he readily tantrums, it happens often, and the duration of the tantrums could be "extended."

I knew that his tantrums had been an oft reinforced behavior. In other words, tantruming got him what he wanted. Often, when children are doing well cognitively but not verbally, they are easily frustrated. A typically developing two-year-old may tantrum if he doesn't get what he wants, but at least he can say what he wants. When someone cannot say what he wants, he has two problems: he is not getting what he wants, and he has an inability to negotiate.

Angel's mother, like most mothers, always knew what he wanted: candy, iPad, favorite video. If he was not given these things, he would tantrum, and Mom would give in. In fancy ABA terms, the child's tantruming was positively reinforced (tantruming got him what he wanted), and Mom's "giving in" was negatively reinforced (he'll stop crying if I give it to him). And so, the cycle gets stronger. His tantrums took the form of falling back on the floor and hitting his head while doing so, pulling out his hair while screaming, and kicking wildly.

There was no table or chair for us to work on, so I brought a set with me. He readily sat in the chair and engaged with me using my magic toys. I always began with toys that most children liked: tops, wind-up toys, magnets, and image captors. His evals said that he had no interest in toys or people. From our first visit, I found this was not accurate. But he did tantrum when he didn't get what he wanted quickly enough. He'd slip out of the chair, fall on his back, and scream. Mom said, "Just leave him alone, he'll stop." It was hard to watch! This would have to be addressed right away.

We had been working for a few weeks when they got his schedule arranged for him to begin going to the Center. This was great for Mom, as she could get her homework done and go out shopping for food. I was also happy that he was in the Center-based program with other children and other adults and could work on social skills and patience. However, after a few weeks at school, they reported that he tantrumed a lot and would not respond to instruction.

I also found this, but I was sure of the reasons for it. Angel did not take well to "discrete trial teaching," wherein you present a stimulus, "touch your nose," and get reinforced (toy, candy). If you tried to prompt him physically, he'd physically retract and begin to cry.

The programs were not fun for him, they were not functional (pushing a button makes music is functional; touch your nose get a cookie, is not functional), they were boring, and he had no patience. This is a bad combination. On the occasions when he tantrumed with me, which was far fewer than a few months ago when we'd started, I had a strategy: I would introduce a new toy and tell him, "Quick, go to your chair," and we'd begin again. He was learning that he didn't have to tantrum, but there was nothing I could do about his programs. As his home therapist, I was obliged to follow the programs as written by the team leader, which was the classroom teacher. I knew that he would not do them; in fact, he'd tantrum if I tried to "prompt" him through them. My job was to do them and take data on the programs as written. My plan was to carry on until the winter break and hope I could convince his teacher, in the meantime, to make his programs more functional and interesting to him.

There was one other thing I wanted to try but was considered a big mistake at that time in ABA land. He did not like sitting in the chair. A therapist is supposed to get "stimulus control" and reinforce "good sitting." I decided to let him stand if he wanted. This produced amazing results. Our changing to working out of the chair, not in such a highly structured condition, made the sessions much more fun for him. I could even squeeze in some non-functional programs. This would not happen at the Center, as working out of the chair was unheard of in ABA classrooms.

By January, after the break, a few things were well established as far as I was concerned. Angel did not like doing the non-functional discrete trial programs. Like most of the higher cognitive level kids, he was bored to death with them. His teacher kept writing them, and he kept tantruming. The only way to get cooperation of any kind from him was to find things that he enjoyed playing with or that interested him. They had to be on the table and readily available or he would fall on the floor, bang his head, and pull his hair. That meant that everything had to be set up before we began our sessions. You can't expect a child such as Angel, who doesn't understand time, to come to the table, sit nicely, and listen to the instruction, "Wait."

The other thing that appeared to be the case with Angel was that he was acting more and more like a normal child—it's just that he was not talking. No words at all. It was clear he understood language and social interaction. His speech teacher was getting nowhere with him verbally.

On January 10, exactly three months after we'd started working together, a surprise was waiting for me in their cute, little apartment: they took in four puppies! What the..? It seems that Dad decided, suddenly, to start breeding dogs! Wow, are you kidding me? This was beyond belief! They put up a little partition to keep them in the kitchen, which connected to the tiny living room, but the four of them had little trouble breaking it down. They were all over us. I told Mom that this couldn't go on. She didn't need it, and we absolutely could not work under these conditions. A few days later, they were gone. Whew!

Another nagging problem was that the TV was used as a baby-sitter. Mom was always at the kitchen counter, whereby she could watch Angel and do her homework at the same time. She was working hard on her degree, but it was hard for her to do that and attend to a two-year-old with a diagnosis at the same time. The TV was the perfect solution. Unfortunately, that meant that when I came in to work with him, the TV had to go off precipitating tantrums. One other problem was that he always wanted his bottle, empty or full, in his mouth. Take it away, and there was going to be trouble.

I was pushing at the Center for them to drop the discrete trial teaching and move him into the advanced class, where children were taught in a more typical pre-school environment with children of all different levels. Except for speech, he was acting more age typical now. In fact, he was doing great and became a joy to work with. But I could not justify working with him anymore if it meant sitting at a table and doing discrete trial teaching. The Center agreed, but this made a problem for Mom's schedule, as I would have to see him at nine a.m. for two hours. Mom went to college in the mornings in very early hour classes. I suggested to her and to the Center that they replace me with someone who could see him later in the day. I had other kids, so I couldn't change my afternoon schedule.

I officially left the case at the end of January. The Center sent another man to replace me. Unfortunately, all they could find to replace me was Alex. He was Russian and had no experience with children on the spectrum. Aside from that, he just wasn't "child friendly." I felt terrible, but what could I do?

On February 2, I got a desperate call from the Center. Mom did not like this new guy and wanted me to come back. I told them that I could work one hour late in the morning, squeeze in an hour in the afternoon, not work Fridays, and see him on Sundays. This meant driving all over Brooklyn every day, but me and Angel had come so far, and I couldn't live with him losing his home services. Mom agreed, and so we set up our new schedule.

Angel did not like the morning sessions, but he got used to the new routine. The good thing was that he was switched to a more normative classroom environment, and henceforth I would write his programs. I would concentrate only on language.

Two months later, Mom had to take afternoon classes, and that ended our afternoon hour. Angel was going to lose an hour a day of therapy. On Sundays, I could do a two-hour session with him, so he was actually losing four hours a week. Nothing to be done.

He continued to work well, but his tantruming was still his preferred way of communicating. Tantrums were rough: falling to the floor, screaming, head banging, hitting, or scratching. It could take a long time until he calmed down. Usually, the only thing that calmed him down was getting his bottle or turning on the TV neither of which I wanted Mom to use. I told his parents that I might have to stop working with him, as his tantrums were, like the old days, interfering with his progress. Telling them that was actually a warning. If they continued to give him a bottle or turn on the TV every time it happened, he'd never stop it. I had to convince them that, as bad as his tantruming was, and how much it hurt them to see and hear it, they had to stop giving in to him. He was smart enough to learn now that tantruming was just not going to work.

I taught them to "reinforce other behaviors," as they say in ABA land. "Catch him when's he's good" and replace the tantrum with some kind of communication, whether verbal, pictures, or sign language. I learned this from watching the movie *The Miracle Worker* about Helen Keller, wherein Ann Sullivan had to remove Helen from the parent's house to prevent their reinforcing her tantrum behavior.[24]

Something changed in late March. He started talking! Not communicatively, but he began to name pictures I showed him. He began to repeat words. He began to sing along with his favorite songs on my cassette player. His eye contact increased, and he was more sociable, that is, friendly. Here is what seemed to change everything:

One day, I found a street vendor selling blow up dolls of Spiderman and Batman. They stood about two feet high. I bought a few to try with Angel. He loved them, and in order to play/work with them, he had to sit at the table and do his work. I used these dolls as his instructors. They would tell him what to do. His verbal language also increased, as he tried to communicate with them! Spiderman was my miracle worker.

Throughout April, May, and June, it was a guessing game with his working at the table and learning the kinds of skills he needed. We had two months left to work together. His verbal skills were still way below age level, but it was obvious that he was on the way to catching up. One day he would sit, "like an Angel," and the next, scream for an hour. One day, he would do all of his work, no problem; the next, he'd refuse and run away or scream. I threw away his program book, and for the next two months, we would work only on language and communication at the table or away from the table. This behavior, it was now obvious to me, was simply his way of getting what he wanted or refusing to engage in unpopular lessons. It had to stop. It was obvious by now that "replacement" behavior and "catching him when he is good" was simply not working. If he had been a typically developing child, we would readily have said, "he's spoiled." But when a child is diagnosed as "autistic," we assume that it's a "communication problem" or a "sensory issue."

With Angel, I was convinced that it was simply him wanting to do what he wanted to do and refusing to do what he didn't want to do. I began to not allow him to escape anymore. If he cried or tantrumed, he would still have to do his work. I would, "work him through it," which is a technique I don't recommend but felt that with Angel, he was smart enough to understand that he had to do his work and that tantruming would no longer help him get out of it. That was an unorthodox change that I made.

The other was that I tried to use only things that interested him. If we had to do non-functional programs (because we have to learn a lot of things, and some of them simply can't be taught in a functional manner), or use things that he didn't like, I would do it quickly and highly praise him for doing them. I knew that it would take a while until this approach would work—if it would work.

It's painful for a mother to listen to the tantruming in the meantime. I bit my lip and stayed consistent in this approach. I begged Mom to also do it with him when I was not there. It was hard for parents to do this, for sure.

By August, there was a complete change in behavior, attitude, and attending. He was using words now to make requests, there were no more tantrums, he became very sociable, and looking to interact both at home and at the Center. Our last session was August 31. In September, I was told that he began to attend a school in regular education.

Angel Across the Street

Could it be? A child needing services right across the street from me? The worst part of my job was the travelling between children. Brooklyn is big! It could take more than an hour to get from one part of town to another in good traffic. Usually, the service coordinators try to find children in the same parts of town where the therapist lived. If I had a kid an hour away, that was two hours in my day that I could have been working. I was only paid for the service, not for the travelling (or insurance, or anything else for that matter!). Finding a kid right across the street meant I could see him anytime, day or night. Great!

Another Angel. For some reason, I've lost the notes on him, but there are a few things that I remember quite vividly, as these things were so strange. The first one was that a Spanish child was in the Jewish area in Boro Park, Brooklyn. It was not unheard of, but most of Boro Park was Orthodox Jews. The area was first established immediately after the Holocaust, with the residents primarily survivors from the war. I lived on the very edge, and different ethnicities began across the street. Brooklyn is known for having the most diverse ethnic neighborhoods in America. Part of the charm, as it were. On Seventh Avenue, you spoke Spanish; on Eighth Avenue, you spoke Chinese.

Angel lived in a two-bedroom apartment with his mother and two brothers. The older brother was diagnosed as ADHD. He was a wild kid but charming. He loved Pokémon toys and clothes and bed sheets. He loved to show me his cards, over and over again. I got a sense that there was more than ADHD going on, but that was not my concern.

Angel also had a baby brother. There was no father on the scene. What I heard through the proverbial grapevine was that the father lived with his "other" wife and children in another part of town! Supposedly, he was the leader of some local gang. Who knows if it was true or not. I didn't care and never discussed him with Mom. One day, however, I did have the pleasure of making his acquaintance.

I was working with Angel, and he was progressing so well, so fast, that I found it easier to get out of his cramped little bedroom and work around the house. I would follow him around and engage him in things that he liked and push his verbal language. One day, he ran into Mom's bedroom. The door was open. There was a big mattress on the floor. I went in to get him and bring him out of her room. I learned a lesson that day. Two lessons, actually. One was that according to New York State regulations, a therapist is forbidden to enter any room in a house other than the designated therapy area and the bathroom. The other was that it was, rules or no rules, a stupid thing to do.

As soon as I grabbed Angel and brought him out, I came face-to-face with Dad in the doorway. He did not look happy—not at all. He was covered in tattoos, and there was lots of gold hanging from around his neck. I said, "Hello," and he sort of grunted. He was gone in a few minutes. The next day, Mom told me that Dad was very angry that I entered the bedroom.

"What if I had been nursing?"

What indeed…

I really don't remember too much more except for the fact that he really learned well and quickly. By the end of our time together, he was talking and acting pretty much age appropriately. After our time together was over, I would see them, without Dad, on the street. One day they were washing the car in front of my house. I quickly ran to the store and bought three ice pops. I came back and told Mom, "Can you help me? I have three ice-pops, and I really don't want them."

Her eldest spoke up. "I'll take one!"

I said, "Oh, really? Thanks so much."

I asked Angel if he wanted one, and he answered like a typical child. The littlest got some in his mouth and most on his shirt. I liked this Mom and could not understand how she could live the way she did with a part-time husband who was married to another woman.

Angel R

His name was Angel, but they called him Gabi. I could put him in the cutest chapter or the successes chapter, but since his name is Angel, he'll go into the Angel chapter. They didn't tell me that they called him Gabi. What difference does it make? Well, when you're trying to get someone's attention, and you're using the wrong name, he probably won't respond. Fortunately, that little problem was resolved quickly. But I had to call the school and let them know, as they were also using Angel. Everything matters in Autismland.

We began working together in early September. Gabi had an older brother, Davy, about four years old, who was in the hospital battling leukemia. Mom was often at the hospital with him, and so there was usually a babysitter with us—either an aunt or Grandma. Nobody spoke English. This made communication between us difficult. If I had to cancel or change a time, I had to call the school, talk to the teacher, who spoke Spanish, and get her to call Mom at the hospital, and then she would call the babysitter. There were no cell phones in those days.

If Mom needed to cancel my session, I was often not informed and drove to his house only to be told, in broken English, "No today, Gabi sick." He missed a lot of school, especially during the winter months. Every other month, he'd lose at least a week, and when I was sick, he lost more days. Fairly often, he'd lose a day here and a day there, and that meant that he missed going to the Center also. He could not afford to miss, but when it's very cold out, and there is a child in the hospital with leukemia, priorities were set by what they could do.

Dad was home on and off. He was a day laborer when he could find work. It was obvious that the family did not have much money. They had to move once during our time together to a smaller, cheaper apartment. The move was only a block over, but like all moves, it was expensive and a major hassle. It interrupted our work, of course.

One day, there was an official letter on the floor that I accidently sat on (I always sat on the floor when working with children). I picked it up. It was confirmation that Dad had a job that paid seven dollars an hour. I had no idea how a family of four lived on that! Social services in New York were, no doubt, helping them with food and maybe even rent. It was heartbreaking to see how they survived. Life is hard enough without a child whose life is on the line and another diagnosed with autism. Yet, both Mom and Dad always had smiles on their faces when I was there.

Gabi was a difficult child to figure out therapy-wise. He could not talk, flapped his hands, and made no eye contact. He could readily tantrum, and they were intense—the usual kinds of symptoms associated with autism. Yet, he seemed more intelligent to me than his evaluations suggested. His teacher had written beginning programs for him, and he did them easily enough. He did not like sitting at the table and doing these programs. They bored him. That, as always, was a good sign. The worst sign is when a child sits at the table and never objects to anything. That usually indicates that he just doesn't know what's going on and is not at all interested. Most people use food to get the attention of kids like that, but I never liked using food.

Another "famous" Center in another city had built-in video screens on their table and would use that to get the child to work. Do this, watch ten seconds of video. I really objected to that. Last thing I want is a child to learn that therapy is a drag and watching TV is fun.

If I made it fun, and used things he liked, he would do programs that bored him. I did them rapidly just to get the scores and let them know at the Center that I was following their plan. By late October, we had a good rapport, and he was more willing to sit with me and do the programs. I was getting straight hundreds for scores. The Center was getting low scores. This was often the case with children. Children respond different ways in different environments. I don't know how they were working with him at the Center, but I ran through their programs quickly just to avoid not being called a "team-player." As a team, we should all have been working on the same things. But he was beyond the programs they wrote. They bored him to death.

In late October, he was switched into a different class at a different time. I had to change the times that I could see him. It also meant rearranging bus schedules for him. I was hoping his new teacher would write more appropriate programs. As we went through November and the beginning of December, his verbal imitation increased, spontaneous words would pop out. He was still beyond his new programs, but all was going well.

On December 10, Davy came home from the hospital. He had a catheter in his nose, held on by bandages, and often had a bloody nose. He was bald due to the radiation therapy, but the good news was, he was in remission. Thank God! He was such an unbelievably happy child. He was heavy due to the medication, short and bald. Very cute. He spoke perfect English and was often my translator for Mom. He and Gabi played together well and obviously much enjoyed each other's company. That made a bit of a problem, as now that Mom and Davy were home, Gabi absolutely did not want to leave them, sit with me in another room, and do his work.

It took a lot of ingenuity and new toys to get him to come and engage. I broke my golden rule of never using food. Using cereal, he was easier to convince. His tantrum and aggressive behavior, unfortunately, continued. Still, it was hard to get him to come and work because aside from me, he also had an OT and a speech therapist, and this meant a lot of time away from Mom and Davy. However, I was greatly encouraged, as he was making really good progress when he wasn't tantruming!

We'd now been together three months, and he went from nonverbal to using words to request and to name objects and pictures. Excellent! It was as if all the switches in his brain were being turned on. He was a different kid. Yet, the tantrums continued, and by late December, it was apparent that he used tantrums to get what he wanted, or to "escape" what he didn't want.

Usually, children on the spectrum, who have no communication skills, tantrum. Often, there is nothing to do other than "differential reinforcement of other responses." It's a "behavior reduction" method but doesn't give the child a replacement behavior as far as communicating goes. With Gabi, it was apparent that he could readily use words, so I felt that Gabi understood well enough to know that he could ask for a break when he needed it but would no longer get one by tantruming, hitting, or throwing objects. Fortunately, he learned quickly to request a break.

At the Center he was still scoring low. I asked them to put in a "receptive picture/object ID" program. That is, to show him things in groups of three and ask him to point to each. They did it but with only one object at a time. At home, he was doing it with three items, no problem. At the Center, for some reason, he wasn't. I knew his poor performance was due to poor teaching techniques at the Center. They used trainees or assistants to implement the programs—rookies who did not understand the importance of or a correct way to incorporate error correction.

Davy had to go back to the hospital before Christmas. We were back to babysitters, and that made it easier to work with Gabi, but too sad for the family, as they had hoped Davy's hospital days were over. Apparently, the remission stopped, and the cancer increased again.

I had to remember that Gabi's tantrums might also be due to the stress of not having his mother around again. Behaviorism is concerned with "the function of behavior." I had to remember that there's more to children than simple stimulus-response and "functioning." Skinner was wrong.

In any case, I decided to increase his break time and to break the rule of following his boring programs. He did well when challenged and interested in new things. Though, he also tantrumed when frustrated. I had to teach him how to ask for help. People with aphasia know how frustrating it is not to be able to use words that they understand. It is the same for non-verbal children who understand well, but for some reason, can't get the words out. We also worked more often out of the chair.

One day, while Mom was home with us, she watched a full session. She was very happy about all the new words he was using and his overall progress.

In February, there was a change. The agency brought in a new therapist to work with him on speech, as his old one had to quit. I popped in early to see how she was doing with him. I could not believe what I was seeing. She was screaming at him for not responding, and he closed his eyes and covered them with his hands. You don't see me; I don't see you—you no longer exist. I asked Mom what this was all about. Mom's English was not good, but she managed to tell me that they couldn't find another speech teacher, and though they didn't like her (she'd been previously taken off this case), they had no choice but to bring her back.

If an agency is mandated to give speech services, they must fill those hours or be "out of compliance." Paperwork over children, as it were. "Out of compliance" are the most feared words in an agency's heart. It was a good thing that he only got speech twice a week for a half hour. I usually pushed for kids to have it every day, but in this case, it was a blessing.

It was all going well now, with the occasional outburst. Davy was home again and so was Mom and often, Dad. Gabi was improving day after day, month after month. By June, he appeared like a normal child but still was not understanding a lot of concepts that he should have by his age, such as spatial relations (under, in, behind), amounts (how many?) and "wh" questions (where, when, who, why). Was this a cognitive or a language problem? Hard to tell at his age.

In June, a speech evaluator came to evaluate him. He did very well on receptive objects, pictures, and following instructions. His major problem was his expressive skills. She did remark that his progress was incredible. She said that I had done good work with him. Thanks, but it was obvious to me that he was simply one of those kids who was going to do well regardless of therapy.

Gabi was doing great, but, unfortunately, his brother Davy had a resurgence of leukemia. I was told that he was not going to live much longer. Dad explained to me that Davy could either go through another year of chemo and a transplant with little chance for success, or he could fade away within a month. They chose the latter. Davy grew weaker by the day. He slept a lot, and his nose was continually bleeding. It broke my heart to step into that house every day.

On July 2, Davy passed away.

Do you understand what poverty is? The family was Catholic and wanted a proper burial. There was no money for it. Maybe if they'd had money, Davy could have gone to Seattle, where they are famous for treating leukemia. But no, that wasn't an option here. There was also no money for a burial. Davy's ashes came home and sat in a tiny urn on a mantel in the room where we worked. I will never forget the vision of seeing his father staying with him in the bedroom, day after day, as Davy lay dying, blood ever present in his nose, and rubbing his back for hours.

Through July, August, and the middle of September, Angel was progressing slow but sure. He still had difficulty saying three-syllable words or sentences, but it was obvious that he understood and just couldn't get the words out. His ability to comprehend amounts and "wh" questions and other concepts also improved. It was obvious to me that he really was on his way to complete "recovery," as they say in Autismland.

The new school year begins in September, and the children who turned three "aged out" of the program. I'd lose some kids; I'd gain some new kids. Gabi was not three yet but would be in five weeks. The new school year and schedule changes made it impossible for me to continue with Gabi. His mother was hysterical on the phone when a Spanish speaker called to tell her.

The service coordinator called and told me that I had to continue, if only for a few hours a week. I hated giving up Sundays in the summer, but what could I do? I agreed to do two hours on Sunday. By this time, I really loved this little boy, and his mother had been through enough.

Gabi really hated these sessions now. An excellent sign! He didn't need them anymore. His only problem now was his speech, and that was moving along. He was a normal kid as far as I saw. On October 7, he would begin a new program in a school for children with speech delays. No more autism.

This chapter is lovingly dedicated to the memory of my little buddy Davy. Another of the nameless little heroes swallowed up in the belly of the big city.

CHAPTER TWELVE

The Very Cute

Some are cute and some are very cute. Some have to grow on you; others, it doesn't matter—you're there to service them, like them or not.

I have my list of cute: Jimmy, Luki, Kenny, Kyle—forget it, there's too many. Most of them were Black and from Bed Sty, Crown Heights, East New York, Brownsville, or Bushwick—the so-called "bad neighborhoods."

The "bad" neighborhoods had all been very good to me.

Shaybok

My favorite was probably a little boy named Shaybok. His family was first generation Bangladeshi living in Queens. I'd never had a kid in Queens before or after him. It was very far from Brooklyn. Evidently, there weren't any other therapists available. It was worth the travel time because it was a two-hour session. When the session was over, I drove them to Brooklyn for his Center-based sessions. I was paid for that.

Their world was a small, one-bedroom apartment in a working-class neighborhood. Oh, it was clean enough. Tidy, as they say. There was no view from the windows except for the bricks on the wall of another apartment building a few feet away. "Clean" in New York means no cockroaches, no mice, no fleas, and no chipping lead paint. This place was clean—or so I thought.

One morning as we worked, a mouse darted across the living room floor. His mother, Santana said, "I know, I must call the landlord." Weeks later, I had to move a TV cabinet to retrieve a puzzle piece Shaybok had thrown there. Behind and underneath were two mice. They were stiff and flat and very dead. So much for "clean."

Mom was young and looked like all those posters you see for foreign travel to Bangladesh. I met the father only once on his way out to work. He worked at Rite Aid. Santana told me that he was the manager. He asked no questions about Shaybok. Fathers seldom do.

Shaybok was typical of most of my kids—first born son, didn't talk, repeat sounds, or babble. He was completely silent. He didn't understand much either, in any language. He was short, dark, and had the biggest black eyes and cutest smile, with teeth that shone like a beacon in this dismal environment. He walked on his toes.

I worked almost a year with Shaybok. He also attended the Center for a day program. Unfortunately, we made little progress. Speech therapy, occupational therapy, physical therapy, special instruction, the works. Nothing. His eyes appeared to take it all in, as if he understood, but he did not learn to speak, or imitate vocal sounds, or communicate via alternative methods. He did not imitate or respond to his name. He could not identify an object or picture. If I were to say, "Give me the bottle," he would just stare.

Although I wasn't able to teach him anything, he was able to teach me a few things. He taught me that sometimes, only miracles can change situations. His mother taught me what unconditional love is, what patience is, and that there is no such thing as "false hope." That's an oxymoron.

There was one incident where Mom lost it, however. I'm bringing this up only to show that even mothers who love their child to death, who are beyond the scale of patient, can sometimes lose it.

It was after the session, and I was sitting on the sofa writing up the paperwork. Shaybok stood facing his mother. He was crying. As he could not speak, it was difficult to know what he wanted or how to console him. His mother tried.

"What do you want?"

He kept crying, looking into her eyes, but, of course, saying nothing. She repeated her question a few more times. She knew he couldn't talk, but what else could she do? I hadn't tried a communication board with him yet. The speech teacher was working on speech production instead of communication training, as they usually do when knowing nothing about autism. Suddenly, Mom raised her voice. "Stop it!" she said, and then slapped him in the face.

She repeated it and was about to slap him again, but I grabbed her wrist and said, quietly, "Santana, no."

That seemed to calm her down, and she put her face in her hands and then pulled Shaybok to her and hugged him. Frustration had gotten the better of her. It brought back a memory of the exact same thing that happened to me when I was a kid with my mother. I cringed. People aren't perfect. They lose it sometimes.

He was such a beautiful little child, like a doll. When he laughed, it filled you with such joy. The fact that neither I, the other therapists, nor the work at the Center helped him improve at all was devastating.

Janni

He looked like a Samoan. He had walnut-colored skin, slightly curved eyes, jet black hair pulled into a ponytail, and was two feet tall. He was such a beautiful child. His name was Jannar, but it became Janni, as all my kids acquired nicknames as I came to know them better.

Janni's home conditions were classic Dickensian. He lived on the third floor of an old dinosaur carcass of a brick apartment house. Mom shared the apartment with her sister. There was no elevator, as this was not the rich side of town. This was Bedford Stuyvesant, known locally as "Bed Sty." Bed Sty was tucked into a small triangle between Crown Heights, Brownsville, and Bushwick. Most therapists would not go into any of those areas. That is, none of the usual special education or speech teachers. A typical therapist in Brooklyn was female, White, upper middle class, and college educated. The hoods were just something they passed through trying to get to somewhere else. Black female therapists had no problem going into those areas. Unfortunately, there are very few Black male therapists in ABA or speech. In my nineteen years in New York, I met only one.

Gaining entry into the building was not easy. My first obstruction was a heavy red door with a thick, black glass window about eight inches wide. The door was always locked. There were no electronic buzzers, as these were old apartments. One needed a key to enter. Fortunately, the doorbell worked, a rarity in this part of town. Unfortunately, neither Mom nor her sister often answered the bell. I would find out why after my first visit.

My first visit was memorable because it revealed so much of another world that most of us can't even imagine—especially people from my small hometown in Wisconsin. On that first visit, Mom finally answered the bell, after repeated ringing, by poking her head out of the window three flights up and screaming down to determine who was ringing. I looked up and shouted, "Therapist!"

She said, "Okay, wait a minute."

I waited, but it wasn't a minute. Or two. When she finally arrived downstairs and opened the door, I saw why it had taken so long. Mom weighed, easily, three hundred pounds. She was about five foot seven. She was in her mid-twenties and had two kids, Janni and an older boy about seven years old. There were two different fathers. The other brother was also a very handsome child, and he, too, had a label: ADHD. He ran wild in the house, listening to no one and still wearing diapers due to "accidents."

Mom had tattoos on her massive arms. She had a very pretty face that always had a look of depression, worry, anxiety, and fear on it. She told me and the other therapists, and the social workers who appeared occasionally, that she suffered from manic depression and wanted to finish school and become a gourmet cook. She never evidenced any affect in her speech or facial expression. She did not laugh, did not cry, did not react to anything said, positive or negative. It was hard to tell if she was listening when you spoke to her.

She was breathing heavily as she let me in. Going back up the stairs was going to be a challenge for her. I pitied her. Going up these steps was like walking through an Escher painting. Every other post in the handrail was missing. There was a huge crack where the steps were supposed to butt up against the wall. As we walked higher, the crack seemed to grow larger and larger. By the time we got to the third floor, the steps fell away from the wall about a foot. They seemed to have been hanging there by sheer willpower or some kind of magical magnetic influence.

Once on the third floor, there was a sort of platform about three feet wide and ten feet long. The railing was very loose. On the right there was a door, sealed tight. Turn to the left, and there was another door that led to Janni's room, and then one more door sealed tight with nails and screws. I noticed a gap between the hall's floor and the entrance to Janni's room. You had to step over it. If you dropped anything down there, you would never see it again.

In this tiny hall, there were also boxes filled with old B-movie cassettes, boxes of diapers from the City, and steps leading up to the roof. The ever-present smell of marijuana wafted up from the apartment below.

We would do our work in the bedroom, which I entered through the middle door. Consistently, whenever I arrived to work with Janni, after having caught the key thrown down from the third floor, I had to wait in the hall for a response from inside. I was rarely let into the room immediately upon knocking.

The daily ritual was that I would knock on the door and after five minutes, a harried voice from deep inside would say, "Wait a minute." That minute could be anywhere from five to twenty. Standing outside of the room, I would hear the sounds of sweeping, arranging, moving, and hollering at one of the three kids who lived there. Every day, without fail, we went through this ritual. I learned to bring a book. I did not have a smart phone in those days.

In the adjoining room, separated by a single door, was another two beds, a TV, more junk scattered about and Mom's sister. The door was usually closed. Mom's sister lived in that room and was always on a bed with the TV on. The reason that Sis stayed on the bed was that she weighed, at least, four hundred pounds. She got off her lonely bed fortress for the bathroom and then occasionally when she gathered the gumption to walk down the three flights of steps to smoke a cigarette. She also had a son. He was a very cute little boy in diapers who was just learning to speak but should have been speaking a year ago. It was obvious that he was headed for special education as well.

Finally, there was Grandma. She was a quiet, pleasant woman of average weight. She did not live with them but came often. She supported her daughters and grandchildren with all the patience of all the saints combined. Grandma had gotten this rental apartment via "Section 8." Section 8 in New York City is a government subsidized apartment for those who are indigent. It can take years to get approved for a Section 8 subsidized apartment, and the usual route of doing so is to be on the street or in a homeless shelter as a prerequisite. The City has rules, they have inspections, and they pay the landlord most of the rent.

Janni's mother, brother, aunt, and cousin were all living in this apartment under the good graces of Grandma, in whose name the apartment was registered. They did, that is, until Section 8 found out. Their living there was against regulations. They were ordered out. I had come one day, and Mom was in a particularly passionate panic.

"We have to get out. Where we gonna go? What we gonna do?"

Fortunately for them, the agency I worked for gave therapists the name and number of a man in Manhattan who knew all the numbers to call, all the people to reach, if you had a child diagnosed as "PDD/NOS." The man was able to push off Section 8 for an indefinite period of time. Of course, the landlord also wanted them either to get out or pay more money. Again, the magic man in Manhattan got them a letter from a lawyer informing the landlord that it would not be worth his while to try evicting them. Not at this time anyway. Status quo for now.

It was loud in there. The TV was blaring in the sister's room, and Mom had loud music on her computer. The seven-year-old boy was jumping from mattress to floor, up the wall, down the other, screaming. Mom had to physically remove him to the sister's room, as he would not listen to her when she told him to go there. Then, she would lock the door. On the floor in the sister's room was a pile of empty soda bottles, wrappers from McDonald's, empty pizza boxes, etc. The rumor was that the seven-year-old was really hers, but then, who knew? Didn't make any difference to me in any case.

Janni was an amazing child. From day one, he was highly "echolalic." He repeated the last word in any sentence I uttered.

"Do you want the car?"

"Car."

"Can you pick it up?"

"Up."

He'd also repeat short phrases. "Do you want me to wind it up?"

"Wind it up?"

This was a good sign, as most of my children were completely non-verbal from the start. Janni's problem was like so many of the others: He had speech but no communication skills. He would not ask for food, for TV, for a toy, for anything because he did not initiate communication. In response to questions, he would just echo whatever he had just heard. He made no eye contact. If we did a puzzle together, he would look only at the pieces, pick one up, and then place it on the spot where it went. He did not cry; he did not laugh. He was happy to do nothing all day and that's mostly what he did at home, in front of the TV with the other two boys.

His diet consisted primarily of what his mother ate: fast food and soda. He was definitely the most echolalic of any child I ever worked with. This made communication and learning language difficult because when trying to teach a child a new language, I would begin by demonstrating names of items like this: "Say bottle." A typically developing child will soon learn to reply, "Bottle." An echolalic child will respond, "Say bottle." So, you'll drop the word "say" and just show him the object and either say, "What is it?" and then prompt the correct response, or just say the word when he reaches for it.

The trouble with this approach is if you say, "What is it?" he'll simply repeat the question? "What is it?" If you use the other approach, just showing him the item and labeling it, he might understand that the object and the sound he just heard have something in common. It's hard to break echolalia, and the research has no definitive answers on what the purpose of it is for the child. Some say it's an affirmation, like saying, "Yes, I want the bottle." Trouble is, they'll echo for things they don't want as well. Some say it's a "verbal stim"—self-stimulatory behavior. They do it simply because they like it.

Our first session was to be January 8, but Mom put it off for a week. He was sleeping when I got there. Mom woke him up. He did well after he woke up, but he was hungry. He ate while we worked. Mom gave him a McDonald's hamburger and a fried egg! He ate by himself with his fingers while sitting on the floor.

During this first session, he repeated things like, "It's a red rectangle." Despite his echolalia, within a month he was making spontaneous requests such as, "Wind it up" when I showed him a top; "Open" when I put a candy in a clear jar that he couldn't open; and "Go" when I wound up a toy. I would wait until he said something to make me operate it, like, "Ready, set…"

By the next month, he was making spontaneous requests for items that were not visibly present. He also learned to correct me! We used to build a bridge or a tunnel for his favorite toy train. One day I helped him, and I declared, "We built a bridge," when it was actually a tunnel. He said, "We built a tunnel," in response.

Janni attended a school for children on the spectrum in "early intervention" designed for children between ages zero to three. I never worked with a child aged zero, but I imagine it would present some problems. At the school, they wrote programs of skills for him to learn, and my job at home was to make sure that these skills "generalized across environments." More fancy talk meaning that any skill acquired in one place (school) should also be used in other places. Any skill exhibited to one therapist, or parent, should be exhibited to another. Often kids on the spectrum will do something here, but not there, will do it with this person, but not that one.

Janni went through his programs very quickly. He learned by observation and hand over hand instruction. He never forgot a thing he learned, even if he did not use or practice it. His programs from the Center were too easy for him. They worked like this: The teacher writes up a skill, such as imitation. "Janni will imitate clapping, pointing, waving." The teacher will demonstrate the action and say, "Do this." If he responds correctly, the teacher scores a plus; if not, a minus. Then the teacher will average the amount of correct responding and score from zero to one hundred percent and graph it.

Janni's problem was that his scores were too low at the school to advance his programs. At home, he did these things easily! The teacher told me that the reason for this was that he missed a lot of school. Mom didn't send him because she didn't get out of bed that morning. Or the next, or the next. If I asked her why not, she'd invariably reply, "Janni was up all night, and I couldn't sleep."

"Why was he up all night?" I would inquire.

Either she responded, "I don't know," or "he slept all afternoon."

If I asked, "Why did you let him sleep all afternoon?" there were a myriad of excuses. "My sister babysat, and she let him sleep while I was at the laundry," or "I couldn't attend to him, and he fell asleep." But I dared not criticize. It wasn't professional. Despite this, by the end of January, he was increasing his verbal skills. He was using one-word sentences to ask for things: juice, open, wind it up. His eye contact was better, and he laughed a lot. He was so cute when he laughed. He had big black eyes and pearly white baby teeth—all framed by a jet-black ponytail. His belly bulged over his diaper. It was obvious that he was on the spectrum, but it seemed also to me that he was not as cognitively delayed as his evaluations suggested.

At school, they also assumed that he was very low functioning and wrote basic beginner programs. I suggested to the teacher that Janni move on to higher level tasks, but she said she couldn't move him because he didn't have the scores, and he didn't have the scores because he did not get to school enough. Grr.

After two months, he was applying learned phrases appropriately. Here is an example. One day, as we did the ABC puzzle, he put the N in the wrong place. I told him, "Nope, doesn't go there."

He replied, "Where does the N go?"

On March 25, there was a spring break until April 7. Things were a little different after the break. He began to exhibit some temper. He had always been so passive before, so this surprised me. Maybe it was the break in schedule that was annoying him. Hard to tell. I'd made a mental note to keep an eye on this and try to see what was causing it.

Things were going well enough considering the conditions and a Center-based teacher that did not see the higher level of this boy. Maybe it was because he missed a lot of school, and each time, they felt that they had to start over. At home, his programs were a waste of time. He did them in seconds.

Soon enough, another problem reared its annoying head to interfere with our work. It seemed that the mayor of New York suddenly remembered that there were people living in squalid conditions. He started having city officials make inspections all over the city. Some say it was because of the horrendous accidents that had recently happened in Manhattan when cranes collapsed and people were killed. The TV and papers were filled with it! In any case, inspections for lead paint in old buildings was now solidly on the mayor's agenda. I came to work one bright sunny day in late April, and Mom was frantic.

"We have to be out of this apartment tonight!"

Sure, no problem. They weren't exactly able to book a room at the Hilton, nor anywhere else for that matter. I called the social worker. She called the City, and they arranged for the family to stay in their apartment while the men worked on removing the lead paint. I found that shocking. Lead paint removal is a dirty business. Vapors, fumes, scraping off the old paint, sanding, repainting. The workers were covered in protective gear and wore masks. I wondered how a bunch of kids and two ladies were supposed to stay in the apartment with all that dangerous stuff floating in the air? But they did! The workers kept everything covered behind hanging sheets to keep the dust away from them, supposedly. I doubt it was within legal limits, but what could I do? Even if the City paid for temporary housing, moving a family like this for a few weeks would be insanely difficult, and, as far as the City was concerned, very expensive. Imagine if all the families in the hood demanded temporary housing. Hard to balance your city budget.

While the men worked on paint replacement, they noticed the dangerous condition of the electricity in the apartment. They warned her that it was not safe. The very day they told her, that night, sparks came flying out of the ceiling fixture. The fire department informed her that she must evacuate! Again, emergency calls to the City, and electricians were sent the next day. All this happened while I was on spring break. When I came back, the electricity was updated, and all the walls were freshly painted.

In May and June, Janni's language continued to improve. He was still missing a lot of school, but there was nothing to be done about that. It was just too overwhelming for his mother. She had to come down all those steps with Janni and an equipment bag full of materials. Going down was bad enough, but bringing him up was just too much for her, so his attendance at school slowly dwindled. Despite his lack of attendance, he was doing well.

At the end of May, we were finally back to work, and he went back to school. It seemed to me that he was fast approaching normal. Mom said that he was talking a lot. It was unusual, but after five months, I strongly recommended that he be reevaluated, as I was not sure he'd meet the criteria for autism anymore. I suggested that he be moved out of the ABA classroom and into the advanced class, where children did not get such intensive one-on-one therapy.

I continued our work at home but without the programs. They bored him to death. I took data on goals that I wanted to see improvement in, mostly language. He didn't disappoint me. He was now saying things spontaneously like, "Where is it?" when I hid puzzle pieces. Or he might say, "Pieces missing." Or "We built a bridge!"

His programs were tougher. Things like matching by associating (shoe with sock, brush with toothpaste); categorizing by function, feature, and class (give me something you drink with, give me something that has a handle, give me an animal); following two step instructions; and answering questions in whole sentences without echoing. He was doing so well, yet when something went wrong, he couldn't do something, or he did not understand something, he would angrily throw pieces instead of saying, "I need help." He still might tantrum when I introduced something he didn't like. He also continued to stare off suddenly into space for extended periods. I was afraid that he was having petite mal seizures, but all I could do was suggest to Mom to have that checked out.

On those occasions when he did tantrum, I just held him and sang until he calmed down. I don't know. Are they still teaching in Autismland that when a child has a tantrum you should "work through it?" Fancy term for it: "extinction/interruption." I found with some children, you could do that, and they would recover and go right back to work. But not Janni. I could not tell why a child as bright as him would tantrum instead of tell me something was wrong. One thing was obvious: he didn't know how. To hold him in my lap and sing until he calmed down was violating ABA guidelines! Any respectable ABA text will tell you that the therapist when doing this is "reinforcing escape behavior." Maybe with some kids but not with Janni. He would simply calm down, and we would go back to work.

I worked with him for a total of eight months. By the end of that time, he scored close to a normal child for cognitive ability, some delay in language and self-help skills, but he was well on his way to regular ed. He was given an evaluation for his next school, and he scored seventy-four on the cognitive—low normal. He would be going to a special education school but not one specifically for autism.

It would be hard to leave a family like this. I had become attached to the child and wished so much that I could do something for his mother and maybe even convince his aunt that if she didn't change, she would die on that creaky bed. These women were only in their twenties. Grandma enabled them, as she took care of so many things. She did not know how to help them other than to shop, cook, and babysit. Too sad. My only legacy to them was arranging for free diapers and delivery via the City after I left the case. Love 'em and leave 'em.

Jeannie

She was too cute. Like a little wind-up doll. So cute, in fact, that I put up with two cats that I'm allergic to. She was only seventeen months old when I started to work with her. Her father was Italian, and to look at her mother, you'd think she was Scandinavian. But she wasn't. Actually, her people were from one of those small Muslim towns on the Russian border somewhere. I would have never known that if I hadn't had to work with Jeanie at her grandma's house.

Grandma was called Prutah, which means "little" in their language. Her name was fitting, as she only stood about five feet tall. Prutah was not in very good shape, so they had a full-time caretaker named Beulah who lived in the apartment next door with her daughter and two grandkids. Beulah took very good care of Prutah and Jeanie. I called her Gigi. It was the end of February, and she had just been diagnosed at age seventeen months. A baby.

The building was in a huge apartment complex on one of the busiest corners in Brooklyn. Parking would be a problem. Working during "alternate side parking" would make that problem almost impossible. In nineteen years working in Brooklyn, I never got used to that "alternate side parking" thing. People hated it, but then, how are you going to keep the streets clean in a city of eight million people? What it meant was that four days a week, I would have to run out of the apartment, move my car to the other side of the street, and run back up. And if there was nowhere to park on the other side of the street? I wrote a letter to the senator of New York, named Hillary Clinton, and told her of the problem and asked if the state couldn't issue permits for state-sponsored therapists so they would not have to interrupt or cancel services. Afterall, New York was paying for these services! I never got a response.

I worked with her in New York by her grandmother because Mom worked in Brooklyn but lived in Staten Island. Mom would drop her off by Grandma and then go to work. Grandma's apartment was a beautiful apartment in a well-to-do neighborhood. I was not used to such surroundings, as most of my work was in cramped, neglected NYCHA houses. Here, the elevator always worked! That was also something I was not used to!

I entered the apartment through a hall, and on the immediate right was the kitchen pantry. On the left, directly across, was the living room, where we were to work. As soon as Gigi saw me, she would burst into tears. Her evaluations said that she cried a lot. Well, she was very young, an only child, and spent her days at Prutah's house playing or watching videos. Not unusual to cry when a stranger walks in. But her crying was pretty intense. She cried, almost non-stop, for forty minutes and then fell asleep. I had made no attempt to approach her. I could see that this case was not going to be easy.

After the first day, I became ill and was out for a week. When I returned, it was the same story: as soon as I walked in, screaming, crying, wailing. I knew that this could occur for a period of time if something was not done, but I had no strategy. I noticed that if I walked out of the living room, directly across to the kitchen, she would stop crying. I was out of her fear zone.

On my second day there, I tried an experiment. I entered the apartment and immediately went to the kitchen with Beulah. I sat on the floor in the kitchen (shooing away the cats), pulled out my toys, and began to play by myself. Gigi could see me from the living room. She continued to cry for a half hour until I asked Beulah to bring her to the kitchen door, but not inside. Gigi was brought and continued to sway. I just kept playing with my toys. Music, spinning tops, saying, "Wee, this is fun!" I was completely ignoring her. After a half hour, she stopped crying.

I "accidently" spun one of my tops toward her. She picked it up. I spun another one toward her. She picked it up looking at it, me, it, me. I reached out my hand. "Gigi, give me the top." To our amazement, she brought it to me. Now we were both sitting on the kitchen floor, playing with my toys. So much for day two of therapy.

The next day, I brought a small table and chair and put them in the living room. I sat on the floor and put all the toys on the table. Initially, she cried when I came in, but soon, she approached the table and we played. By the end of the first week, she was able to sit at the table and engage with me. She even laughed a few times. I was thrilled with this progress and did not expect it so quickly. I tried to pick her up and dance or spin while singing, "The Wheels on the Bus," but she was not ready for this. I had to slow down!

By the beginning of the following week, I saw that she was ready to do formal programs. I probed a bunch of skills, such as imitation, eye contact, joint attention, pointing to desired objects, object and picture ID, and simple puzzles. I brought her a five-piece shape puzzle, and she did it, alone, immediately. Doing performance skills were usually easier than communication skills with kids on the spectrum, so I didn't think much of the fact that she had done so well on the puzzle. That was my mistake. Instead of thinking, *She's on the spectrum and therefore does well with performance tasks*, I should have thought, *Hmm, nothing's wrong with this girl!*

She was so young, perhaps the evaluators simply couldn't get her to do anything and so, "PDD/NOS" was the diagnosis given. Hard to tell with a non-verbal seventeen-month-old. Soon, she would show me what the truth was.

By the end of the first three weeks, it was obvious that her abilities were far beyond what the evaluations suggested. I wrote a program book for her, and she mastered all of the programs within days. I had to write harder programs, like following one step instructions and matching three cards depicting objects, animals, and two step imitation. Soon, she understood exactly what we were going to do every day—i.e., sitting and working—and she was not thrilled with that idea. She refused to do any program upon request. That is, if I said, "Show me your nose," or "Stand up and jump," or "Give me the blue cup," she'd get angry and refuse. Not "escape," as they say in ABA land. She knew what and how to do these things and just didn't want to do them. They were boring!

This showed me that she was intelligent. She obviously understood me, knew what I wanted, but being non-verbal, she couldn't say, "No! I don't want to! This is boring!" Yet, I had to get her to do programs in order to advance her to more complicated skills.

So, instead of doing straight, "discrete trials," as they call it in ABA land, I "embedded" the trials in playful events that she enjoyed doing, like taking out, arranging, and putting back plastic dishes in her cabinet. We did all the same work but in a different format. Unfortunately, your average ABA therapist was never taught to do this, and many times, it just becomes a struggling match with the child. The therapist then writes in her progress notes, "Child is resistant to instruction."

I was working with her six hours a week. That means she was missing four hours a week of special instruction. A new ABA therapist started to work with her on Sundays at her mother's house in Staten Island. I was anxious to see how it would go. Children on the spectrum often do not generalize their learning. That means, she might do something for me but not for anyone else; or she may do something in one environment but not in another. I was worried about this.

The following Monday, I was told that she had done great with the new therapist. The other therapist was supposed to follow my programs and use my materials, which Mom would take home with her on Fridays. However, after two weeks, Beulah told me that Mom had said that the other therapist and I were not on the same page! This troubled me. I had not yet even met Mom! I called her.

"Oh, no, there's no problem."

"Hmmm, what does this mean?" So, I called the other therapist, and she told me that when she tried to do the programs, any programs, Gigi would tantrum or try to run away from the table. I suggested to her, "Play with her and try to make her use words. Just have fun with her."

ABA is insistent that therapists take data on the programs, chart them, and make decisions about future programs based on the data. I decided, however, that while I would continue to follow the programs and take data, the weekend therapist would not have to, as she obviously did not know what to do when a child refused discrete trial teaching. And I didn't want Mom to sit through screaming sessions.

For three months, things had been going well enough. She would work with an occasional crying fit of short duration. In early May, I made a big mistake. She was tantruming in the chair, and I said loudly, "Stop it!"

She threw up.

Therapist error! Idiot! She taught me something I never learned in ABA courses. You can't push a child to work, and you can't "reinforce" them to work if they are not interested in what you're doing. They've got to want to do it. There is no, "work them through it." If they don't like what you're doing, change it!

I would work with Gigi for another year and a half. My notes throughout that time were pretty much the same, day after day: She refused to sit. She refused to do her work. She was not gaining any language. Then, there would be days when she did all her work with excellent responding for the entire two hours. What should I have learned from this? There are a few things I can think of:

One, for sure, was that she was capable of working, progressing, laughing, and learning far beyond what her evaluations suggested. Another thing I should have learned, but was never taught in ABA school, was that if she demonstrates the ability to follow programs and she doesn't, that means that my technique was not right for her. Old school ABA taught a therapist to "work her through it," or "don't let her escape because that reinforces escape behavior." Well, there is some truth to that. Obviously if someone learns that screaming or hitting gets them out of doing something they don't want to do, they'll continue to use that strategy. Every time it works, it reassures them that if you hit the teacher or parent, and they say, "Oh, gee, okay, you don't have to," you are reinforcing that behavior. And there is some truth to "working a child through it." Children have to learn that they must do things in life that they don't want to, and there is no escaping responsibility. Sure, both are true. But… but what? When you are working with a child who cannot talk and does not seem to understand language, and is not even two years old, will these "life strategies" make any sense to her? Is there a "one size fits all" approach in ABA land? Did Skinner make the pigeon finish his work whether he liked it or not?

By the end of May, I had learned my lesson. When she refused to work, instead of "increasing the level of reinforcement," or "working her through it," or "using errorless" learning, I did the unthinkable. We left the table, and I let her do what she wanted. I needed to see what she wanted so that I could use that activity as the reinforcer.

She liked to go in the back bedroom and bounce on the bed. I introduced her to pillow fighting. She thought it was hysterical when I threw a pillow at her. Now, we would work on requesting.

"What do you want?"

"Pillow."

"What do you want?"

"Jump."

I put balloons up in the chandelier in the bedroom and asked, "Where is it?"

"Up."

When entering the room, "Turn on the light." When leaving, "Turn off the light."

I rewrote the programs such that the goals were the same: verbal communication. "Why" questions, object ID, but instead of, "sit in table facing child," I wrote, "Find activity child enjoys and proceed with program using reinforcers that she is interested in."

She turned two in late July. We were finding our way. I knew when to back off and when I could push without causing a tantrum. She was doing well, but unfortunately, her verbal language and verbal imitation were not moving. The speech teacher never communicated with me. While anyone in the field of autism knows how vital it is that all therapists work on goals as a team, this never seemed to happen much in reality.

I called the service coordinator and told her that I had no idea who was on the team and what they were doing. I wanted data on a new behavior. She had begun hand flapping. This bothered me because I was not sure if she was autistic or not. She didn't talk, and she liked being alone, but other than that, I didn't see it.

Things went well on and off, until September. By now, words would pop out and she would imitate oral movements, like open mouth, tongue out, blow raspberries. She might say, "Clean up" one day and not the next. She would make animals sounds according to the pictures of different animals. By the middle of September, I wrote in my notes that her progress now was excellent. Her sessions were extended to two hours.

At the end of September, some genius decided to introduce her to an iPad. Big mistake. From the first day, it was a disaster. As soon as I walked in the room, she had to turn it off, and this led to major tantrums. Worse, the babysitter tried to intervene in order to get her to calm down. I did not want that, but the babysitter ignored me and went to comfort her. I called Mom and told her not to let her use the iPad, ever.

It is clear to me that the iPad—for children with developmental delays, under five at least—is the worst thing anyone can give them for two reasons. The first is that once they have it, there's no taking it away. It's addictive for children (and adults). That is the same for all children, typically developing or not. Second, for children with developmental delays, the iPad makes it seem like they are little geniuses hidden behind the silence and the unaccountable behaviors. How so? Let's use an example: There are two logs on the screen, and the question comes up in writing or verbally, "How many logs do you need to add to cross the bridge?"

So, the child hits "one," and nothing happens. The child hits "two," and the logs immediately make a bridge over the little creek. Lights! Music! "Good job!" He will remember that, and henceforth, whenever that question comes up, he immediately hits, "two." Did he learn that two plus two is four? No. He learned that when these logs come up with this picture, you hit the two, and then the screen will change to something else. Take two clothes pins and ask him how many more does he need to make four, and you will immediately see that he has no idea what you are talking about.

Another example: The voice says, "Touch the red circle." He touches the blue one. Nothing happens. He touches the green one. Nothing happens. He touches the red one, and bells ring and lights flash—it screams, "You're right!" Did he learn that the word "red" signifies that color? No. He learned when that screen comes up, and he hears the word, "red" or "blue," he should touch that one, and it'll work.

But isn't that learning to put the word to the color? No. It's a good memory enhancer perhaps, but it is not teaching him about colors. How do you know? Put a red cup and a blue cup on the table and say, "Touch the red cup." His response will be in the "chance" levels. He will, if lucky, get it right 50% of the time. And even then, he's not getting it right. He's just lucky.

When parents see that he is getting all the answers right on the iPad, they do not realize that he's not learning. They don't realize that it is just memorizing, and the skills do not generalize, which means, he hasn't learned it. For typically developing children, they will be able to generalize, and they can learn this way. For children on the spectrum, who are notorious for not generalizing, it is the parents who are overgeneralizing. That is, they assume that cognitively delayed and/or speech delayed children are learning the same as typically developing children. It's good for pigeons, not for children.

The last week in September, the iPad was seriously interfering. I would walk in, she had it, and I, naturally, had to take it away to do our work. She would scream for hours. And in this case, she did generalize! She now knew that when I walked in, the iPad had to go. My mere presence now triggered tantrums. I called her mother and told her that I could not continue if she let Gigi play with the iPad. Even when I'm not there. She reluctantly agreed.

I was leery the next day as I walked in. Immediately, I saw that she was going to behave like the previous day—crying, tantrum. I moved to a different part of the living room and made a barricade such that if she came to sit, she would not be able to see anywhere else in the room.

I did not bring her to the table though. I just sat and played with my toys, and Beulah did not let her have anything: no electronics, no toys, nothing. The strategy worked, as eventually, she came over to see what I was playing with.

The next few days, we just played. It was like starting over. To my great relief, this worked. I let her break anytime she wanted, slowly introduced things that she did not like to do but had to learn, and made sure I presented them in a way that did not upset her. Also, she started, in mid-September, to repeat words and sounds. This was big! When we finished her favorite activity, putting letters in the ABC puzzle, she suddenly said, "Clean up."

One day, the speech therapist was there for her half-hour sessions, and I saw that she had Gigi in the highchair. To my surprise, Gigi was actually comforted being in it! After the speech teacher left, I kept her in the chair, and she did great work. This was a fine short-term solution, but I knew that she was smart enough to be with regular education children, and once her language came, I was sure that she'd be ready to join regular education. That meant sitting in a chair. So, yes, she worked well while in it, but it was not a long-term good idea.

She stayed in the highchair through November and into December. I would let her out for breaks. One of her favorite things to do was stand in front of a full-length mirror and do, "If you're happy and you know it" with me. One of the signs of autism is "rigidity of routine." We had to do the song the same way every time. First was clap your hands, and then stomp your feet, then shout hurray, and then jump. For "jump," I would throw her into air, and she laughed hysterically every time. If I tried to change the order or add or subtract the order, she would tantrum. We had to do this at least once a day. Every day.

Her language was increasing. Words would pop out. We had been working for a long time on "receptive picture/object ID," where she pointed to things that I named. She started to repeat the names on her own. By the end of January, she was using one-word sentences to request: "juice," "fish" (meaning fish crackers), up, down, and other simple words. By mid-February, they were reporting at home that she was using words to ask for things. She was spontaneously naming things that she saw. She could recite the alphabet.

The months of winter passed, and by spring, her verbal skills were much improved. She could name things; she could sing songs. She counted, said the alphabet, and named shapes and colors. But still, while she had words and responded, there was no verbal communication. She knew words but did not use them to communicate with people. And her stubborn streak was still strong. If I introduced something she didn't like, she would turn away from me or close her eyes. It's a good strategy: I can't see you; you can't see me. Once she found that closing her eyes worked to get me to stop, she used it often. I had to break this habit.

Here's how I broke it quickly. I would stand her up on a table and sing. She enjoyed that, and then I would introduce something she did not like, and she would close her eyes. Because she was standing on a table, this was scary for her, and she realized she could fall and so opened them right up. That was the end of the "eye closing" strategy for getting out of work. This little girl, with the big blue eyes and brightest smile, was also the most stubborn kid I ever had.

"Oh, oh, but she has autism. That's why she refuses." Nonsense. (Hellen Keller taught me that having a disability is no excuse for bad behavior.) Gigi would just refuse to do anything she didn't want to. I had to decide, work on "compliance training," that means, trying to reinforce good responding and ignoring any other behavior, or just let her do what she wanted and work on increasing language in the "natural environment." I chose the latter. By April, she was using three-word sentences to make requests yet still would not respond to her name. Aside from that, however, she seemed like a typical child to me.

Our last day was to be June 2. I decided to work on "wh" questions. "Where is it? What color is it? Where does this go?" I brought in new pictures of things and toys for her to verbally identify. The only "wh" question we did not work on was, "Why?" That would have to wait for her to get older. I was surprised to see that she really wasn't good with "wh" questions. Was it language, or was it cognitive? Or both? Or neither? She still seemed to be in her own little world.

When our sessions ended in June, she appeared to me to be age appropriate but still very aloof. She had the residual signs of autism, like preferring to be alone, lining things up and counting them over and over, not responding to her name or other kids, and no reciprocal verbal interaction.

After our work was done, her mother kept me informed and sent pictures. The last she reported was that Jeanie was in regular education indistinguishable from the other children.

Kyle

Kyle was one of my first children, and I could not find his file! Drat! I do remember a few things, however, that make this case worth a word or two. Kyle was Japanese. His parents seemed to have this wild idea about giving him an Anglo name and speaking only English to him. He had an older brother named John. His parents also spoke only English to him. Both parents worked in high tech.

Kyle was too cute! He was autistic, and there was no doubt about that. He had all the usual signs: non-verbal, toe walking, limited interests, no communication skills. But I saw some kind of awareness in his eyes. He did not seem to be "detached" from the world. It was more like he was very well aware of the world, just not interested.

As he was one of my first children, I made a lot of the usual beginner mistakes. As all those old training ABA videos showed, circa 1970–2000, a therapist must get "stimulus control." That's shorthand for, "Get him to sit at the table and pay attention." The very two things an average two-year-old with autism does not want to do! In those days, there were no BCBA's, no autism courses, no manuals except for one: *The Me Book* by Ivaar Lovaas,[25] and I worshiped it like my own personal Bible.

The procedure was straightforward. "Kid at table, present stimulus, child responds, reinforce response." To this day, in 2022, they are still teaching new therapists that if the child does not respond, or exhibits escape behavior, "increase reinforcement schedule." Sure. One M&M doesn't work, so give him two or give them more often. Physically "prompt" him through it and reinforce his attempts to perform the "response." It drove most of the higher cognitive level kids nuts.

It drove Kyle nuts. He would scream the entire time I "redirected" him to his chair. "Redirected" means forcing him into it. Many times, when his father was home, he could not stand the screaming. He would leave the house until the two-hour session was over. He used to ask me how I could stand listening to that screaming for two hours, every day. I had to admit, it was not pleasant.

Eventually, I found things that Kyle really liked to play with or that got his rapt attention, and at those times, he would engage with me happily. Once I found these things, the whole operation changed. Screams turned to laughter, and eye contact was greatly increased. Then he began making joint attention, which was the beginning of real progress. He progressed well and quickly after that. Even though Lovass had written in *The Me Book*, "Make it fun," in the introduction, you didn't see so much fun in any of his early training videos!

Kyle had two cowlicks on the back of his head. You know, those places where the hair on your head turns direction, causing a little circle. We all have one. Kyle had two. His father told me that in Japan, people believe that if you have two cowlicks, you will never be normal. That was the problem according to Dad. Uh, I never saw any research on two cowlicks and autism, so all I could say was, "Uh, I'm not sure that's the problem."

Another thing that I remember was that his mother toilet trained him easily! If you have a child on the spectrum, you know how difficult this particular little task can be. Mom would simply hold a bucket in front of him, pull down his pants, and he would go! When I saw this, I knew that there had to be intelligence in this boy because he knew exactly what to do, and this behavior had not been modeled for him. It had to mean he understood language at some level. He did. We used to go for walks, Kyle me and Mom, and he'd see a dandelion and say, "Flower."

Mom told me that he was attracted to anything colored yellow. I found over the years that there is something magic about the color yellow. Whenever I tried a new toy, I looked for it in yellow. There were no studies on it that I'm aware of, but I'm sure that the color yellow attracts children.

One final thing I remember. Kyle was the first child to make me question whether this "discriminative stimulus, operant response, reinforcer/punisher" method was really the only, or the best, way to go. It was the golden rule in ABA: "The Three Termed Contingency." Here's how it is supposed to work: With the child facing you in a chair, say, "Clap hands," and model clapping your hands. That's the Sd (discriminative stimulus), and then the child will do that (the operant response). Next, you "reinforce" that behavior. Food, access to toy, hug, whatever your reinforcer assessment suggested that you use. Works great with pigeons. Works well with kids on a lower cognitive level unless they're too low.

Most children you work with in early intervention will respond well. They will learn skills, names of objects, names of actions, imitation, joint attention, and lots of other important pre-learning skills that are lacking in so many children on the spectrum. However, children on higher levels, like Kyle, get bored quickly with this procedure—especially with non-functional tasks, such as touch your nose, look at me, touch the ball. Reinforcement only goes so far. Boring is boring no matter what the reward. How can a kid learn if he's bored, screaming, and miserable?

Today, almost forty years since Lovaas introduced this method, these mistakes are not made. ABA has learned how to modify teaching such that the rigid structure of the "three term contingency" is still used, but in a child friendly way to make the learning fun (as he suggested all those years ago), interesting, and "reinforcing" for the child. Check out the book, *Let Me Hear Your Voice* by Bridget Taylor,[26] who is one of the big people in the field today. You will see that when she first started working with children, she made the same mistakes. She was honest enough to admit it, and the authoress of the book describes the agony she had of being outside the room, listening to her kids scream. So, I'm in good company.

After a while, I realized these mistakes and felt like a traitor, but I changed the way that I presented things to Kyle. I started over and simply played with him. He loved to run, jump on the sofa, and kick balls. So that's what we did until I felt that we had a rapport. I became his "reinforcement." At this point, I would introduce the things that he had to learn, in his chair. Ten minutes in the chair, ten out. We had an unwritten deal! Once this rapport was established, he learned quickly and well. He went on to regular education.

CHAPTER THIRTEEN

Hood Happenings

There's no question that working in the hoods in Brooklyn is a far different experience than working in Appleton, Wisconsin. I had experiences in Brooklyn that certainly would never have transpired in small town Wisconsin where I grew up. I had a small-town mentality and expectations about the world that were "broadened" when I began to work in Brooklyn, New York.

Here is just a brief description of small-town Wisconsin in the sixties and seventies. There were no Black people. There were no Latino people. Everyone spoke English. Everyone was white, as in WASP. There was one Chinese family who, as the stereotype goes, owned, and operated the Chinese restaurant. But I never saw their children. There were a few Indians (Native Americans, for the sake of being PC). Gus was one. He's still there. His being an Indian never made much difference to anybody. My being Jewish was more of a negative diversion.

In any case, crime was low, people worked mostly blue collar in the mills—such as Kimberly Clark or the famous Wisconsin paper mills. There was one high school and one Christian high school. There was a separate school for special needs children. You hid them in those days. Teenage pregnancy was unheard of. I only knew one girl who got pregnant in high school, and she "disappeared."

Being a labor state, the Democratic Party was always the preferrable way to vote. Young men accused of serious crimes had two choices: go to prison or go into the Marines. Vietnam was going on, and we all believed whatever our government told us. Domino effect! Today, Vietnam, tomorrow, Oshkosh. There was no dope, no hippies, no peace signing, no long hair, and skirts covered the knees. In public school, shirts had to be tucked in, you had to wear a belt, and you could not wear Dingo's (suede shoes). And of course, despite the Beatles appearing on Ed Sullivan in 1964, boys' hair had to be short—off the collar and above the ears. Wisconsin always had two establishments in every little town: a church and a tavern. I grew up in that idyllic world. The "formative years," as they say.

To say the least, Brooklyn was nothing like that! Brooklyn, being only one section of greater New York City, was bigger and more populous than Green Bay, maybe even Milwaukee. It has the most diverse population of anywhere in America. It was not uncommon to hear five different languages every day. If you walked down forty-ninth street, for instance, (where I lived) in an easternly direction, you would begin in a Yiddish-speaking area, cross over into a Spanish-speaking area, go through a small Korean area, into a Chinese-speaking area in less than a half hour. The signs were all in local languages. The products in the stores, the signs in the stores, different foods, newspapers, and magazines were all in the language of the area.

In a car, you'd drive through Russian hoods, Black hoods, Syrian Jewish hoods, Irish, ad infinitum. I lived in an Orthodox Jewish section, not to be confused with the secular Jewish sections. There were mostly Chassidim, like those guys in "Fiddler on the Roof." I did not dress like them, however. I was more preppy. Only a beard and skullcap, worn under a ball cap, hinted at my being Jewish.

I'm going to relate some things that happened in the course of my working in the Black hoods that were a new experience for this small-town Wisconsin boy. None of the following are earthshattering, but they were new to me.

"Come on in!"

On two occasions, someone simply jumped into the passenger seat of my car as I stopped at a red light or stop sign. The first time, I was driving through East New York, which was completely inhabited by Black people. At a red light, I saw a fight between teenagers. A garbage can was thrown at one of the attendees. It looked like three against one. Okay, this had nothing to do with me, so I didn't pay much attention until suddenly, my passenger door flew open and the kid who was being attacked hopped in and said, "Go! Go! Go!"

I turned to look at him and asked, "Uh, can I help you?"

He said, "They trying to kill me."

The light turned green, and I drove through the intersection. On the other side, I pulled over and told him, "Get out." He began to protest, and I repeated, "Out." He got out and took off running.

The second time was in Brownsville, also primarily a Black neighborhood. As I came to a stop sign, I didn't see anybody and was about to step on the gas when a young lady, maybe twenty, hopped in. She was Black, short, heavy, and would most likely not win any beauty contests. She said most joyfully, "Wanna party?" I looked at her stunned as she sat there smiling.

I said, "Uh, no, I don't."

Not put off at all, she said, "Hey, can we go to your place?"

"What? Can we what?" I queried.

"Go to your place and party," she repeated. Big smile.

"No, sorry. You'll have to get—"

She interrupted. "Oh, ok. How about my place? Wanna party at my place? I have some pot."

"No. I don't want to party. Please get out of the car."

She looked at me with great pity for passing up such a fortuitous opportunity. She got out. I drove to my next child.

"Role me another one."

There were two smells that were usually present whenever I worked in a NYCHA building. One was bacon, and the other was marijuana. How would a nice Jewish boy know what bacon smelled like? I grew up in a non-observant home, and bacon was on the menu. How would I know what marijuana smelled like? My fellow Navy buddies and I smoked enough to sink the aircraft carrier we cruised on during the Vietnam War. But that's for another book.

I saw pot very often in the hoods—on the streets, in the halls of the buildings, in cars. It was everywhere. I saw it real close one time, as I was working with a little girl at the coffee table and there was an open pouch full of pot sitting on the table. I handed it to the mother and suggested that maybe she should keep this out of the reach of her two-year-old, autistic daughter. Mom said, "Oh yeah! She could spill it!"

One other time I came to that apartment, and no one answered the door. But I heard sounds and knew someone was inside. Mom had not called to cancel the session. I knocked. No answer. The scent of smoke in the hall was thick with marijuana. It was coming from this apartment. I knocked again, as I knew the little girl was home and figured Mom had fallen asleep in the back bedroom. Finally, I heard a young male voice at the door, but he would not open it.

"Man! Whatchu want?"

I told him, "I'm the therapist for the little girl, and now is time for her therapy." I wasn't sure he heard me. Truth is, he probably had no idea that there was even a little girl in the apartment. It was her fifteen-year-old sister he was more interested in.

"She ain't here," he said.

I knew she was. I also knew that whatever they were doing in there, they were not about to interrupt it for me. I told him through the door to please tell the mother that I was there.

I didn't want Mom to think it was my fault the girl did not get her therapy that day. "You hear me? Tell the mother."

No response.

I walked away, mumbling.

Another time, I had just left a building and found, in the outer entrance, a small, plastic zip lock bag about the size of an average adult thumb. It had some kind of spice in it. I picked it up and smelled it. Sure enough, marijuana. I had a few options at this point: Sell it and risk getting caught for selling drugs. No, not worth the gamble. Smoke it: No, I hadn't smoked pot for over thirty years and had no interest in it anymore. Leave it alone.

While I held it, contemplating my options, a young "Rasta-Man" walked by. He was about twenty years old, with long dreadlocks. I stopped him and said, "Excuse me. I found this on the ground and have no idea what it is." I handed it to him. He took it and looked at me with a bit of a smirk on his face. He never said a word. I left it in his hands and went off to my next child.

Something similar happened in another NYCHA building. I had a child on the fourth floor, and in the adjoining apartment, the smell of pot was always thick, rolling up from under the door. None of my concern. One day, as I was leaving, I found a small bag of pot in front of that door. It had obviously been dropped accidentally. A crazy idea came to me. I'd turn it into security, just to see their reaction. Security was in a small trailer outside of the building.

I entered, and there was a young Black lady and two Black, uni-formed men behind a counter. I put it on the counter and said, "I found this in the building. I think it's pot."

There was a look of astonishment on all three faces. No one said a word. They just looked at each other wondering what this idiot was doing. I left it on the counter and walked out.

Truth is, I saw small bags like this often on the streets and usually just ignored them. Still, it reminded me of when I lived in California during the Vietnam War. As mentioned before, I was in the Navy and smoked a lot of pot. In those days, they had "nickel bags" and "dime bags." A nickel bag filled half a baggie for five dollars, a full baggie for ten. You could buy an entire kilo for two hundred and fifty dollars. It would cover a kitchen table. I wondered what the going rate was on this tiny, thumb-sized bag nowadays. Just curious.

"Guns."

Growing up in small-town Wisconsin, I saw guns, mostly rifles, every day. All my friends grew up hunting. Deer, bear, pheasant, duck, grouse, moose, and wild boar were all hunted according to season. People proudly displayed gun racks in the living rooms, usually with a bust of a deer's head or a boar's head hung proudly on the wall in proximity—maybe next to the forty-pound musky that was mounted nearby. Every kid (girls, too) knew the difference between a deer rifle and a shotgun, or which kind of arrow to use for turkey versus which kind to use for deer. If you saw an article in the local newspaper with the headlines, "Joe Blow was shot!" you knew it was a hunting accident.

Truth is, I never saw a gun in New York unless it was strapped to a policeman's waist. However, the results of gun violence I saw all the time. I'll list a few examples.

The one that sticks out most vividly because it was the first time I'd been aware of such an incident, was detailed in the chapter on "Different Kinds of Mothers" in the case of Corey's mother. Just to recap briefly, Corey was a two-year-old, non-verbal Black boy living in a dilapidated building. He was the one who'd blurted out, "Daddy" when I walked in one day. His mother stopped and said to him, "Boy! Dat ain't yo Daddy. Yo Daddy's daid!"

As mentioned in that chapter, I'd noticed the picture of a young man on a shelf in the living room, and I asked Mom if that was her husband. She said, "Yeah."

Like an idiot I asked, "What happened to him?"

Mom explained that he had been shot dead while sitting on the steps in front of the building with friends. "He was mistaken for someone else." I learned never to ask how or why someone died in the hood if he was young.

Another child, another picture on the wall of a young man with a black ribbon around it. I never asked Mom who he was. Mom never mentioned him. He was not in the child's records. I was looking at the picture one day as the child's grandmother was home babysitting. She noticed me looking and simply said, "That's my son. This boy's father. He got shot by accident. They thought he was someone else."

Whenever I heard this, "shot by accident" story, it would remind me of all the times I had met men who were in the German army in World War II. If I asked them what they did in the war, invariably the answer would be, "I was in a Russian prisoner-of-war camp." But that's also for another time, another book.

I mentioned another gunshot in the chapter called, "The Ones I Couldn't Help." Kathy's father was "lucky" because he didn't have to work. He was drawing disability because he'd been shot in both knees. In part two of that chapter, I mentioned a shooting death a few houses down from where I worked with a little boy named Davy.

In the chapter on "Twins," part two, I mentioned a Black teenager who had been shot to death on the sidewalk near a house I was working in. I remember seeing it on the news that night, but I don't recall what happened.

Previously, I had made mention of the shooting death of Akai Gurley by the police in the Pink Houses in Brooklyn. He was simply walking up the steps one night, and a rookie cop shot him. There were no lights. I had just started working in the Pink Houses and had done no research on the history of the place. Drugs and violence were common. Unfortunately, these things continue to this day there.

Then there was the robbery and shooting death of a UPS man while delivering a package in Brownsville. I worked in the building next store.

As I worked with a little girl in one of the hoods inhabited by Bangladeshis mostly, there was a ruckus often heard from the next building over. This particular ruckus happened one to three times a week. I would hear, loudly through our window, about twenty yards away from the other building, a man screaming the following words, rather consistently: "Shut the f***. F you, you no good MF." The F word, the N word, violence, the sound of things banging, and the continual verbal harassment of what I gathered was the man's "Soulmate." It could go on for an hour. I asked the mother of the girl that I was working with why no one put a stop to this? She told me that the man had a gun.

On one sunny day, as I walked down a brick path from one of the buildings toward my car, I noticed a shiny brass object between the bricks. I picked it up. It was the shell of a 22-caliber bullet. I wondered whether I should bring it to the police. I couldn't think of any reason a casing for a spent bullet should be there unless it had been used for some illegal purposes. But I decided to just drop it. Should I have? I'll never know, I suppose.

"You're under arrest!"

I saw quite a few undercover cop arrests. On the street, in the buildings. Handcuffs I had never seen used before, but over the years in the hood, I saw them often being placed on people. One guy I felt sorry for. He was a little Black guy pushing a shopping cart full of junk metal down the street. Obviously, he was foraging for metal that he could sell to places that melted it down and recast it. He had a lot in his basket and was simply pushing it down the street, not bothering anybody. Suddenly, a cop car pulls up and orders him to stop. He stood there while they made a call into the station. Seems this guy was wanted for something or other, and they cuffed him and took him away, leaving the shopping basket full of junk metal in the middle of the street.

I did learn something though. I learned to tell the difference between a domestic violence arrest and an undercover drug bust. In the latter, the cops all looked like long-haired hippies in torn jeans. When the bust was made, the badges were immediately hung around their necks as they escorted the man off in cuffs.

"Vermin."

"Vermin: Wild animals that are believed to be harmful to crops, farm animals, or game, or that carry disease e.g., rodents." Well, that's what Google says anyway. I always thought they were anything that moved that you didn't like. In any case, there were tons of such creatures in the hoods. Most of the NYCHA houses stood there for years. There were creatures in the walls, in the floors, on the roofs, and under the buildings. Everywhere. Their very names conjure up disgust: cockroaches, rats, mice, and the occasional opossum. Lots of them, and not to forget, raccoons. Such pests are not uncommon anywhere in the world, but it seemed that some of the apartments I worked in were just infested with them.

In the fancier apartments I worked in, there was always a readily available manager to make sure that the exterminator kept the buildings pest free. But in the hoods, there was only a "super" who wasn't around much. One super for seven hundred apartments. The NYC Health Department was not much help, unfortunately. All of the NYCHA houses had a manager's office, and there one could find complaint forms about such things. Many of the occupants did not speak English, so they never complained, and others simply didn't want to "make trouble."

For some reason, the apartments of people from Bangladesh had the biggest problems with mice. In one apartment where I worked with a Bangladeshi girl, I would watch the mice scurry from the bedroom closet, past the bedroom door, and disappear into a hole in the bathroom somewhere. I opened the closet door to see that it was packed from floor to ceiling with all kinds of clothes, papers, and assorted junk—the kinds of things mice love to live in.

I informed the mother, and the next day, that closet was cleaned out and things were put in plastic bins. The mice never came back.

In another Bangladeshi apartment, mice would run across the floor, over my legs (as I always sat on the floor), and off behind some furniture. I asked Mom why she didn't tell the super. She replied that she had, many times. As mentioned before, one day while there, the child had thrown a puzzle piece behind an open cabinet that held the television and other things. It was heavy, but I had to move it, as I was forever losing puzzle pieces from expensive wooden puzzles. I looked down to see two dead, squished flat, dry mice. It seems that unlike rats, mice don't give off an odor when they die. They just dry up. Mom handed me a broom and a dustpan. She was disgusted and told me that her husband would get on the super again.

The third apartment not only had mice but also armies of cockroaches. Everywhere—in the kitchen, the shelves, walls, floors, ceilings, but the worst was the single bathroom. You'd open the door and watch whole armies move away across the wall in formation. Their super was Korean and not real interested in the tenant's problems. Mind you, he kept the front of the building immaculate, with trimmed lawn and flowers. Likewise, the entrance was clean, painted, and shiny. But the apartments were another story.

I took care of their cockroach problem, however. I brought them a bunch of little round tins containing poison, which they would carry back to the nest, and it would wipe out the whole herd.

The parents had never heard of such things, as Mom's English was nonexistent. Within days, they were all gone!

The worst mice infestation, however, was not in a Bangladeshi apartment but in one inhabited by Puerto Ricans. I worked with twins there and related the situation in the chapter on twins, part two. I was amazed when I told the male caretaker of the twins that I saw mice all over the kitchen, and his response was, "Ya, well, we got most of them."

In one building in a downtown Brooklyn hood, there were huge holes under the outer concrete stairs in the sidewalk leading up to the side entrance. There, rats flourished. It reminded me of the groundhogs I saw in Wyoming by Devil's Towers. Miles of them running freely from hole to hole. It was the same here. These were very busy rats going about their business and apparently unconcerned with the comings and goings of the people.

I had seen the same thing in Chinese parks in Manhattan, where the people gathered to play mahjong, eat, and generally just hang out. The Chinese seemed to see the rats as a good omen. When I first saw them, my first thought was immediately of "the plague." The great plagues of the world were brought by parasites riding on the backs of rats. You may have noticed that on ships tied up in ports, there are cones placed on the ropes to keep the rats from climbing up and entering the ships. The "plague" is what killed the famous Arizal, the famous Kabbalist who taught in the "mystical city" of Safed in the Galilee in the sixteenth century. That's what rats meant to me.

I went to the office to complain. They handed me a form and told me to call the health department. I did. The rats are still alive.

In one particularly small apartment in the poorest part of Brooklyn, I worked for a short while with a little boy "from the Islands." His mother seemed very strange. She did not talk to me. Shortly after I started she reported to the Center that I was swinging her little boy around by one leg! I had to go to the office and explain myself. When I got to the office, I told them that after all these years of working for them, I was shocked that they would actually believe such a wild story. They told me, "Yes, well, when a mother complains we have to check it out."

The next day I went back there and asked the mother why she'd said such a thing! She didn't respond and left the room. I quit that day. What's this got to do with vermin? That apartment was crawling with ants. Everywhere. As I left every day, before I put my ball cap on, I had to shake out the ants. I think it was "from above" that the mother made this wild call, as it gave me an excuse not to go back there.

Thankfully, I never saw rats in an apartment, just mice. But I must say, I never had any idea how big rats could grow until one day, in Manhattan, down by the harbor, I saw rats that, at first, I thought were beavers. They were huge! I remember there was a police car down there with two cops in it. They saw my reaction to the rats, and both broke out in a hardy laugh. "Welcome to New York."

I suppose every place in the world has their vermin problems. In Wisconsin, we had bats flying in and out of the house. In Israel, there are snakes, scorpions, and "jukkim," aka, cockroaches to deal with. The only good creatures I ever saw were the geckos on the walls in houses in the Philippines. They ate bugs, so the people wanted them there.

I fear that the descriptions above may sound racist. The vermin did not care what your race was or where you were from. Poverty was the reason for poorly kept broken-down apartments full of creatures. It is probably more racist that I have to explain that in my nineteen years working with minorities in lower socio/economic areas, the vast majority of apartments and rooms were very clean, tidy, bug free, and the people were honest, working-class people living in very poor conditions. Having grown up in small-town Wisconsin in the sixties and seventies, I simply never had any experiences in other environments.

I'd read books like *Manchild in the Promised Land* by Claude Brown, and of course Dickens, but never considered that such conditions actually existed. There were drugs, and shootings, and all the other kinds of things you read about, but these were the exceptions, not the rule.

"Another NorEastener."

"NorEasteners" are what they call storms in New York. In the summer, it could be hurricanes, like Sandy, that shut the state down for weeks. In the winter, it was blizzards with "eight to twelve inches expected tonight." I had a jeep, so the winter storms were always great news for me. When there was a blizzard of snow falling in New York, the city panicked. Everything was shut down before the snow even began to fall—businesses, schools, factories, buses, trains, grocery stores, and restaurants. You could not drive. Consider that, as of the year 2020, the population of Brooklyn was 2.59 million people. The population of greater New York City was nineteen million! A population that size made two things very difficult: driving and worse, parking. I've explained in other chapters what "alternate side parking is." The snow solved this problem. When there was a blizzard, the first thing that happened was that alternate side was discontinued for the duration of time it took to clear the streets. Days or weeks if it was bad enough.

The other thing was that having a jeep, I could park in two feet of snow, where other cars could not. When I went looking to buy a car in New York, I looked only for cars that had four-wheel drive and a high frame off the street. In other words: a Jeep. I was proud of the fact that I never missed a day in nineteen years in New York due to weather conditions. Except for Hurricane Sandy. That not only shut down the whole town, but it also made getting gas impossible. My mother was lying, near death, in a hospice on the other side of New Jersey, and I could not get gas to go see her.

There was one particular day that the snow was really heavy. I was in Brownsville, which is considered, "a bad part of town."

(Wasn't to me; I didn't see any difference.) In any case, the snow was so bad that even my little jeep got stuck. I could not get out of a spot. This was going to take some muscle. I went to one of the small stores that are dotted all over Brooklyn. Seems there's one or two on every block. They sell stuff like drinks, sandwiches, and hot food. You did not see too many White people in those places in Brownsville. I walked in and simply announced, "I'm stuck and need a push." I didn't say anything about paying for help. That's all I said. Three young ladies responded immediately, "Hey, we'll push ya'll."

We walked out to my car. I got in and began to "rock" the car. "Rocking the car" is a technique we all used in Wisconsin to get out of snow. It usually worked, but in New York, no one ever seemed to have heard of this technique. Even with the rocking and three ladies pushing, I was still stuck. A young Black man walked by and began to push, too, and suddenly, I was free. I was so relieved because I had more kids to get to. I opened my wallet to see how much cash I had, intending to give them twenty dollars. I took out three twenty-dollar bills and SNATCH! A hand reached in and grabbed all three twenties. Shrieks of joy ascended as these ladies were overjoyed at their new fortune. Wow! Sixty dollars!

I sat there thinking, *Uh, ok, what you gonna do?* I said, "Please give some to the guy who helped," as I pulled away. Whether they did or not, I'll never know. Actually, I found this whole escapade very amusing. I had no intention of giving away sixty dollars, but hey, for them it was like hitting the jackpot. Their shrieks of pure joy sent me off down the road to my next kid.

Hurricane Sandy was different. I had never experienced any-thing like it before. There had been hurricanes before in New York City. After all, it's on the coast. But nothing like Sandy. My house was on a one-way street, and a huge tree had been ripped up and thrown across it, making it impossible to get out. Fortunately, the people on the street did not have to wait for the city to move it. We all brought saws and went to work. Still, it took a few days. Almost every street had trees across them and sidewalks ripped up where the tree roots had been.

Far worse, however, was that gasoline was unavailable. The trucks that brought it either couldn't get through or the refineries were shut down. There was plenty in New Jersey, about a half hour's drive away, but my gas tank was on E, and I was afraid to try to make it there. It wasn't the kids I couldn't get to that bothered me. It was the fact that the hospital in another town, Port Jervis, was continually calling me to tell me that my mother didn't have much longer to go, and I'd better get there soon. In order to get to Port Jervis, New York, from Brooklyn, you had to drive through New Jersey.

I took the chance, and immediately after going over the New Jersey border, gas stations were plentiful and well stocked. How it could be that just over the border in New York, people were fighting in the streets over gas is beyond me.

When I got to my house in the Poconos near the hospital, there was no electricity, no running water, and no stores open, as Sandy visited there as well. It was December, and the cold was adorned with extremely deep snow everywhere. To use the bathroom, I'd have to walk to the lake with buckets to bring water to the house. It was freezing. Mom was in hospice and died December 24 in a room down the hall festively decorated with Christmas decorations, a little tree with lights, and all the nurses wearing Santa hats.

"Is you da super?"

Naivety has its virtues. Growing up in small-town Wisconsin sent me into the world with a naïve view of life. When I moved to New York, the thought of danger, or violence, or drugs, never entered my mind. I had been acquainted with racial strife and all the stereotypical things you hear about when I lived in Baltimore, Maryland. But in Baltimore, "those people" lived over there. My only exposure to poor Black people was when I worked in the

Baltimore City Jail as a teacher (kids in jail have to go to school to!). But there, I felt no threat, as there were cops everywhere, including the classrooms.

Actually, I really enjoyed working there. The students and I had a great rapport despite our differences. I tried subbing in the inner-city schools, but there I felt very threatened. And I was, often, so I quit that quickly. Unfortunately, racism hangs in the air in Baltimore like fungus. I never felt that in New York. Why, what was the difference? I do not know. I can only surmise. Baltimore was below the Mason-Dixon line. There were even houses there connected to the "Underground Railroad" that hid escaping slaves. Maybe the racism was a carryover. People tended to live in sections. Blacks here, Jews there, Whites here. No doubt there was plenty of real estate "steering" going on over the years. I applied to work with autistic kids in a public school there and was told, point blank, "This is a Black school, with Black children and Black teachers." I pointed out that it was actually a public school. The Black lady principal and her Black male vice-principal looked at me like I was an idiot. I didn't get that job!

In New York, there are every kind of people in the world. All colors, all religions, any and all different kinds of people can be found there. They all seemed to get along. Initially, it reminded me of London, where I also never felt any threat but was enthralled with the diversity. It never occurred to me that there were "bad neighborhoods" or dangerous places to be. Not in Brooklyn anyway. Maybe the Bronx. Maybe Manhattan in parts. But I didn't live there and never worked there. So, when the Center offered me a child to work with, if my schedule was open, I took the kid no matter where it was in Brooklyn.

One of my first kids was in East New York. That's the name of the area, not a location. When one of my White friends asked me where I worked and I replied, East New York, he was visibly shaken! "Are you crazy? How can you work there?" I had no idea what he was talking about. Such was to be the common response when I told my Jewish neighbors or White friends where I usually worked: Bed Sty, Brownsville, Crown Heights, East New York, poor side of Coney Island, Bushwick. I never had problems except once.

Indeed, the most common experience I had when walking through the hoods was someone approaching me, usually a woman, who would see a White guy carrying bags and ask, "Scyuzz me. Iz you da super?" It was automatically assumed that if you were White, with materials in your hand, you hand to be the manager or owner of the apartments. That happened often, and it was, except for the one time, the only "threatening" thing I encountered.

There was that one time, however. I was waiting on top of the four steps that rose to a door in an apartment. There was a fence I had to pass through to get to the steps. At this house, the front door was far away from the kitchen and living room. Mom could not hear me knock, the doorbell did not work, and I had no cell phone in those days. Three teenagers stopped by the gate, and one said, "Hey, man. Give me five dollars." I turned to look at him. He had a cane. They were about fifteen years old. I responded, "Why should I give you five dollars?"

"Because I'm hungry." The other two never said a word.

Again, he said, "Look, man. Give me five dollars." They were still behind the fence four steps below, and I was still banging on the door.

I'm not sure what caused me, I said, "You think I have money?" You're right. You know why?"

He's starting to get angry. "No, why?"

"Because I work for a living. You know how I work for a living? I went to college."

He was thoroughly unimpressed. He opened the gate and came up the steps. He said, "Man, you owe me five dollars!"

I asked him what he could get for five dollars. He told me, "A hamburger."

I responded, "Hmm. Well, why don't you go home and cook some hamburgers?"

All three of them laughed at this suggestion. It never occurred to me that having hamburger always available in the freezer was not something these guys would be used to. In any case, it appeared to me like violence was the next step. However, just at this moment, the father of the child drove up. He was a big man, very well fit as a rugby player, and immediately got the sense that something was not right. He got out and said, "Everything all right here?"

I said, "Yeah, no problem. Your wife doesn't hear me knocking." The three boys just walked away. I worked with my little student, and when I came out, those three guys were still there! As I walked to my car, the kid with the cane swung it over my head, as if to hit me.

I ducked, and they laughed. I got into my car but before pulling away, I motioned for the cane bearer to get in the car with me. He got in. I gave him five dollars and told him, "Look, man, if you use your head, you can also make a hundred thousand a year. Go to school!" He nodded and got out. I never saw them again.

"Naivety."

In an elevator, taking me to the top floor in a six-story building, were two young Black men. It was small and pitch-black inside. I noticed that there was a fixture in the roof for a light bulb. As we rose, I just mentioned, "Uh, how come they don't put light bulbs in here?" They both broke out laughing. I didn't get it. Then one of them said, "Man—dey steal 'em." Oh.

I had been warned never to take the steps in any of the NYCHA houses. I wondered why not? If the apartment I needed was on the first or second floor, why take the elevator?

I learned. There's a few reasons. One is that they usually wreaked of urine, or worse. There were always large stains on the floor, and it was anybody's guess what had caused it.

Graffiti, of course, was ubiquitous, some of them marking gang areas. The other reason was far more insidious. It was a good place to get "trapped." If you met someone there who was not someone you'd like to be alone with, you were in trouble.

I was "privy" to a serious, private conversation as I passed two young men in the stairwell one day. They were discussing the advantages of their gang joining forces with another gang nearby and making themselves invincible by the merger. "Ain't no one gonna F wit us."

At the apartment of one of my angels, I left a brand-new umbrella outside the door to dry off. When I came out an hour later, it was gone. There were four apartments on that floor. Two of them were either vacant or the people were never home. It was obvious who had taken my umbrella on this eighth floor. But what was I to do? Knock on the neighbor's door and suggest that they return the umbrella they'd stolen? Chalk it up.

Glossary

ABA: Applied Behavior Analysis. A therapy based on the science of learning and behavior based on the work of B. F. Skinner.

Discrete trial teaching (DTT); also, discrete trial instruction (DTI): A method of highly structured (often one-on-one) teaching technique that breaks down learning goals into smaller, or discrete, steps. Correct responses (behaviors) are "reinforced" with tangible reinforcements, such as a favored toy.

Picture exchange communication system (PECS): A communication system that utilizes pictures to help children with communication difficulties to express themselves. Developed by Professor Andy Bondy.

Facilitated Communication (FC): A discredited technique utilizing keyboards or letter boards for non-verbal children to write their thoughts to express to others.

Natural environment training (NET): A teaching technique that utilizes the child's environment to engage them in learning opportunities instead of relying on reinforcement provided by the instructor, as in DTT.

Verbal Behavior **(VB):** 1957 book by B. F. Skinner. Skinner's analysis of language based on function. For example, if a child says, "Apple," the function of his saying this could be a "mand" (request) or a "tact" (simple identification), etc. The book explains how analyzing the function of the words uttered or written, etc., can guide a therapist to utilize and reinforce language or "verbal behavior."

Verbal Behavior (method): Verbal Behavior therapy uses similar concepts to Applied Behavioral Analysis. It is a method of teaching communication to people who have not yet acquired language using operant conditioning. It consists of four "contingencies": Motivational Operation, Discriminating Stimulus, Response, and Reinforcement. These four factors ensure that students are motivated to acquire language to meet their needs. (Description taken from: **"Applied Behavior Analysis Programs Guide"** https://www.appliedbehavioranalysisprograms.com/about/)

REFERENCES

Introduction

(1) Dr. Lauren Elder. Autism Speaks.org. December 5, 2018. What is discrete trial teaching?

Some Successes

(2) O.I. Lovaas. 1987. Behavioral treatment and normal educational and intellectual functioning in young autistic children. Journal of Consulting and Clinical Psychology, Vol 55(1), Feb 1987, 3-9

(3) E. G. Carr and V.M. Durand. 1985. Reducing behavior problems through functional communication training. Summer; 18(2): 111-26. Doi; 10. 1901/Journal of Applied Behavior Analysis. 1985 18-111.

(4) Andy Bondy and Lori Frost. 1985 Picture Exchange Communication System (PECS) First edition. New Castle, Delaware, Pyramid Educational Consultants.

(5) Yoyo Ma and Bobby McFerrin. HUSH. Sony Masterworks. 1992.

Some Successes 2

(6) C.C. Park. 1982. The Siege. The First Eight Years of an Autistic Child. Later printing edition. Little, Brown, and Company. New York, New York.

<u>The Ones I Couldn't Help</u>

(7) Craig Schulze. August 1993. When Snow Turns to Rain. Woodbine House. Bethesda, Maryland.

(8) "Bklyner" Magazine. 2013. "List of City's Worst Housing Projects, Marlboro Houses list 41st out of 349."

(9) SpaghettiOs. Campbell Soup Company. Camden, New Jersey

<u>A Few More I Couldn't Help</u>

(10) Facilitated Communication. Douglas Biklen developer of Facilitated Communication. Facilitated Communication Institute. Syracuse, New York. 1992.

(11) Mark Sundberg. August 2014. The VB MAPP. AVB Press. First edition Concord, California.

(12) B.F. Skinner. 1957. Verbal Behavior. First edition. Copley Publishing Company. USA

(13) Why "Sensory Integration Disorder" is a Dubious Diagnosis. Peter Heilbroner, M.D. Ph.D. November 9, 2015)

(14) Premack. D. 1959. Toward empirical behavioral laws: l, Positive Reinforcement. Psychological Review, 66(4), 219-233.

<u>Twins</u>

(15) Film: "Lorenzo's Oil" 1992. Directed/Written by George Miller. Ben Avon, PA.

(16) Mozart for Babies: Various Cd's of music available on major book and music sites.

(17)   Charles Hart, 1989. Without Reason. 1989. Arlington, Texas. HarperCollins.

More Twins

(18) Philos Trans R Soc Lond B Biol Sci. 2009 May 27; 364(1522): 1351–1357. doi: 10.1098/rstb.2008.0326   PMCID: PMC2677584 PMID: 19528017 The savant syndrome: an extraordinary condition. A synopsis: past, present, future Darold A. Treffert1,2.

(19) Treffert DA (May 2009). "The savant syndrome: an extraordinary condition. A synopsis: past, present, future". Philosophical Transactions of the Royal Society of London. Series B, Biological Sciences. 364 (1522): 1351–7. doi:10.1098/rstb.2008.0326. PMC 2677584. PMID 19528017.

(20) Lorna Selfe. 1979. Nadia: A Case of Extraordinary Drawing Ability in an Autistic Child. Harcourt. First edition. San Diego, California.

Savants

(21) Early Lovaas tapes. https://www.youtube.com/ watch?v=qtRod0V57HU&list=PLm0-s9RXo5gAuUfjJLaqgWmdt4_Y-Afne&index=11 8:24-8:55

(22) The Playdoh Factory. Hasbro Toy Company.

Grandmothers

(23) American Psychiatric Association. Pervasive Developmental Disorders. In: *Diagnostic and Statistical Manual of Mental Disorders.* 4 ed.-text revision (DSM-IV-TR). Washington, D.C: American Psychiatric Association; 2000: 69-70.

Angels

(24) The Miracle Worker is a 1962 American biographical film about Anne Sullivan, a blind tutor to Hellen Keller, directed by Allan Penn. The screenplay by William Gibson is based on his 1959 play of the same title,

which originated as a 1957 broadcast of the television anthology series Playhouse 90. Gibson's secondary source material was The Story of My Life, the 1903 autobiography of Hellen Keller.

(25) O. Ivar Lovaas. Teaching Developmentally Disabled Children. 1981. First edition. University Park Press. University of Pennsylvania.

The Very Cute

(26) Catherine Maurice. 1994. *Let Me Hear Your Voice*. First edition. Random House Publishing. New York, New York.

www.ingramcontent.com/pod-product-compliance
Lightning Source LLC
Chambersburg PA
CBHW040735120726
48007CB00008B/93